Brilliant! Fabian Schwartz dazzles with playfully precise writing rarely seen in top-rate business literature. The best book on agility yet.

— **Joe Justice**, CEO of Wikispeed, creator of Extreme Manufacturing and Scrum@Hardware

Having lived with the failed central planning of totalitarian East Berlin as a child and then embracing big planning in development through work, Fabian at first thought there was no other serious way to manage. Then he discovered success with Scrum.

Embracing Scrum's underlying principles led Fabian to find that teamwork and serious problem-solving were the road to better outcomes and a better life. Yet, Fabian also found that dogmatically following Scrum is not a recipe for success. He added his own interpretation of Scrum and enjoyed even better outcomes. If you want to find your own success, Fabian's experience and story serve as both inspiration and pragmatic primer.

— **James W. Grenning**, coauthor of the Agile Manifesto, inventor of Planning Poker

You'll learn from your own experiences when practicing Scrum journey. But you don't have to go alone. Fabian's book recounts his wisdom and practice of Scrum, providing you with a good companion for your own journey. Enjoy!

— **Kiro Harada**, Scrum Pattern Group, CEO of Attractor Inc.

Weaving in his experience as a young boy when the Berlin Wall fell and a new, unimaginable world appeared, Fabian Schwartz draws the reader in and shows the reader the new world Scrum can reveal. Come along for a riveting tale of a Scrum skeptic turned convert turned enthusiast. Learn that you, too, can conquer your healthy skepticism and learn how to work in a more agile manner. There is hope!

— **Jon Kern**, coauthor of the Agile Manifesto

Fabian Schwartz helped us with the implementation of Scrum since the beginning. His practical approach has guaranteed that the effort returned the immense value. Through him, Scrum has been a very valuable tool for our organization. We have implemented the discipline across all departments in the company, so we are now focused and strategically aligned. Thanks to Fabian and Scrum, communication is effective and teamwork is the norm at our company. It hasn't been easy. It is a cultural change. But it has worked for us.

Our own experience proves it: Scrum works and Fabian is the strategist to bring it to your organization. His book *Your Scrum Playbook* is a must-read for anyone who's interested in diving into the Scrum framework and for everyone who sees Scrum's experiential side. We are thankful to Fabian for his continuous contribution to our organization and for his experience with Scrum. We hope you will find his work as valuable as we have.

—**Alberto García**, country manager of Drummond Energy Inc.

YOUR
SCRUM
PLAYBOOK

YOUR SCRUM PLAYBOOK

IT'S POKER NOT CHESS

FOREWORD BY
DR. JEFF SUTHERLAND

FABIAN SCHWARTZ

Cover Designer: **Lucas Vargas**

Editorial and design services
www.roundtablecompanies.com

Editor: **James Cook**
Interior Designer: **Christy Bui**
Proofreader: **Adam Lawrence**
Project Manager: **Keli McNeill**

ISBN hardcover: 978-958-52689-0-6
ISBN paperback: 978-958-52689-1-3
ISBN digital: 978-958-52689-2-0

First Edition: March 2020
10 9 8 7 6 5 4 3 2

To my parents, Doris and Hartmut, who taught me that integrity is worth more than any amount of money.

To my brother Tobias, whom I deeply admire for the way he takes action while others are still deciding.

To my sons Alejandro and Juan Andres: always remember that I will love you for the rest of my life. I send you into the world with my love and deep belief in all the incredible things you can accomplish; I hope you take that faith in yourself with you throughout your life. Take beautiful risks, stay safe, and live your lives to the fullest. No matter how far you travel, I will always be here to welcome you home.

Love, Dad.

Contents

Foreword

In 1993, when I launched the first Scrum team at Easel Corporation, we tuned the implementation until it performed ten times better than traditional project management both in speed of production and quality of product. When I asked Ken Schwaber to take a look at this team in 1995, we saw very quickly that Scrum's lightness and agility could enhance value in surprising ways and agreed to formalize Scrum as an open-source framework and write the first paper on Scrum for my first book, *Business Object Design and Implementation: OOPSLA'95 Workshop Proceedings*. My fifth book, *Scrum: The Art of Doing Twice the Work in Half the Time*, described the essential lean practices and patterns (later published in my sixth book, *A Scrum Book: The Spirit of the Game*) that allow any Scrum team to achieve the level of performance of the first Scrum team. When implemented correctly, Scrum can supercharge a company's performance, giving developers more freedom and agency so they can accomplish more in less time, working with more motivation at an easily sustainable pace. Scrum can be magical, allowing companies and teams to perform feats of great strength without breaking a sweat.

The key phrase, of course, is *when implemented correctly*. Scrum is not business as usual. It's based in values, insight, even intuition—it makes actuaries uncomfortable and intrigues martial arts devotees. It requires a change of mindset that can make transition tricky. When I work with Scrum teams, I find that they implement a third of the components poorly and completely fail to implement another third.

Fabian Schwartz is one of the most knowledgeable Scrum trainers I've worked with over the years. He has an encyclopedic understanding of project management in the twentieth century, and he can apply that to almost any situation. Because he was himself wary of Scrum at first, he has a natural ability to help those who are having difficulty adopting it. But, particularly, he is a learner who enjoys navigating complexity and finding innovative solutions. His motivation is contagious, his experience is vast, and he can not only explain Scrum but *show* how to put it into action.

It's been exciting to see Fabian bring Scrum to new markets in Colombia and across South America, and there is no one better to instruct leaders in the *shu* stage of implementation. At the *shu* stage, most teams understand the pieces of the framework but need practice putting them together, getting them working, and making good use of all the component parts. Then, Sprint by Sprint, Scrum gains momentum toward high performance, profit, and even pleasure.

Scrum at Scale is designed to take basic small-team Scrum and scale it up to be used by tens or even hundreds of teams, with productivity rising proportionately. Scrum at Scale is designed to be used in all parts of the organization, across the organization, and in any domain. And it measurably improves the organization's value.

This book brings a new voice to the Scrum conversation, discussing Lean principles and patterns as well as the tenets of Scrum. It speaks to stakeholders from all industries, offering a primer for productivity-focused change that can work in every sector.

It's not enough to know Scrum; you actually have to know how to play Scrum and win. You have to live its values, play by its rules, work within its structure to slice through bureaucracy, allow your team creative freedom, learn through each Sprint, and, finally, deliver great value to your client. *Your Scrum Playbook: It's Poker, Not Chess* is the manual you'll want by your side as you take advantage of this framework that has been doubling value for all types of organizations and those who work within them.

— **Jeff Sutherland**, inventor and cocreator of Scrum and
author of *Scrum: The Art of Doing Twice the Work in Half the Time*
https://www.scruminc.com/
October 2019

Preface

> *You can't expect to meet the challenges of today with yesterday's tools and expect to be in business tomorrow.*
> —Anonymous[1]

Business is often compared to a chess game. It's complex, with lots of pieces to move, and every move changes the story, offering new opportunities and closing off others. In theory, a chess player can calculate every possible scenario before each move. They may sometimes think for an hour, analyzing the situation, breaking complex problems apart, considering different scenarios, then, finally, moving a pawn one square.

While earning my MBA, and over the course of my long career in project management, I learned to think like a chess player. Business leaders are taught to analyze situations, break complex problems apart, plan for different contingencies, then select the best solution and execute it. I believed I could foresee every step if I consulted the right experts. My Gantt charts felt like works of art—so many departments, each with so many goals, all coming together finally in a smooth flow, a waterfall. I've worked on projects where the planning phase lasted two years before we opened the dam and the actual work began.

Unfortunately, in business, you can't see all the pieces laid out on the board, and the moves are unlimited. Everything you do is based on the assumptions you made at the beginning, but by the time you deliver the project, a new queen may have stepped onto the board and flicked half the other pieces off the edge.

According to Peter Senge, founder of the Society for Organizational Learning and senior lecturer at MIT's Sloan School of Management, today's problems come from yesterday's decisions, and business decisions are more like bets on the future than chess moves. There *are* rogue queens out there: things you depended on may suddenly disappear, and pathways you never dreamed of may become discernible in the new landscape.

---

1   Alan J. Stolzer, Carl D. Halford, and John J. Goglia, *Safety Management Systems in Aviation* (Burlington, VT: Ashgate, 2008), 219.

Traditional project planning worked very well during the first Industrial Revolution—the age of the steam engine. It was perfect for the second revolution, the era when Gantt charts were invented and assembly lines created every kind of machine. In the third revolution, the age of robotics, it proved essential. But any manager who started planning a large project in the mid-1990s finished it in an entirely new era, one very few had foreseen.

Business decisions predicated on assumptions are difficult to track over time. Many years may pass before a result is seen, making it nearly impossible to track that result back to the original decision. The longer the gap is between the decision made and the results delivered, the more difficult it will be to determine which decision delivered those results. Therefore, minimizing the time from decision-making to decision impact should be a major goal of any organization. Shortening the gap between making decisions and seeing the consequences makes for more accurate future predictions and assumptions and provides immediate feedback to help team members improve their game.

The Gantt chart was developed in 1910 and is still the preferred way to illustrate project planning within businesses. The idea is that you break a complex problem into smaller ones, hoping that by solving each small problem, you will have solved the big one. This approach leads to localized optimization: each unit (person or team) remains focused on a small part of the problem. They never have a view of the overall picture or understand their connection with the rest of the project. Still, managers desire an exact plan that is as accurate and predictable as they can get. Creating this chart can take months of effort, demands a high level of detail, and is not flexible to changing environments. Since life isn't predictable, these charts rarely, if ever, hold true. In today's fast-changing environment, playing chess just doesn't work. We're playing poker now. The fourth industrial revolution—the Internet of Things (IoT)—and digitalization have us hurtling through changes at warp speed. We gained access to a universe of information, which would have been a Tower of Babel if Google hadn't slipped it into harness. Google's development of Google Maps allowed Uber to change the landscape of ride-sharing, and Amazon is using breakthroughs in artificial intelligence and machine learning technology to rapidly transform the customer ordering and fulfillment experience. Change isn't linear anymore; it's exponential. And anyone who blinks, opens his eyes to a new world.

Things are changing so fast we need a shorter feedback loop just to keep up. The way we used to do business doesn't work anymore. Our assumptions are based on past experiences and metrics, but what has worked in the past is rarely true for the future, especially when the landscape changes so swiftly. Even when we do it right, and our assumptions are true, the very basis we made them on may have changed by the time we deliver. We work on complex projects in a complex environment; our only certainty is that there will be many obstacles, many changes, and a constant flow of new information to be absorbed and reacted to.

The traditional way of working can no longer be relied on to deliver the expected results. Huge teams, separated by specialty and adhering to long-held bureaucratic standards, can't react to quick developments and sudden changes. A lightweight, elastic approach was necessary, so Scrum was born.

Was I a visionary, early adopter of Scrum? Did I read Scrum creator Jeff Sutherland's *The Scrum Guide* and realize that Scrum would revolutionize software development? Unfortunately, no. I had done well on three different continents with the skills I had. Why would I change? Then—absolute failure. A year of careful, Gantt chart–organized planning on a major project where, out of hundreds of our deliverables, not one worked. On the precipice of financial disaster, I remembered this thing called Scrum and thought I'd rather try it than go broke.

With Scrum, we turned that project immediately around, gaining the ability to deliver more completely and more quickly. The client was getting exactly what they needed, and my team was working with a new kind of dynamic energy. It felt like a miracle, or at least like a royal flush.

I've made up for my early skepticism by immersing myself in Scrum, becoming certified, teaching it, working with Joe Justice to write *Scrum in Hardware Guide*, which takes Scrum beyond software delivery, and helping Jeff Sutherland develop the *Scrum@Scale Guide*. By now, I've used Scrum in almost every domain from retail to oil and gas mining. I've seen that although Scrum works wonders for the bottom line, it creates those wonders through shared values in the workplace. A team of up to nine people, freed of Gantt charts and bureaucracy, committed to courage, commitment, respect, openness, and focus, are motivated to generate more value with less effort. Scrum makes a project more exciting, more creative, and more satisfying—naturally that leads to more success. People feel better when they have more agency— they do more and take more pride in their work. They don't have to guess at the future; they expect to meet impediments and work to overcome them. Everyone works better in an atmosphere of trust and psychological safety, where mistakes are expected and quickly remedied. A team works together and supports each other almost like a family, and they can respond with confidence to the unforeseen.

In the last ten years, I've worked with teams across North and South America and Australia who were learning to implement Scrum, and I've seen again and again the results the technique can produce. One gas company I worked with took an average time of nineteen days to drill one well. The fastest well they'd ever drilled took ten days. After adopting Scrum, their average drilling time went down to six days. And they accomplished this with the same staff, no complex infrastructure, and, probably most important, a strongly motivated, comfortable, agile team.

Of course, with all major shifts in thinking, there exists a lag between understanding the basic concepts and being able to process the new thinking almost subconsciously. *Shu-ha-ri* is a Japanese martial arts concept that outlines the stages of learning from absolute beginner through that level of subconscious mastery. This book is intended for those in the *"shu"* state—those who've seen that Scrum is a lightweight, responsive approach that changes with the shifting conditions we face, and who want to implement it in their business processes. If you are ready to play business in a more agile, fast-paced, even more enjoyable way, pull up a chair and I'll deal you in.

—Fabian Schwartz, MBA

CHAPTER ONE

A New Reality or the Gantt Hits the Fan

Business is a combination of war and sport.
—Andre Maurois[1]

Twice in my life I have discovered an alternate reality—a new, different, and exciting world just outside the one I lived in. The first time was when I was ten. I grew up in East Berlin, where everything was owned and operated by the state; they decided how much milk was needed, how many eggs. The government would plan everything for years in advance, and we lived according to the plan, although it was usually wrong. If the state ran out of bread, we did without bread. I assumed this was how everyone lived. At the edge of the city was a wall, which had been there all my life. I could no more go through the wall than I could fly, and I didn't question these boundaries.

Then, in 1989, the wall came down. I crossed, with my family, into a technicolor world I'd never imagined I'd see. The bright signs, the shop windows were dazzling. The different packages in the grocery store, all designed to scream "choose me, choose me," made me dizzy with their colors and variety. My father bought me a little Batman figurine, souvenir of a thrilling experience.

The second time I had this stepping-through-the-rainbow feeling was in 2014. I was a grown man, of course, living in Bogota, with an MBA and years of successful project management under my belt. I was working with a client, leading one arm of a $70 million program, working to replace almost all the backend software tools for a multinational Ecuadorian-based telecommunications company. We'd been working for a year, through layers of stringent

---

1   Roger LeRoy Miller, *Business Law Today, Comprehensive: Text and Cases: Diverse, Ethical, Online, and Global Environment* (Stamford, CT: Cengage Learning, 2015), 810.

advance planning, pages of Gantt charts, different projections undertaken by experts in their fields. We'd filled a huge reservoir of understanding that we expected would produce the results we wanted. The final month was wildly stressful as such times tend to be—late nights, pointless meetings, frantic emails, and far too much coffee. But we delivered on time—two hundred test cases that would form the basis of the company's internal software infrastructure—and sat back to await the results.

None of the test cases worked. Not one, out of two hundred. It felt like we were the Titanic—brilliantly designed, proudly put to sea, but nevertheless sideways and sinking fast.

The client refused to pay (of course). Fines, notices from lawyers, and heated phone calls followed. We had to lay off more than half of our staff members, and still we had to produce everything we'd promised, with only a few months to bankruptcy.

At this point, we couldn't just make a minor shift in operations. We called an emergency meeting, and it was there, in a room full of anxious faces, that I remembered Scrum.

I had reluctantly tried it years before, in 2007, when a group of entrepreneurs asked me to help them create a car-sharing company, a new idea for Germany at that time. The partners wanted to try Scrum. I'd spent years in the methodical, carefully charted world of organizational planning, and invested thousands of dollars in my certifications. Scrum seemed like a kind of Wild West approach, okay for such a small project, maybe. After all, they were only paying me in shares. By some stroke of luck, it worked. In three months, the project was up and running—much more easily than I'd expected.

Now I wondered, what if that wasn't just luck? What if Scrum would be a better approach now as well? The thought made me queasy. This wasn't a little start-up but a major project for a multinational company. And I'm not a Wild West, shoot-from-the-hip kind of guy. I'm well-organized, some might say inflexible. I was heavily invested in traditional project management, not just in money and time, but at an emotional level. I saw two ways to manage a project: my way, or the wrong way. In fact, I had once engaged in a heated argument with a supplier because what they had estimated for the project had changed. My thinking was so rigid that I insisted he had to change his problem to match my plan.

I was still playing chess in a world that was changing; planning my moves, my strategies, keeping every piece accounted for in my head. Unfortunately, my game board had just been obliterated. I felt I was about to plunge the whole company into chaos, but better that than accepting bankruptcy without a fight.

Scrum uses a very small team—no more than nine people, and that was about the number we had left on staff. Scrum goes one step at a time, so if something went wrong, we would know it immediately and be able to get the bugs out before we went on to the next step. And quite honestly, Scrum was my only hope. The company I contracted with was my only client and my fortunes were tied to theirs. I had to bite the bullet and try it if I didn't want to go broke.

One thing I had learned about Scrum was that you can't try it begrudgingly. We couldn't just dabble in Scrum; we had to fully embrace it. But as I looked around the room, I saw the gloom dispelled. My team was relieved to have a plan, and ready, even excited, for the adventure.

We snapped out of anxiety and into action. Jeff Sutherland, Scrum's cocreator, had just published *Scrum: The Art of Doing Twice the Work in Half the Time*, and we read it cover to cover. I invested in Scrum training for myself and for the company's head of operations. Then I trained the rest of the group. With this modest framework in place, we approached the client and convinced them to join us in using Scrum.

The next day we formed our Scrum team, determined who would act as Product Owner (the "visionary" in charge of determining and maintaining the Product Backlog and keeping the client's needs as first priority), and Scrum Master (the "servant-leader" responsible for ensuring adherence to the Scrum framework.) I took the job of Scrum Master, and meanwhile the Product Owner got to work populating the Product Backlog (list of the work to be done), determining what to undertake during our first two-week Sprint, and defining what would count as "done." The client gave us a list of priorities, and we took them on, one test case at a time. The executive who had trained with me became a key member of our team. This was the first sign that Scrum was working: we had switched up the conventional arrangement and simply done what was best for the project.

It wasn't perfect. We screwed up many times as we forsook our old ideology. In poker parlance, we bluffed when we should have folded, and called when we should have doubled down. But we were able to identify the causes of the original project issues, and, one by one, we addressed them.

When we were in waterfall mode, every worker was focused on their individual task, to the exclusion of all others. They were more concerned with checking off their to-do list than making sure the project actually worked. We were working in virtual silos, each group ignorant of the others' progress, and unaware of how their actions—or lack of actions—affected the other parts of the project. This wasn't their fault; they were merely working in the framework we'd built.

1.1. Waterfall vs. Agile

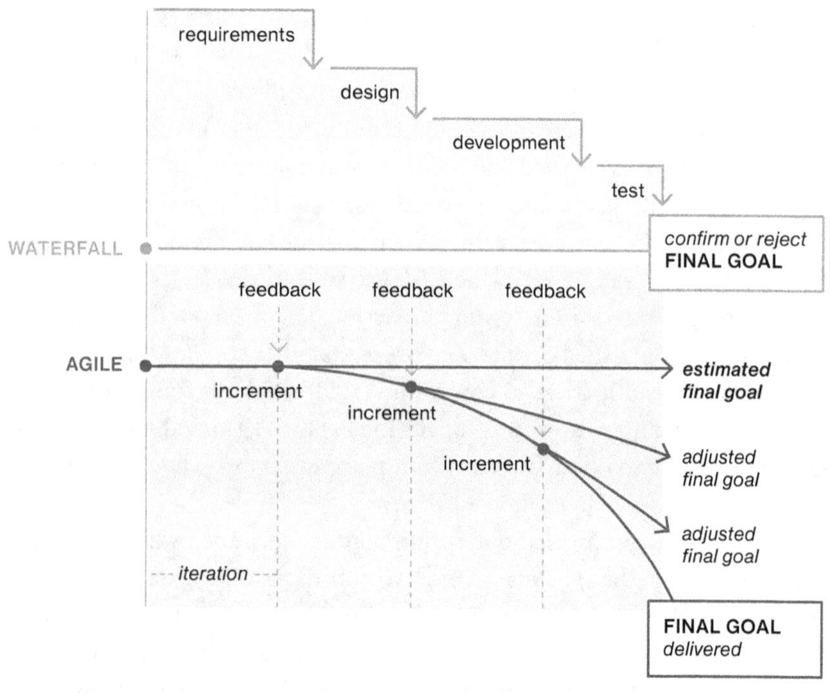

For example, we had Cecilia (we've changed names throughout this book to protect anonymity) working on a tool to monitor the process flow of all other tools. Meanwhile, Carlos was working on the integration of all tools, including Cecilia's. Both kept asking for more time. As soon as we switched to Scrum, the walls came down and we saw that while Cecilia's code would output some variables that were true, it would also output many exceptions. She had no way to know that those exceptions would interfere with the integration into Carlos's tool. Now that we had transparency between the two projects, both the problem and its solution were apparent.

Then another problem was revealed: many team members were waiting for resolution to issues with the software giant whose development systems we were using. Before Scrum, a developer would submit a service ticket and move on to something else while waiting for the problem to be resolved. We were a piddling client to this corporation, and they took weeks to respond to each issue. We were blind to the ramifications of this until they were staring us in the face on our visual board and coming up repeatedly in our Daily Scrums. We were going to miss our new deadline thanks to the software giant's interminable delays.

Fortunately, with the client's liaison unofficially on our team, we had a plan. We might be small potatoes to the software giant, but our client had a multimillion-dollar contract. The liaison got one of the senior VPs involved, and next thing we knew, the software giant had a new task force assigned to solving our issues.

The problems weren't limited to external factors either. Our Ecuadorian-based team had spotty access to the internet and was often unable to collaborate with the Colombian office. You'd think this would be an easy fix, seeing that our client was the internet provider, but no. Over and over, we had to go through the chain of command and levels of bureaucracy just to get back online. Finally, I decided to invite the guy at the top of that chain to lunch, to "fill him in" on our project. From then on, we had internet access.

Again, without Scrum showing us that this impediment was becoming a major priority, we might have wasted weeks trying to solve the issue another way.

And as we solved each problem, we had more confidence going on to the next. We were now delivering products—test cases—to the client systematically every two weeks. We'd test, get client feedback, and either make a new iteration or cross the item off the backlog. Under the old system, we had no chance for client review until the end. Think about that: in one year, under the traditional framework, we got feedback once. Now we consulted with our client over twenty times a year—more communication, more understanding, and much less pressure to get everything right. The emphasis was on learning and improving, not on readying a project for one big make-or-break moment.

The atmosphere within our office changed. It crackled with an electricity of excitement as the team pushed forward Sprint by Sprint. There were still risks, of course, but they were smaller risks and we were facing them, and resolving them, together. We started having fun.

This change wasn't easy. Failure was inevitable on a Sprint, but what might have led to blame and finger-pointing before was accepted as part of the process now. If we found an instance of "spaghetti code" (overly complex and lengthy code), we simply worked together to refine it. Working side by side fostered a new camaraderie, a sense of safety that allowed the team to flourish together. Innovation came with ease: someone would have a wild idea, and the team would vote on whether to try it. Some pretty outlandish suggestions ended up working perfectly. Some were duds but helped us learn. Yes, we still had some personnel issues, some challenges we hadn't anticipated. But we were moving forward every day, cutting through red tape, finding solutions, and each Sprint informed the next.

Scrum, at its best, functions like a well-ordered system of stem cells. Teams of people work cohesively, step-by-step, toward a unified end. Instead of decisions made in isolation by a select few, they are made quickly and organically by the people on the ground. A collective consciousness develops that allows faster decisions and better results. Those results get nearly immediate feedback, the team can respond accordingly, and the iteration cycle is drastically shortened. In the end, Scrum, like business, is everyday people working in collaboration. These are not "superstars" either. On that telecom project, we had lost some of our best people and others had to step in and take up the slack. Good Scrum requires strong, knowledgeable folks who have deep knowledge in their field of expertise, but also have a broad, working knowledge of what other team members do. We call them "T-shaped people": they fit tightly together, each able to do his or her own job as well as many communal tasks.

1.2. T-Shaped People

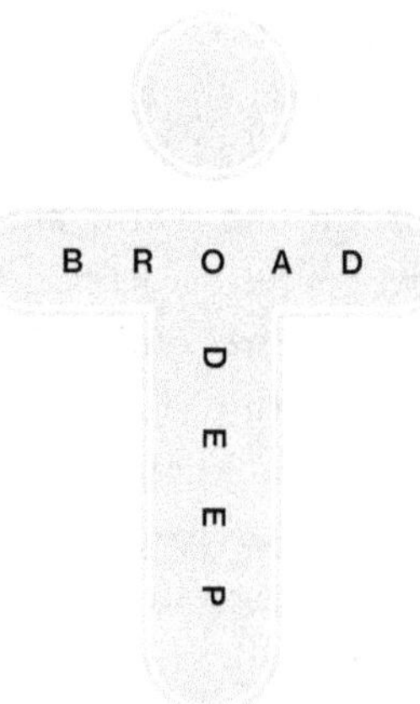

Smaller collaborating teams of T-shaped people can determine the best course of action within predefined limits without the wasted time and energy to bounce ideas "upstairs." Such collaboration requires psychological safety, which allows for a complete commitment to the goal from every team member. Psychological safety "is defined as a shared belief that the team is safe for interpersonal risk taking."[2] In other words, they believe they can safely take risks that in other situations could jeopardize their career.

---

2   Amy Edmondson, "Psychological Safety and Learning Behavior in Work Teams," *Administrative Science Quarterly* 44, no. 2 (June 1999), 350–383, http://www.jstor.org/stable/2666999.

But did our last-ditch effort work? Every two weeks I traveled to Ecuador to test each tool and meet with the client. This is technically not good Scrum because tests should be part of the Sprint, but this was an additional user acceptance test that the client ran outside our Sprints. Almost every two weeks, we had more successful test cases. It turns out that not everything the client thought they wanted was needed. That's the value of a rapid feedback loop and of providing a fully functional product with each iteration. I'd been a preacher in the church of Traditional Project Management, but my eyes were seeing a new light. All the color-coded charts on earth can't replace real-world results.

Our client's test team and our team were now working together in real time. As soon as we finished a test case, we'd perform our tests and then deliver it immediately for them to test on their platform. If it worked, great. If they had an issue, we worked on the issue until we solved it.

We walked back from the precipice and accomplished what I'd thought was impossible. In only four months—a third of the time, and with less than half of the workforce—we had produced 100 percent functionality for the client, saved our business, and, not least, we'd had a wonderful time. We knew and liked each other better, we each had a sense of true agency, and we came to work each day with a belief that what we were doing really mattered.

For the second time in my life, I had crossed into unknown territory and found an entirely new world that operated on principles I couldn't have imagined before I experienced them. I had always approached my work as a form of chess, where my first move was to study my opponent intensely, trying to precisely predict his future moves. Then I would plan out my future moves based on that analysis. But life is not a chessboard. You can strategize and might even calculate the next potential three or four moves, but you can't see every single possibility through to checkmate. By the time you reach the game's end, the board may have tilted, the usual moves may have become obsolete.

Now I was learning to play poker. Gather the players, set the rules, and deal. Each hand will present its surprises. No one can guess where every card is held, but the players are well-versed and ready to respond to each situation as it arises. When playing well, a poker champion can be nearly unbeatable.

I should have realized sooner that Scrum is no fluke, but a reliable framework. Some luck comes into play on any given project, but according to the Standish Group's studies, "The results for all projects show that agile projects have almost four times the success rate as waterfall projects, and waterfall projects have three times the failure rate as agile projects."[3] I'd worked on a mixture of projects, most of them traditional, but a few of them used Scrum. The Scrum projects had far better results. Despite the evidence, I continued to think it was just luck—like playing slot machines in Las Vegas. Sure, you might be ahead for a short time, but eventually the house wins. The house *always* wins. Little did I know that it was poker the Scrum people were playing, not slots. No poker player reaches the high-roller table in Vegas by just being lucky. There's a method to his apparent madness—strategies, ploys, and a systematized approach that allows the player to react quickly to every change and surprise.

As Albert Einstein said, "We cannot solve our problems with the same thinking we used when we created them." But people change for only one of two reasons: Either they are already very good and are always looking to improve, or they realize that if things don't change, they will die. We were lucky in that we were forced to try Scrum. You may not be so lucky—maybe your business is humming along, unimpeded by bureaucracy, unlikely to be challenged by a surprising new development, just a bunch of highly motivated workers delivering complex projects like stacks of hot pancakes. Then your decision will be more difficult to make, and you may miss out on learning the new framework that energized and empowered us, cut bureaucracy, fostered innovation, allowed us to react quickly to change and to deliver successfully and on time.

GOING FORWARD

I wanted this first chapter to show that I was no easy convert, because if you are reading it, you may well have your own doubts. My eyes have been opened, and while I still find the waterfall method useful in some situations, I do feel strongly that Scrum is the answer to many organizational problems.

In the pages that follow we will look more closely at the various aspects of Scrum: its values, the structure of its teams, and the role each member plays. How do scrum teams prioritize work for Sprints? How do they decide what constitutes a successful sprint? We will dive deeper into the terminology and approach in upcoming chapters. We'll look at Scrum's best practices and how to implement lightweight, values-based approaches into your particular organization.

---

3   The Standish Group, *CHAOS Report 2015*. Yarmouth, MA, 2015.

For now, I want to prepare you for this journey you've embarked on. Implementing Scrum can be frustrating, especially without a knowledgeable guide beside you, but it is completely doable, and even the stodgiest, most stubborn traditionalist (like me) can come around to a new way of thinking. What will serve you going forward are optimism, flexibility, and agility.

I could not see what awaited me past the Berlin Wall, nor how my traditional project management skills would fail me in Ecuador. I was (sometimes with difficulty) able to open my mind to the new worlds I stepped into, and to develop the flexibility and agility to succeed and even to expand the application of the framework. My colleagues and I found great pleasure in working together, thinking on our feet, resolving one issue after another as we pushed toward our goals. And I've been able to spread some of that joy as I helped take Scrum beyond software and into mainstream project planning in a variety of industries. Scrum liberates organizations to produce more value in less time, but that is not its only focus. It's not just a collection of tactics and techniques, but a system, a framework, and a culture. Done well, you will produce far more value faster, in an energetic, collaborative atmosphere that increases motivation and satisfaction for everyone involved. It also makes work more satisfying for all involved.

None of us knows which cards life will deal us next, but Scrum can give us the tools to be ready for the next surprise and to turn it to success.

CHAPTER TWO

Language of the Game

Business is a game, played for fantastic stakes, and you're in competition with experts. If you want to win, you have to learn to be a master of the game.

—Sidney Sheldon[4]

Because Scrum was first brought forward by software developers, much of the language sounds like it applies to software. This major challenge is why I believe many other industries have not readily embraced Agile and Scrum and therefore dismiss the opportunity to add tremendous value to their organization.

The terminology tends to be very technology-oriented. I'm working to change that impression. In a surprising number of cases, the real problem with using Scrum outside of these sectors is nothing more than a matter of language. For example, Scrum refers to Developers, but what if you don't develop software? What if your company drills for oil and gas instead? Believe it or not, there are many nontechy, nonsoftware projects that do very well with Scrum, as you will see.

WHERE SCRUM WORKS BEST

There are some Scrum practitioners who are as passionate and fanatical about Scrum as I was about traditional PMI project management. And while I have since "converted" after witnessing near-miraculous changes in several situations, I do not agree that it is always the best practice. (However, I will say it is most often the best approach.) I believe there are a couple of models that can help you and your organization determine if the Scrum framework is the best approach for you.

---

4   Johnnie L. Roberts, *The Big Book of Business Quotations: Over 1,400 of the Smartest Things Ever Said About Making Money* (New York, NY: Skyhorse Publishing, 2016).

David Snowden created the Cynefin framework (pronounced KUH-nev-in. Hey, it's a Welsh word). It is used to identify problem complexity and to aid organizations in finding solutions and making decisions. While the framework and its application are incredibly involved, I'll briefly overview the four systems within this sense-making framework.

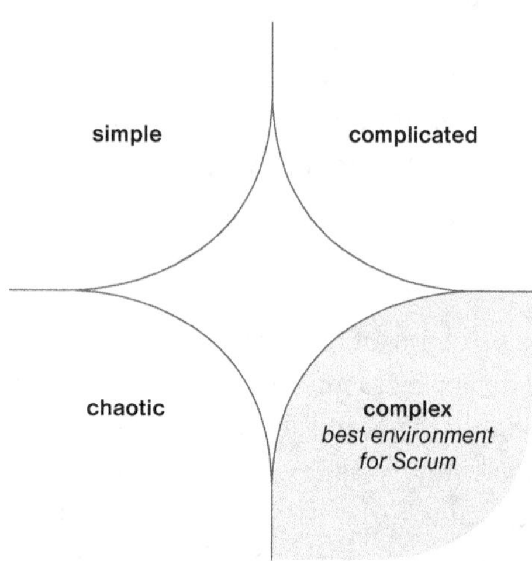

2.1. Cynefin Framework

As you can see in the above example, there are four systems: simple, complicated, complex, and chaotic. Snowden proposes that the decision-making framework you should use depends on the system your organization or project is in. If your project is as simple as painting your house, you exist in the simple system whose decision-making framework is sense, categorize, and respond. You *sense* that your home needs painting, you *categorize* the steps (surface prep, color and paint selection, masking, etc.), and then you *respond* by following the steps.

If only all organizations and projects were that simple. If you think you exist in the simple system quadrant, though, I would challenge you to reconsider. When all the factors are considered, few organizations exist here. You may look at your typical day and assume you're in a chaotic system. I doubt that, too. Though your workday may be hectic and stressful, it doesn't mean the entire system is in chaos.

For our purposes, Scrum works best in the complex system. It can work in a chaotic system as well (as I found with the Ecuadorian telecom). But first we should define what a complex system is.

Consider what might happen if you introduce a new species to an ecosystem. In that situation, cause and effect are rarely apparent and often are only obvious in hindsight. When variables are not known, rapid iteration is necessary to hypothesize and test different solutions. As a result, Snowden says the decision-making process for a complex system is probe, sense, and respond. This is exactly how Scrum works in Sprints and Increments.

As shown in the chart, complex products, projects, and organizations possess a great amount of uncertainty. Uncertainty exists about timing, issues, solutions, and outside changes like market demands, changes in technologies, client scope changes, and even economic or political disruption. For instance, plans to construct a five-mile long bridge should be halted if a flying car is created that runs on water instead of gas and costs only $100 to manufacture.

Scrum's usefulness is not limited to complex systems only. My first experience with Scrum (as a skeptic) was a pretty straightforward project: developing the backend web platform for a car-sharing startup. It wasn't necessarily simple, but it wasn't a multimillion-dollar project with thousands of moving parts either.

2.2. Uncertainty vs. Cost of Change

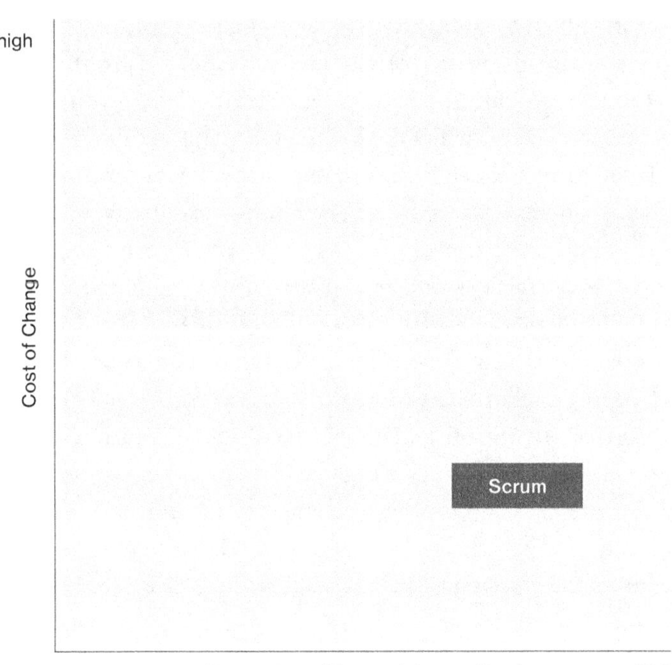

2.3. Uncertainty vs. Cost of Change in a Project

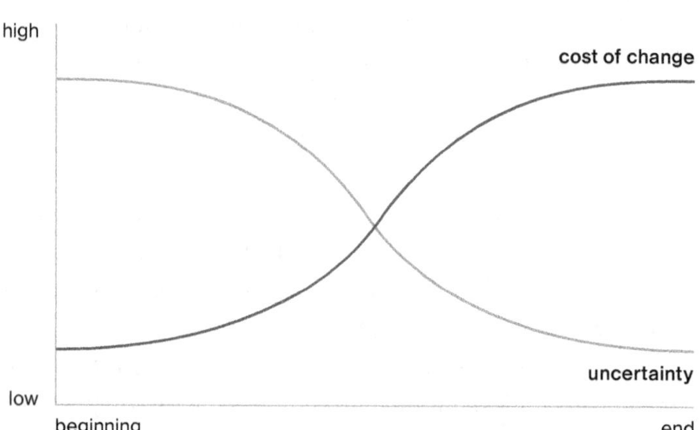

The above graphic represents the stages of many projects and product lifecycles. If you were building a mansion, for example, early in the project you might be collecting many different ideas, designs, and concepts on Pinterest or in an old-fashioned binder. Next, you could contract an architect to work up some preliminary sketches. You would then pick the one you like, commission full blueprints, hire the general contractor you've selected, and, assuming you already have a piece of land, you'd break ground. When would it be best to change your mind about some detail—before you even set foot in the architect's office, or when the last coat of paint is drying? Of course, the answer is the former. Deciding at the end that you want the main archway to face east instead of south would be exorbitantly expensive.

In the beginning, uncertainty was high—you weren't sure exactly what you wanted. Maybe a sleek modern twist on a Mediterranean style or possibly a gothic revival, complete with a tower. Over time, as the work is done, the uncertainty lessens—you just need to pick out moldings and hardware—and the relative cost of change rises.

Because of short Sprints and built-in feedback/adaptations, Scrum is ideal for projects where uncertainty is high and where there is a relative low cost of change. For the mansion project, you could have multiple digital models created to "walk through" the various designs at relatively low cost. In major civil projects like subterranean tunnels, computer models can be constructed and multiple scenarios tested at comparatively cheaper rates than after one speck of dirt is disturbed. Scrum is practically designed for such agile environments.

But why is Scrum best suited for complex systems and high-uncertainty, relatively low-cost scenarios? As Snowden has shown in the Cynefin framework, the best way to move forward in a complex environment is to probe, sense, and respond. This is precisely how you accomplish work on a product or project in Scrum. You probe (hypothesize a solution); sense (perform work and complete a minimum viable product based on the hypothesis); and respond (test, deliver the product, and adjust based on feedback). Either it worked and you get to move to your next part (Sprint), or it didn't work and you must iterate based upon the feedback. We will cover this in more detail when we outline the full Sprint process and its implementation. For now, it's time to get acquainted—or reacquainted—with the language of the game.

GAME TERMINOLOGY

Perhaps you are well acquainted with the terms already. Maybe you've studied *The Scrum Guide* and possibly have read numerous other sources. However, some terms have developed outside the core practices of true Scrum. I want to clarify not only which terms are essential to good Scrum but also demystify some of the terms by adding plain language. When learning any language, a word is just a word until you have something to compare it to. I could repeat *mesa* to you a thousand times, and that will not further your understanding. But if I point to the table while saying it, you have complete understanding.

Throughout this book, we use analogies such as chess and poker to make it easier to understand some of the concepts. These analogies may not always reflect a perfectly correct literal comparison.

I do not intend to invent new terminology and add to the confusing soup some so-called Scrum experts are creating. Instead, I want to review the terms as simply as possible and quickly highlight how these might relate to other industries.

If we are playing poker here, we still need baseline procedures. Players can't just draw cards, look at other players' hands, take their bets back, or play out of turn. Such a game would be chaos.

THREE PILLARS

Scrum is based on three pillars: transparency, inspection, and adaptation. An organization lives or dies by how well these are implemented. That may sound a bit grandiose, but as a Scrum consultant, I've worked with dozens of organizations who desired to implement Scrum. Without the right sponsor in place (more on sponsors later), many business units attempted to create a hybrid system, which is like trying to practice two religions simultaneously. Anyone who tries to implement Scrum without honoring these three core principles will almost certainly have great difficulty and will possibly fail.

1. **Transparency.** You may be familiar with this term in everyday use, such as the media talking about transparency within political organizations, and it has the same meaning here. Transparency in Scrum means that everybody can see what work is being done. Many organizations have chosen to place the Sprint Backlog on a board in a space where everyone can see it. In addition, everyone must agree on terminology and the definition of "done," which we will cover later. But the best part is when your work is done, you show your result and this Increment is provided to the client for inspection. In other words, transparency assures that the entire team sees what's happening and where there's progress, and they can immediately see any impediments to the work that need to be solved.

2. **Inspection.** Thanks to transparency, everything is visible and can be inspected by team members, the Product Owner, the client, or any stakeholder. This might be best explained from the perspective of an artist commissioned to paint a landscape of the Rhine. In this example, though, the patron who commissioned the painting is brought in every so often to make sure each part of the painting is to his liking. The client makes sure all is as he hoped—the lighting, shades, the shimmer of the sunlight in the boat wake. In Scrum, any stakeholder can inspect the work. They look at their own work or the work of others to see if it contributes to the Sprint's objectives. Like the artist, they are ensuring that what's being captured reflects the desired end.

3. **Adaptation.** Adaptation means ongoing assessment and recalibration. Going back to the complex system's decision-making process of probe, sense, and respond, adapting is the response. During the Ecuadorian telecom project, developers were having issues with a third party's software. They'd submit support tickets and then work on something unrelated. We didn't know how much this impacted the project until the switch to Scrum. With transparency, the issues were listed on the Scrum board for everyone's inspection. Only then were we able to adapt and seek a work-around to the problem of unresolved software issues. Adaptation provides continuous improvement not

only in the product but in the team's process. This ties everything together. When everyone is transparent with their work, struggles, and impediments, an inspection by all parties helps the team learn quickly and adapt based upon the results of inspection.

These principles support each other. If one falls, they all do. Some think these principles apply to just the product, while others apply them to the process. But the pillars are critical for both the product *and* the process in Scrum.

For example, I was consulting with a Colombian company. A topic came up during a Sprint Retrospective (more on that later in this chapter). There were issues getting things completed from the IT department. The department ran on a traditional model and wanted all requests made in advance of the next fiscal year so budget requests could be made. Because both the product and the process were *transparent*, every member was able to *inspect* how this situation affected their Sprint, and they were able to *adapt*. In the end, they hired their own developers, so they were no longer dependent on the IT department. Because of these principles, the problem was solved quickly, and they were able to continue their Sprints unimpeded.

SCRUM VALUES

Values define what you prioritize as an organization and how you respond to challenges. Often, an organization goes to great pains to create a list of values by bringing in consultants, going away on retreats, and locking themselves into boardrooms for marathon planning sessions. In the end, they present a list of values to their employees and stakeholders as if the act of writing values alone transforms their organization. Of course, the values only work as they are expressed in action. For example, a company could say they value quality above all else. But when they choose to ship an order of items they know fall outside their quality specifications so they can meet month-end projections, they are only fooling themselves.

In Scrum there are five values: commitment, courage, focus, openness, and respect. I will outline the values below, and we will later go into more detail with how these are practiced within the Scrum framework as we explore implementation.

- ▸ **Commitment.** The first and perhaps most essential value is commitment to the Product Goal created by the Product Owner and to the objective of each Sprint.

- **Courage.** With any worthwhile work, courage comes into play. It takes courage to do the right thing—not to do the easy thing, but the *right* thing.
- **Focus.** There's an old expression attributed to Confucius that says a man that chases two rabbits catches neither. However, if the man chases one, his odds of a good dinner are increased. Which would you rather have at the end of a year—eighty projects at 5 percent completion each, or twenty projects 100 percent completed? That's the power of focus.
- **Openness.** The meaning of openness is that you must be open to address difficult things. If you see a problem, you must mention it. You can't keep quiet and expect the problem to go away. It also means being open to receiving feedback.
- **Respect.** This is a value that is fairly self-evident. If a team can't foster a level of respect for all involved, I don't know how it could work. This doesn't mean you have to like or be friends with your teammates, but respect must be cultivated if the team is going to accomplish anything of value.

2.4. How the Pillars Support the Values

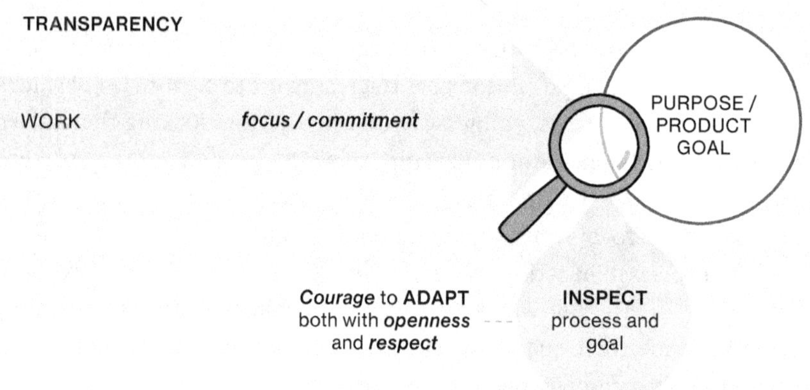

At the heart of the pillars and values is the need to create an environment of psychological safety. First coined by Amy Edmondson of Harvard University,[5] psychological safety is defined as "a shared belief that the team is safe for

---

5   Edmondson, "Psychological Safety and Learning Behavior in Work Teams."

interpersonal risk taking."[6] Though psychological safety isn't a value or part of the Scrum framework, I feel it is just as important as any of the other five values. In fact, without creating an environment of psychological safety—of the ability to take risks within reason—the Scrum team can only be impeded. Imagine working in an organization where you feel free to take chances for the good of the team, explore new possibilities, or freely question accepted assumptions without fearing for your place within that organization. Does it sound like a dream? It doesn't have to be. I'll be touching on this term in future chapters and offer strategies for creating a space of psychological safety as you implement Scrum.

SCRUM TERMS AND DEFINITIONS

You can't play a game when you don't know what things are called. Imagine playing poker and referring to the joker as "laughing man," the king of spades as "stabby crowned guy," or a royal flush as "series of five." Maybe you could get the game done, but it would be awkward and confusing, especially when experienced outside players join your table.

Though you probably have a working knowledge of the Scrum language, I'd like to outline the terms again here just in case. Plus, I want to add a little nuance that might be helpful in understanding how these terms work in implementation.

There are three parts of Scrum: Scrum Roles, Scrum Artifacts, and Scrum Events. I've broken them up below. Later, we will discuss how they interact.

Scrum Roles: The Players

You can't have a game without players. After all, you need to know who is going to deal the cards. Each role is critical to the success of Scrum. These are the roles:

- ▸ **Product Owner.** The Product Owner is the visionary for the team— think of someone like Steve Jobs or Jeff Bezos. This person knows the industry, the client, and the product, and is ideally selected from within the organization. The Product Owner doesn't need to be a Scrum expert, but she does need to have basic knowledge. As we'll

---

6   Edmondson, "Building a Psychologically Safe Workplace," May 4, 2014, TED video, 11:26, https://www.youtube.com/watch?v=LhoLuui9gX8.

learn later in more detail, the Product Owner gets input from all the stakeholders regarding the Product Goal and then decides what to say yes to and, more importantly, what to say no to. In the end, they determine and have a passion for the Product Goal.

▸ **Scrum Master.** This role makes me think of Jedi masters in the *Star Wars* movies. No mind tricks here, though. (Sadly, there are no lightsabers either.) A Scrum Master is an expert who coaches the team. The Scrum Master has advanced Scrum knowledge, has adopted the Scrum values, and applies his experience to every project. His job is to ensure the team is working efficiently and following the framework. The Scrum Master is not a taskmaster, but a leader who serves and works to minimize and solve impediments, and ensures the team has everything they need so they can focus on what they do best.

▸ **Developers.** This term sounds inherently like it's describing those who work in software development, but they can develop any type of product in any industry for which they have expertise. These are the team of three to nine people who will be doing the work, creating the Sprint Plan as well as the Sprint Backlog, all while supporting the agreed Definition of Done. If you're used to thinking of workers in various departments, the Developers are a team made up of one or two people from each department so that the team can complete the product from start to finish. They are consummate professionals who are accountable to each other.

Scrum Artifacts: The Card Deck

The term artifact seems strange, as it evokes images of ancient objects unearthed at an archeological dig site. The word literally means something made by humans. And since we're at work making products that add value, the term works. Here are the three artifacts of Scrum:

▸ **Product Backlog.** *The Scrum Guide* states, "The Product Backlog is an emergent, ordered list of what is needed to improve the product."[7] Think of it as a task or to-do list (though it's so much more) for the

---

7 Ken Schwaber and Jeff Sutherland, *The Scrum Guide* (ScrumGuides.org, 2020), https://www.scrumguides.org/scrum-guide.html.

project. It is maintained by the Product Owner and visible to all stakeholders, including the client.

The commitment of the Product Backlog is the Product Goal: the aspired end state of the product that serves as the team's target.

▸ **Sprint Backlog.** The Sprint Backlog is a list of product backlog items selected for a Sprint and usually broken down into more details. The client doesn't usually see this backlog; it's an internal tool very similar to the Product Backlog. Let's pretend it's as simple as an automotive mechanic doing work. You, the client, might just want a tune-up. That's one item. For the mechanic's team, this item gets broken down further and includes tasks such as replacing sparkplug wires, checking engine timing, running a diagnostic, changing the sparkplugs, and making sure the plugs are gapped to specifications, among other things. For a real-world example, I can use my company. A client may have "Train Scrum Master" on the Product Backlog. On the Sprint Backlog, this is broken down into smaller steps: "send client invitation," "travel to location," and "set up training," among other items leading up to "done."

The Sprint Backlog's commitment is to achieve the Sprint Goal— the Sprints singular desired outcome. By having this singular focus, it encourages the team to work together instead of on individual pursuits.

▸ **Increment.** An increment is the total amount of work—Product Backlog Items (PBIs) on the Product Backlog—completed during a Sprint and includes the value of all the work completed from previous Sprints. In other words, the increment grows as you work through the Product Backlog as each release should work with the ones that preceded it. A common misconception is that if you completed three Sprints, then you have three increments. This is not true. You still have one increment that has grown larger as each Sprint added more value. This concept was a little difficult for me to grasp in the beginning. As we explore the implementation side, things will get clearer.

The Increment's commitment is to meet the Definition of Done, which is when the work meets the quality standards. In short, the Definition of Done is met when a Product Backlog item can be delivered to the end user.

Scrum Events: The Game

Scrum events are exactly how they sound. Poker involves a game time, dealing, betting, etc. Scrum has events for the start, duration, and end. And while I'd hate to add another metaphor, events can be compared to military missions. If the entire Product Backlog is the war, each Scrum Event is a piece of that war. Except this war is defined by periods of time and not tactical objectives.

- **Sprint.** Whatever the product or project, the Sprint is the longest amount of time in which the team should accomplish a releasable product. A Sprint is the mission. As mentioned above, the main difference between a mission and a Sprint is that the Sprint is defined by a time period—think of it as a time box—not a tactical goal. That period can be a maximum of one month, but the shorter the better. Most teams shoot for a one- or two-week period.[8] Work is then completed on the predetermined requirements from the Product Backlog.

- **Sprint Planning.** Going back to the military analogy, Sprint Planning occurs at the beginning of the Sprint and is a bit like mission planning. First, the entire team determines what is possible to accomplish within the time period based upon the Product Backlog, and then the Developers determine how the work will be done. You may want to think of this planning event as a meeting. Please don't. When most people think of meetings, they have images of boring marathon sessions, where much is discussed and little is accomplished. Most meetings waste time. We aim to accomplish the exact opposite in Scrum. So, get rid of the office swear jar and make a "meeting" jar with the goal to never utter that accursed word again.

- **Daily Scrum.** This daily team get-together is crucial to the success of Scrum, especially during the initial implementation of Scrum. It functions as a synchronizing event, ensuring that the whole team is unified in their work toward the goal. The team's Daily Scrum should be at the same time every day and last no more than fifteen minutes.

---

8 Scrum Alliance, *State of Scrum 2017- 2018: Scaling and Agile Transformation*, 2017, https://www.scrumalliance.org/ScrumRedesignDEVSite/media/ScrumAllianceMedia/Files%20and%20PDFs/State%20of%20Scrum/2017-SoSR-Final-Version-(Pages).pdf

One more thing: everyone who is able to is encouraged to stand—sitting only invites wasting time on nonessential tangent issues.

- **Sprint Review.** This is the general product review in which a full discussion of the product takes place. In the Sprint Review, the people who have done the work show the product to the users and receive feedback. We discuss the current product state, end-user risk, opportunities, and problems, and then forecast the completion date.

- **Sprint Retrospective.** Once the Sprint has concluded, this session serves to assess the effectiveness of the process and the team. Relating back to our military analogy, we might describe it as a debriefing like the military's after-action review (AAR—the military loves their acronyms). This review is not about the product; it's about the process and how the team worked together. It's a time for team feedback, examining what worked and what needs improvement.

These are the core terms of Scrum. If this is your first time seeing them, you may want to bookmark these pages for future reference because these terms will be used frequently as we go forward.

I'd like to take a moment right now and reiterate that while these terms seem like they're exclusive to the software industry, they're not. While it's true that Agile and Scrum both found early adoption within the software industry—the creators were both involved in IT—I have found Scrum to work amazingly well in a broad array of industries. Because many hardware industries had this limiting belief about Scrum, Joe Justice and I wrote "The Scrum in Hardware Guide."[9]

Now that you have a basic grasp of the terms, next we will be looking at where your organization is now and how that can transition into a Scrum implementation. This will happen first with a pilot team (ideally) and then can grow until your whole organization is running on the Scrum framework. This includes the newly defined Scrum at Scale (Scrum@Scale or S@S) implementation. Up until very recently, large organizations were using Scrum across many teams by creating a hybrid monster—part Scrum, part traditional bureaucracy. This was partly due to a disconnect between relatively small Scrum teams and massive departments that run the company's

---

9   Fabian Schwartz and Joe Justice, "The Scrum in Hardware Guide," Scrum Inc., 2017, https://www.scruminc.com/scrum-in-hardware-guide/.

day-to-day operations. S@S allows you to run your entire organization on the Scrum framework in a more organized, integrated way. As the name suggests, it allows your organization to scale easily as it grows.

But enough talk. You now have a better idea of the principles, values, players, and events needed to effectively implement Scrum. Now it's time to start the game.

CHAPTER THREE

Setting Up the Game— The System

The ability to adapt is the truest test of a person's intelligence.

—Thomas Faranda[10]

You are ready to dive into your shiny, new poker set. The chessboard has been gathering dust, and it's time to put it away. That doesn't mean you'll never play chess again. It certainly has a place, but it's just that you're ready to play a faster-paced game with a little more fun. (For the record, I thoroughly enjoy both games.)

But where do you start? Do you totally renovate your game room down to the studs and start over by building a poker room? You could, but that would be long, difficult, and costly. All you need is a place to play, a table to play on, and all the implements necessary to have a successful game night. Box up the chess pieces, clean the table, and let's get started.

First you need a host. Maybe you played chess at your friend Tim's place, and he's willing to try poker. He's read about the game, he is interested, he's not sure he'll like it, but he's willing to do whatever's necessary to have a good time at his house.

Maybe you played chess at his dining room table. But on Friday nights, the night your buddies are available, his kids have movie night in the adjoining living room. You will need a separate space, a table, cards, chips, snacks, someone who knows how to play (ideally, a well-versed player), and a rule book for any disputes. And when you sit down to play, you'll have to change your mindset. No longer will you see all the variables and play out a dozen

---

10 Thomas W. Faranda, *Uncommon Sense: Leadership Principles to Grow Your Business Profitably* (Paradise Valley, AZ: Knowledge Press, 1991), 31.

possibilities in your head before making your move. You now have to make calculated risks and adapt as you go. What cards are still available in the deck that might improve your hand? Is your friend bluffing? Based on the evidence, should you check, fold, or call? It's a new game, and, if you're flexible, it can be an extraordinarily successful game night.

However, if you set up the game badly, ignore the rules, or establish the conditions poorly, game night could be a complete failure. You could end up disagreeing, losing, or spending more time debating the rules rather than playing. Worst-case scenario: you might throw down the cards in frustration and put an end to game night altogether.

When implementing Scrum, it's the same. You need a space—a protected bubble from the rest of the organization within which to operate. You'll need to set up the team, establish a method to create transparency, determine the roles, and determine what you're playing for.

Good Scrum—when it is done well—is everything you've heard it is: fast, motivating, and fun. Bad Scrum, on the other hand, is an unsightly beast—a freak of nature that is not long for this world.

BAD SCRUM

If you've been in the business world for any length of time, you've probably seen good ideas and initiatives fall flat. The larger and more complicated the organization, the more likely this situation happens. Early in your career, you may have bought in to new ideas and been excited by change. Around the third or twentieth initiative management concocted, cynicism set in. But why don't these changes stick? Is it a lack of desire or resources, incompetence, a toxic culture, or laziness?

It might be a combination of all these factors or none at all.

If you're reading this book because your organization is going to switch to the Scrum framework, you might rightly have a hint of this healthy cynicism. You're quite justified to question everything and not accept anything on blind faith.

In all the organizations I've trained, I find it easier to train those who have volunteered to be a part of the Scrum pilot team. People who want change tend to be curious and eager to learn and improve their work. They bring a natural enthusiasm that makes everything go smoother. But sometimes no one volunteers for the Scrum team. Sometimes management selects team members who may not have any interest. I've encountered my fair share of arm-folded skeptics. When I meet them, I only ask that they keep an open mind, give it a chance, and let the results speak for themselves.

But maybe you do have experience with Scrum, or more accurately, you *think* you have experience with Scrum. Maybe you were at a company where they had Daily Scrums, scheduled Sprints, and even had a Product Backlog. Was it really Scrum, though? In my experience, the worst enemy of good Scrum is bad Scrum. For instance, when Scrum is implemented half-heartedly, using all the terms and a few of the techniques but none of the values or commitment implementation requires, it backfires, leaving those involved with an embittered view of Scrum.

There are two types of bad Scrum:

1. Frankenscrum: an attempt to implement Scrum while still using a somewhat traditional framework—a hideous monster that does nothing useful
2. Stunted Scrum: when full implementation is stymied by an impotent Scrum Sponsor (more on that in just a bit)

A case of Frankenscrum usually comes about when a well-intentioned middle manager, the head of a department or unit, gets excited about Scrum. With those good intentions, he reads up on the philosophies, terminology, and roles. Even though a Scrum team is nothing like a single department, the manager announces his department will now do Scrum. The project manager is renamed Scrum Master, a technical supervisor is called the Product Owner. They rename their work breakdown structure a Product Backlog, and begin to have daily meetings, calling them Daily Scrums.

The manager believes he can take items from a work breakdown structure and use those items in your Sprint Backlog. But the very definition of Sprint requires that you have something done at the end, an item that has value. In this situation, all you have accomplished is a few small parts of a larger whole. Without adding value, you can't receive feedback. Without feedback, you can't adapt.

Has anything really changed in this situation? Sure, the manager and team are using the lingo and have the outward appearance of Scrum, but if they aren't focused on accomplishing set work within a time period, if the team can't complete that work from start to finish and end with something of value, and if any team member is on more than one project, then it isn't Scrum. If you do what they've done, you've put a saddle on a cow and called it a horse. And just like that lumbering cow, your framework won't run—it's not *agile* enough. (See what I did there?)

I've encountered a fair number of employees who have ridden this stubborn creature and grown frustrated. Unfortunately, their frustration is misdirected at Scrum, an animal that is still not familiar to them.

More insidious than this form of Frankenscrum, however, is when the same middle manager, with even better intentions, tries to do things right but lacks enough power to make things happen. This form of bad Scrum implodes.

BIG OG: A STUDY OF STUNTED SCRUM

One example of Stunted Scrum occurred at a large oil and gas company whose name you would immediately recognize. For our purposes, let's just call them Big OG because I hate paying for lawyers.

I believe we learn through mistakes. I learned a lot from Big OG. My team was hired by the head of the IT department. They wanted to build applications for internal use faster and knew Scrum would help them. We started as we usually did by training the team. Then we started coaching them as they got started. For transparency, we claimed a big whiteboard on a wall where the whole team could see it. They created columns for Sprint items to do, items being done, and items that were completed. A fourth column was created to list any issues that arose. There are always issues implementing Scrum. As mentioned, Scrum has a built-in process for handling these implementation issues, which we call impediments.

The IT department wanted to build internal applications—their product. Yet, team members were involved in more than just this product. Their involvement in more than one product was an impediment to the implementation of Scrum. Their focus was divided between the Sprint and other projects. This division of focus makes Sprint Planning extraordinarily difficult. We also encountered issues with procurement. The department needed some equipment to complete the work, but procurement continued to be a roadblock. Progress was slowing to a crawl.

The impediment list on the wall was growing. Work was not being done. The Scrum Master whom I was coaching handled many of the impediments, but he could only do so much by himself. The IT head who was brought in attempted to handle the interdepartmental impediments. He immediately ran into a problem: the IT department was attempting to use Scrum in isolation. This is certainly doable with the right leader involved, as you will see. Unfortunately, Big OG's IT head was not the right leader.

The IT head attended upper management meetings where he pled his case. He requested an expedited procurement process. He asked that team members with divided focus be removed from the other projects. It didn't work. Upper management basically said, "But the way we've been doing things works. Why should we change for your department?"

The impediments remained, and I watched the impediment list grow. The IT head told me, "We just have to adjust and adapt Scrum to how we work here."

In the end, the whole idea died. Why? Because the idea of Scrum is that you deliver value faster and handle changes better. With the IT head unable to address the impediments, we then had a team that was using Scrum techniques but were not seeing results—there was no added value. Hundreds of impediments stacked up until the entire team became frustrated and demotivated, and, after a while, started blaming Scrum for the failures.

I said that Stunted Scrum is more insidious. Big OG's IT department tried to use Scrum. They brought in an expert (me) and were excited to use the framework they had heard so much about. From their perspective, Scrum had failed—except Scrum hadn't failed. What failed was the strength of the sponsor to make necessary changes. This experience taught me that, to have a successful implementation, you need an ally in the company who has the *power* to remove impediments. The IT head, well-intentioned as he was, had no positional or even influential power to overcome major impediments. All the good intentions in the world won't get you to where you want to go.

Imagine if you were playing poker with your friends. On the table were little brick-walled cubicles that prevented you from seeing other players or the community cards. You might be okay playing for a hand or two, but eventually the walls would take all the fun out of the game; you'd grow frustrated at these impediments. That's what implementing Scrum was like at Big OG. Walls were in place—the structure of the bureaucracy—that the IT head could not remove. They tried playing in spite of the walls, but eventually the game stopped.

There's a better way.

A STRONG SCRUM SPONSOR

How might have Big OG implemented Scrum successfully?

With the full support of a strong sponsor.

Impediments like procurement procedures and team members on multiple projects are why having a strong Scrum sponsor is invaluable. A Scrum Sponsor is not the same as the Scrum Master, whose function is to coach and aid the team. The Scrum Master can handle many issues within the team.

But when it comes to major items involving other departments or divisions, a Scrum Sponsor is needed to step in and address these impediments from a higher level.

In traditional project parlance, a sponsor is in many ways like a project champion—someone within the company who either sees the value in what you're attempting to accomplish or, better still, is the reason the project was created in the first place. Unlike a traditional champion, though, a Scrum sponsor is not providing analysis or updates to other teams. Where they do function like a champion is by supplying access to resources and removing obstacles from within the organization. While a sponsor is not listed as an official role in *The Scrum Guide* (they are not essential for the practice of Scrum), a strong sponsor is almost necessary for successful implementation.

It's usually the sponsor who hires me and my team to provide training and to consult as they migrate away from traditional frameworks into the Scrum framework. The IT head at Big OG was a sponsor—he just wasn't a strong sponsor.

So what's the difference between a sponsor and a "strong" sponsor?

The IT head did not have the power to change procurement procedures to better meet his team's new needs under Scrum, nor was he able to influence those with the power. When he attended meetings, he lacked the skill to persuade his vice president and others to support his Scrum initiative. Either unable or unwilling to fight for what he needed, he resigned to trying to work Scrum into their other systems. Scrum can be implemented within an existing culture. It should be done with care and inside a protective bubble that isolates the team from the rest of the organization's bureaucracy. Then, full implementation is achievable. Scrum cannot exist as a hybrid inside a team.

A great example of a strong sponsor comes from my time working with a Colombian telecom company we'll call GoTelecom. They hired a new vice president specifically to help them with their digital transformation—moving their physical processes (bill payments, account management, service requests, etc.) to a digital platform. The project had languished for two years without producing any usable results. Here's the bonus: the newly hired vice president was already familiar with the superiority of Scrum for these complex situations. Within months of taking over the digital transformation project, he helped create a new division, hand-selected a number of staff he felt would be great additions to an Agile framework, and brought in me and my team to start training and coaching.

What made this VP a strong sponsor is that he created a separate division removed from the traditional framework. However, even when separated into a protective bubble, no Scrum implementation happens smoothly. If we conclude Scrum training and certification on a Friday afternoon, the trainees have a good grasp of the basics of Scrum in an ideal environment. When Monday morning arrives, reality sets in. To say nothing goes smoothly is like saying the Grand Canyon is a little valley. The real-world application of Scrum is the most challenging (and the most rewarding) part of my job.

At GoTelecom, we worked with the division, trained their team, and implemented Scrum the same as we did with Big OG. As is typical, we soon encountered impediments. One of the most memorable is that the new division needed some software written by the IT department. But that department was one of the more bureaucratic, traditional departments within the company. They wanted our division to make the request in the budget for next year's approval. After that, it might take a year to write the code. In other words, the software needed to help accomplish the digital transformation might take up to two years to develop. Our sponsor at Big OG would have pleaded his case to his bosses. The VP at GoTelecom, however, overcame this impediment by hiring his own IT people. Problem solved!

Now, I don't live in a dream world. I know firsthand that no division or department is fully independent from the rest of the company. Unless we're implementing Scrum within an entire organization and our sponsor is either the CEO or COO, there will always be some interdepartmental dependency. A strong sponsor, however, can usually eliminate a good percentage of the impediments. In contrast, a weaker one, like our sponsor at Big OG, is typically the head of his "silo" with far more dependency. Lesson learned. It's better to have a strong sponsor from the start.

SCRUM IMPLEMENTATION STRATEGIES

Let's go back to the card table. Your friend who knows poker (your Poker Master) has explained the initial rules, procedures, and the basic hands. Maybe he brought a cheat sheet with pictures of the various hands and which ones are stronger.

Using this metaphor, the sponsor is only the person whose house you are playing in. They unlocked the door, set up a table, and removed any impediments the team couldn't (the kids screaming at their video games, for instance). The sponsor doesn't need to play. Maybe he enjoys watching, or he's busy with other things but wanted to help his friends.

Of course, the right sponsor is only part of the equation to having a successful game. At what point do you begin playing? How do you start playing?

There are three implementation strategies:

1. Top-down—when a chief executive forces the entire company to switch to Scrum
2. Bottom-up—when a team with latitude experiments with a pilot Scrum program at a lower level, allowing the program to spread
3. Mixed—a combination of top-down and bottom up where a strong sponsor creates a pilot team

We will discuss each of these implementation strategies, including their advantages and disadvantages.

The Top-Down Strategy

You've been in business for a number of years, you're well established, and you're the CEO or COO or other chief executive, able to make company-wide changes. While you certainly have the power to make new frameworks like Scrum happen, as with all changes, this approach is not without its inherent challenges.

You are your own sponsor with all the power you need. But power alone does not move people to action. When anything is *forced* into an organization by upper management, the level of cynicism and skepticism escalates more than if the workforce had ownership in the decision. In short, there is resistance to the idea among those who will have to implement it. In this case, Scrum can appear as another edict from the "throne," and water-cooler conversation centers around complaints about change, when things were "fine" as they were.

The good news is that with strong, steady leadership, working with those who are willing to learn and reassigning or letting go those who aren't, an organization can transition into normalcy with the top-down approach. Time eventually wins and changes that were once complained about are seen as the improvements they really are. And eventually, Scrum becomes *the way we do things around here.*

The other trick regarding this top-down approach, assuming your company is larger than ten employees, is the scaling of Scrum. We will go into detail about how to implement Scrum@Scale in larger organizations in chapter 11.

The Bottom-Up Strategy

This strategy is fairly self-explanatory, but let's go into a little more detail. With bottom-up, we're not talking about an intern trying to convince her department to use Scrum—that might be too *bottom*. True bottom-up implementation resembles Big OG's attempt: a low-level manager or head chooses to experiment with Scrum in a pilot team.

With this strategy, a pilot team is created in isolation, protected from the rest of the organization. They focus on one "project" or product to bring it from concept to full completion.

This strategy can and does work, but not without great difficulties. It takes much longer to fully implement Scrum when compared to the other strategies, and you will have difficultly removing impediments as Big OG's IT head did. If this is the strategy you are forced to use due to the corporate environment or other factors, it behooves you to either have strong influence within executive levels or to partner with an ally who does.

What's most interesting about bottom-up is that, if it survives the long and slow implementation process, Scrum starts to spread. Once one division or pilot team produces far more value in shorter periods, other managers take notice. Research shows that when around 25 percent of a society or organization adopts a belief, the rest of the organization could be tipped to the belief of the minority.[11] Other studies have suggested that this minority tipping point could be as low as 10 percent.[12] What this means is that when around 25 percent of an organization adopts Scrum, the balance tips in favor of Scrum. Soon the entire company is running on the Scrum framework.

The Mixed Strategy

Mixed implementation is a combination of both top-down and bottom-up strategies. This is the next best option to being a startup that begins from scratch (which is truly ideal but extraordinarily rare). Mixed strategy leads to getting faster engagement and results with fewer impediments. But what does this strategy look like?

In the GoTelecom case, they created value through releases and functionalities while they continued to add new functionalities and releases to the Product Backlog.

As we saw in GoTelecom, the mixed strategy also requires a strong sponsor

---

11   Damon Centola, Joshua Becker, Devon Brackbill, and Andrea Baronchelli, "Experimental Evidence for Tipping Points in Social Convention," *Science* 360, no. 6393 (June 2018), pp. 1116–19, https://science.sciencemag.org/content/360/6393/1116.full.

12   "Minority Rules: Scientists Discover Tipping Point for the Spread of Ideas," *Rensselaer*, July 25, 2011, https://news.rpi.edu/luwakkey/2902.

to remove impediments. An important thing the vice president did for his Scrum team was to protect them from the rest of the company. Within the Agile community, there's a saying—referred to as the "cuckoo effect"—that claims, "Any foreign innovation in a corporation will stimulate the corporate immune system to create antibodies that destroy it." The vice president had solicited some great talent, even some open-minded managers from the PMO who were willing to see what Scrum could do. Many departments were eager to borrow people and resources or outright attack what they were attempting to do. But the vice president was steadfast and shielded his transformation team from the arrows of the corporate bureaucracy.

CHANGING FROM CHESS TO POKER

You and your friends are now sitting around the card table. The chess set has been put away. Only one friend has played poker before; the rest of you haven't played any other card game beyond gin rummy or Go Fish. In fact, the only game you have played together until now was chess, with all its strategy, predictions, and logic.

By its very nature, poker is quite different from most card games and completely different from chess. Learning a new game can be intimidating. You don't want to make mistakes or look foolish. You want to have fun and enjoy yourself. You've enjoyed other types of games, but how do you know if you will enjoy poker?

Simple. You probably know what a deck of cards looks like, the meaning of suits and face cards, and that some cards have more value. From chess you've learned tactics and strategy, if you're any good, and a little bit of gamesmanship. Yes, poker is different from these other games, but there are learned skills and concepts that fit right in.

It's the same with Scrum. It might seem very different at first, but all you need to do is change your viewpoint and mindset a little. Maybe *change* is too strong a word. Sometimes all it takes is a shift.

Yet, whether you are playing a game or in business, change—or a shift, if you will—is inescapable. We either control the change, or it just happens. Sometimes we want to change certain things in our lives without changing our behaviors. We want to lose weight and get stronger without eating healthy food and exercising. We want to get out of debt without changing any of our spending habits. We want our organizations to provide more value and to do it faster while doing the same things we've always done.

However, when we don't eat healthy, exercise, budget, and adjust, we will still change—just not in the direction we wanted. Change happens automatically, especially when we're trying to keep everything the same, and in that case, it's never the change we wanted.

Systems Thinking

I feel remiss if we examined systems and didn't discuss systems thinking. As Peter Senge discusses in his landmark book *The Fifth Discipline*,[13] a learning organization understands that no change occurs in isolation. Changes have a ripple effect. All systems within an organization interrelate: finance, sales and marketing, operations, human resources, and the hundreds to thousands of interpersonal relationships within and without the organization.

Most managers understand the difference between problems and symptoms of problems—how a sharp increase in defects might have multiple root causes. However, I challenge you to look deeper. Understanding how complex and interrelated cause and effect are is important for a successful Scrum implementation. Sometimes solutions fix a team or department's issue but wreak havoc within the whole organization. A highly effective team implementing Scrum and existing within an organization comprised of mostly traditional teams will quickly overload the other departments. This points to a structural problem. If you want to change the culture, you have to change the system; and if you want to change the system, you have to change the structure.

If you have ever lived near a major city, you're familiar with the headache of rush hour traffic. Civil engineers must be careful in tackling this issue. There are numerous causes for traffic snarls, and each proposed solution could have disastrous consequences on other systems. Low unemployment rates add commuters, lack of or expensive public transportation reduces its use, multiple construction projects cause delays, school schedules and seasonal changes affect traffic times, etc. Often, a solution such as widening on- and off-ramps only causes gridlock in the communities those ramps serve. The engineers implementing such a solution don't solve the problem; they move it further downstream.

Even on small, Scrum-sized teams, lack of systems thinking can create issues. When I was in Boston, I used to watch collegiate sculling teams practice on the Charles River. These teams must row consistently with minimal wasted effort in order to move as quickly as possible. Imagine if they could recruit a superhuman rower to their team—someone who had ten times the

---

13 Peter M. Senge, *The Fifth Discipline: The Art & Practice of Learning Organization* (New York: Doubleday, 2006).

strength and speed of the other rowers. It might seem like this would be a benefit, until you saw them making circles in the middle of the race. One person rowing much more powerfully and quickly than the rest throws the balance off. You no longer have a team working together. Instead, you have chaos because no one can keep up with the one person working out of sync.

An organization works much the same as a rowboat.

3.1. People in the System or Team

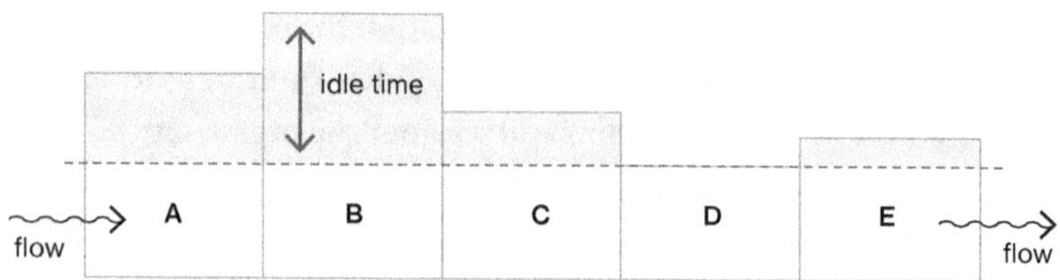

The above diagram shows five boxes lettered A through E. Pretend each letter is a department. The height of each box shows that team or department's capacity. B has the most capacity, and D has the least. Let's say D was testing or quality control. If every department kept their capacity even with D's capacity, you achieve a state of flow. A product would move from A through E without any bottlenecks. But the managers don't like B having so much idle time. So the managers instruct B to work ahead of schedule to produce more. This overloads C and completely overwhelms D—testing. An inexperienced manager would assume the issue is with testing and not with the other flaws within the overall system.

This could be true with an individual Scrum team. Person B could finish their work easily while the person testing the team's work (D) is overwhelmed. Or this could represent one team converting to Scrum, creating value and products faster, and causing issues for the organization as a whole.

In the real world, this might play out in a company with traditional departments. Suppose the coding department through a process change is able to generate four times the amount of code it was able to previously. By optimizing their work, they feel pretty proud of themselves. However, the QA/testing department hasn't adapted. They have the same staff and the same hours. Soon QA will be backed up with work. When bottlenecks like these occur, it's not unusual for the backup to slow the department down further just through having to log and track more items. By optimizing only coding, they have effectively suboptimized the entire organization with less work (value) delivered.

When people think in a linear fashion, they believe every action has a consequence. Instead, every action or inaction has multiple unknown consequences—the ripple effect Peter Senge discusses. Scrum recognizes that ripples affect ripples in a complex structure that isn't always predictable. We will go into more detail on how to solve these problems systematically in the future through feedback loops. For now, it's important to be mindful of how Scrum implementation will affect systems within not only the Scrum team but the entire organization.

These ripple effects are felt in the culture as you implement Scrum. The ripples create shifts holistically throughout the organization. I want to make this clear: you don't have to change your culture to implement Scrum—implementing Scrum influences your culture. Implementing Scrum changes what your teams do, which in turn changes the culture.

Shift Happens

When we're willing to consciously change our behaviors, create systems that support the new behaviors, and diligently pursue the behavior we desire, momentum begins to kick in. Suddenly the man who was a coach potato got sick of letting his days be filled with binge-watching TV and decided to plan his day around the gym instead of Netflix. Now he looks forward to his gym time because he enjoys it.

What changed? Did this guy take out a sheet of paper, label the top "My Values," write down "Health & Fitness" in the first spot? If he did, that alone would not have changed anything—no more than if a stingy miser said he valued generosity, or if a politician vowed to be honest. We can say our values are whatever we want them to be, but what they actually are is what we do.

What may have happened is this man had an awakening—a health scare, or maybe a death in the family—that made him assess who he was becoming. Maybe he realized his vision for his life didn't match his behavior. With great pain and difficulty, he got out of bed an hour early and started going to the gym. He threw out all the junk food and found healthy alternatives he enjoyed. When he woke up late, he made sure he still got in a little bit of exercise. If he missed a day of eating well, he made sure he didn't miss two days in a row.

In other words, this man took action, adapted based on results, and committed himself to a new routine. It began with willpower along with some strategies. Over time, his new behaviors became second nature. To old friends, he changed. To new friends, they can't imagine him *not* going to the gym. Suddenly, the man who once valued rest and entertainment now values his health.

These shifts tend to spill over into other areas of life. In our example, the man might find he is more productive at work and no longer procrastinates on chores like paying taxes, and maybe he's decided to pursue a serious relationship. In other words, positive behaviors are contagious.

But how do you make this shift in an organization? How do we accomplish something so big and complex? As absurd as my example was, many start the same as my hypothetical example—by writing down what values the organization wants. The problem is, as we comically saw, this alone changes nothing. No, it starts by first observing the behaviors—the organization's culture—that already exist.

Changing the Culture

Changing the culture sounds intimidating, doesn't it? Nobody wants to change. I recently spoke at a conference where I surveyed fifty-two people. One of the questions I asked them was "What would you think if someone told you your values are not okay?" Sixty-eight percent responded that they would feel bad (angry, upset, or irritated.) The other 32 percent said they would feel neutral. Nobody said they would like being told their values are wrong.

In effect, when a consultant, new CEO, or whoever comes into an organization and makes drastic changes to how things are done, the perception is not much different from my survey participants. The unspoken message in the proposed changes is *the way you do things is bad*. This is one of the reasons organizational change is so difficult. There's a built-in human resistance to the process.

So how do we change our organization to align with Scrum's values and principles? The same way our coach potato friend turned his life around: by making slow, consistent, and persistent shifts in our behaviors. Ironically, this approach can lead to an organization's demise when the shifts are made in the wrong direction.

I'm going to tell you a story about a majorly successful company. This company has massive amounts of revenue each quarter. In fact, in the year 2000, it created more revenue than Microsoft, Dell, and Goldman Sachs combined.[14]

Money alone doesn't determine success, though, does it? How does this organization operate within its environment? Is it doing good, making an impact, and caring for its customers and employees? Well, let's look at its defined culture.

---

14 Dan Ackman, "Enron the Incredible," *Forbes*, January 15, 2002, https://www.forbes.com/2002
    /01/15/0115enron.html#539ffdfe3c9c

Its mission statement is "[Our] vision is to become the world's leading energy company—creating innovative and efficient energy solutions for growing economies and a better environment worldwide." Okay, pretty impressive.

But what about their values? Are they any good? Judge for yourself:

Respect: *We treat others as we would like to be treated ourselves. We do not tolerate abusive or disrespectful treatment. Ruthlessness, callousness and arrogance don't belong here.*

Integrity: *We work with customers and prospects openly, honestly and sincerely. When we say we will do something, we will do it; when we say we cannot or will not do something, then we won't do it.*

Communication: *We have an obligation to communicate. Here, we take the time to talk with one another . . . and to listen. We believe that information is meant to move, and that information moves people.*

Excellence: *We are satisfied with nothing less than the very best in everything we do. We will continue to raise the bar for everyone. The great fun here will be for all of us to discover just how good we can really be.*

You must admit that their values sound amazing. Maybe you're ready to spruce up your resume, so you can work for this amazing company. But first, let me tell you their name.

Enron.[15]

Yes, the same Enron that imploded from a toxic and greedy culture.

Enron didn't grow into the behemoth that it was by lying, committing fraud, and engaging in abusive behavior. At one time, they might have believed their mission and values. All it takes is some key people—some executive officers—engaging in behaviors that might be considered slightly shady to sink the ship. The proverbial slippery slope is slippery for a reason. One poor decision unchecked can lead to many.

But it works in the reverse, too. You can climb a cultural slope by shifting your organization's behaviors in a more positive way. Let's look at that more in the next chapter.

---

15   Enron, "Statement of Human Rights Principles," https://www.csus.edu/indiv/m/merlinos /enron.html.

CHAPTER FOUR

Shifting the Culture: The Game's Code of Conduct

You will never change your life until you change something you do daily.

– John C. Maxwell[16]

It's Sunday afternoon in early December, and you and your family are awaiting your dinner guests—some new potential friends you met in the stands at a football match. While you wait, your family is putting the final touches on the Christmas decorations, and the doorbell rings.

You greet your new friends and welcome them into your home. Then they stop in the living room and stare.

"What's with the dragon on top of the tree?" Ricardo asks.

"My grandmother made that when I was a child," you say proudly.

"But that's wrong. Dragons are evil. It should be a star to represent the star over Bethlehem. This won't do."

I don't know about you, but the friendship would probably end right there. I am fine with friends having differing opinions and voicing them, but when a veritable stranger enters my home and tells me my traditions are wrong, I don't like it. I imagine you wouldn't like it either.

Changing your company culture is not any different. You might feel like something is off—that the *dragon* isn't what you really want in your organization, but if someone tells you it's wrong, you get defensive. Nobody likes being told they're wrong. However, Scrum isn't easily adopted when you cling to your old way of doing things. An attitude of *that's how we do things here* is tempting but ultimately stifles change and creates a stiff-necked

---

16   John Maxwell, "It All Comes Down to What You Do Daily," John C. Maxwell (blog), January 14, 2015, https://www.johnmaxwell.com/blog/it-all-comes-down-to-what-you-do-daily/.

organization doomed to fall behind in its industry.

To align your organization's culture with one conducive to agile adoption requires care, tact, and deft maneuvering.

It also requires knowing what a culture is and understanding the hidden structure that creates it.

To be clear, you don't have to change or shift your culture before implementing Scrum. When you commit to implementing Scrum, you change how you and your team work. When you change how your team works—their behavior—you shift your culture in the process.

WHY ALIGNMENT MATTERS

Do you know how Scrum got its name? Jeff Sutherland and Ken Schwaber drew their inspiration for Scrum from a 1986 paper authored by two Japanese researchers.[17] The researchers compared highly responsive product development teams to rugby players in their ability to move as a cohesive team, passing the ball up the field of play. One formation in particular is called a "scrum."

4.1. Scrum Formation

---

17 Hirotaka Takeuchi and Ikujiro Nonaka, "The New New Product Development Game," *Harvard Business Review*, January 1986, https://hbr.org/1986/01/the-new-new-product -development-game.

A scrum formation is comprised of nine team members, eight of whom are locked together: three in front, four lined up behind them, and two in the back with the ninth player on the side. The team pushes together as a single unit against the other team. The formation is literally bodies crammed together pushing in one direction to accomplish an objective.

Many managers like this visual—a team of people digging in and using all their power to accomplish a goal. There's no room for being lackadaisical. Everybody must do their part for it to work. And truly, this is how a well-run Scrum team looks in operation. But there's one thing rugby players have that many managers miss: the team knows their objective. They have a clear vision of what they are trying to accomplish. If they had no idea in what direction they should be pushing, it would result in chaos.

A rugby team has to be aligned like a car. If you drive a car with wheels out of alignment or balance, it's a rough ride. The steering wheel shakes, you constantly have to pull on the wheel to keep the car straight, and the issues cause more gasoline consumption and parts to wear out faster. A car needs to be checked for balanced and aligned wheels. Automotive technicians check these against standards for tolerance. Too far out of tolerance, and issues emerge. Ignore the issues, and your car is headed for more work or, worse, an accident caused by mechanical failure. Even if it is drivable, you can't drive as fast as you'd like without dealing with a headache of a ride. Bring it into alignment and get the wheels balanced, and the ride is smooth at any speed (assuming you don't have other issues).

Returning to the poker table, what if there were no standards for fair play? You watch as Miguel pulls an ace from his sleeve and nobody balks. What do you do? Do you hold to the higher ground and play fair, losing your money in the process, or fight fire with fire? Unchecked, some players may begin cheating. It stops being fun and becomes toxic. Isn't this partly what happened at Enron?

Like a rugby team, a poker game, or your car, your organization has to be aligned. There needs to be principles that everyone agrees upon. In short, organizations need vision and values that align with that vision. If your culture is not aligned with Agile's values, implementation comes to a halt. Fifty-two percent of respondents to the *13th Annual State of Agile™ Report* stated that their organizational culture being in conflict with Agile Values was the number one barrier to implementation.[18]

---

18 VersionOne CollabNet, *13th Annual State of Agile™ Report*, May 7, 2019, https://www.stateofagile .com/#ufh-i-521251909-13th-annual-state-of-agile-report/473508.

Before we get too far into this topic, I want to be clear about something. People sometimes confuse Agile with Scrum. *The Manifesto for Agile Software Development* was written and published in 2001 by several software developers studying the lightweight, responsive frameworks available, including Scrum. The Agile manifesto explained the qualities that underlie these frameworks and described the mindset that inspired Scrum. So Scrum is one flavor of the Agile philosophy—the most popular, the one that generates the best results.[19] And agility is perhaps Scrum's greatest strength. Scrum's use of iterations to foster continual improvement is likely the reason it's the most commonly used of the Agile frameworks. Scrum needs a values-driven culture in order to thrive. If your culture is lacking, we can shift it.

STARTING WITH WHY

There are a number of things you must do to implement Scrum successfully no matter the scenario. But successful implementation starts with the desire to use Scrum for the right reasons. Maybe you want to accelerate product delivery, manage changing priorities, and increase overall productivity. Chances are, if that describes you, you have all that you need to implement Scrum. As you follow the behaviors that support the implementation of the Scrum framework, your values will shift.

On the other hand, if you're considering Scrum as a quick fix, a technique that can make you more money, and a nice additional little certification to your CV, chances are your values are misaligned and implementation won't work. That's not to say you can't change, only that until you do change, Scrum implementation will be nearly impossible.

Scores of books, training programs, and even specialized consultants have explored the hows and whys behind the importance of having a company vision ad nauseam, so I will not waste too much time discussing this topic here. I will add that a strong vision inspires responsibility through the company. Employees begin acting like owners—they understand where their actions have meaning and an impact.

Visions are perhaps easier to create when your organization is trying to change the world for good. Dana-Farber Cancer Institute's vision is this: "[Our] ultimate goal is the eradication of cancer, AIDS, and related diseases

---

19 Ibid.

and the fear that they engender."[20] At Dana-Farber, I think any employee with even the most menial of jobs can feel like they're doing their small part to rid the world of these nefarious illnesses.

But what if your organization does something not nearly as cool and sexy? What if you are a custom fabricator building giant parts for power generation? Some employees might love the challenges, problem-solving, and feeling of accomplishment from making a part that functions above expectations, but many more employees will be disengaged, finding no meaning in their day-to-day work.

Salesforce founder Marc Benioff was passionate about creating CRM software that actually helped small businesses without having to download and update constantly. But he and his partners realized that not all employees would fully embrace their mission, which was "The end of software." It was cool, but not life-saving cool. To counter employee disengagement, Benioff and his team created philanthropic ways for their employees to feel a part of something bigger, with activities like charitable contributions, paid volunteer work, and facilitating opportunities where their employees' skill sets could be used to help nonprofits who might otherwise have no access to those resources. The employees saw how they were contributing during the workweek, which allowed them to be a part of something even bigger.

What's your vision? Is it a bloated, corporatese statement that hits all the plot points but stimulates no one? Maybe it looks like this nebulous and bland one:

> **Mission Statement:** *To create a shopping experience that pleases our customers; a workplace that creates opportunities and a great working environment for our associates; and a business that achieves financial success.*[21]

Maybe you don't even have a written vision statement. That may be fine. What's important is that every employee knows what the company is trying to achieve and feels like they're a part of making that happen. When that is clear, and the values align with that vision, changing how you do things—especially when it aligns with the vision—is much less daunting. If you haven't yet defined a vision, I strongly recommend that you do. When you've clearly

---

20 Dana-Farber Cancer Institute, "Mission and Values," accessed July 29, 2019, https://www.dana
-farber.org/about-us/mission-and-values/.

21 Minda Zetlin, "The 9 Worst Mission Statements of All Time," Inc., November 15, 2013,
https://www.inc.com/minda-zetlin/9-worst-mission-statements-all-time.html.

defined your vision, how to achieve that vision will be equally as clear. For further exploration, I recommend Simon Sinek's book *Start with Why*.

IDENTIFYING YOUR CULTURE

A stellar, well-communicated vision is a great start to shifting your culture, but vision alone can't accomplish anything. If vision alone could alter a culture, Enron might still be around and many other CEOs would have a far easier job. Culture is a sum of the values exhibited by the behaviors within the organization. In other words, the culture within your organization is derived from something you can't even see, let alone quantify: the actual values of your people.

Culture has been compared to an iceberg floating in the ocean. Only 10 percent of it is visible. But what you're actually seeing in day-to-day actions are the behavioral results of culture, not the values, assumptions, and beliefs that cause those results.

4.2. Concepta and Percepta

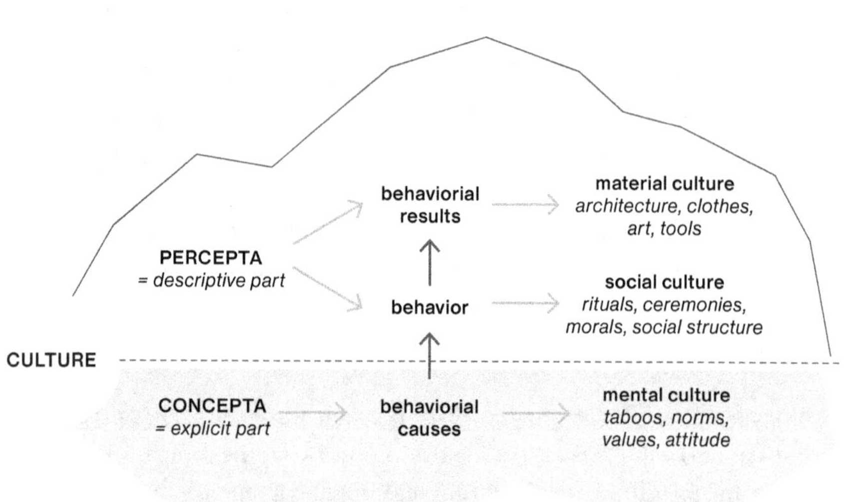

Data source: Müller, Gelbrich: Interkulturelles Marketing

"But, Fabian," you might say, "I *can* quantify their values. Look at Roberto. He's a hard worker who completes assignments on time. He obviously values industriousness and productivity."

It's possible you're right; he does value those things. But how would you know for sure? How do you know Roberto doesn't just fear reprimand? Or what if he values a financial bonus or praise? Take either of those factors away, and his work ethic might vanish too. So can you really measure what someone values? No. You can only see their behavior. We never get a full picture of the values that drive that behavior. Determining what drives our own behavior is often tough enough, even without trying to determine someone else's.

Values do determine behavior, which determines the overall culture of a company. And I don't mean the behavior you see. It comes down to the behavior no one sees. Who are your employees, and what are they doing when no one's looking?

For Enron, despite their bright, shiny mission statement and noteworthy listed values, a much different behavior was exhibited behind closed doors. In the toxic, codependent soup of a culture, bonus targets and profit margins were valued beyond anything else. We can determine that value by looking at the sum of the behaviors: systemic lying about numbers, lack of transparency with the media on fiscal reports, and a culture described as full of fear. When employees perform tasks from a place of fear, you have zero psychological safety. Compliance with procedures, defined values, and maintaining productivity is determined by how much trouble someone thinks they'll have and how closely they're being watched. And forget about employees taking the initiative and making calculated risks for the good of the company. In that kind of environment, people who stick their necks out often lose their head.

You might look around your company and wonder if your assumptions about your culture are true. Worse, how do you go about changing a possibly conflicted culture not congruent with Agile or Scrum so you can begin implementation? Here's the good news: while a culture shift must happen in order to successfully implement Scrum, it can happen with just a small group of people, and the shift can happen *during* Scrum implementation. But a map of where you want to go is only helpful if you know where you are. In order for you to shift the culture in the way you want to go, you must first determine what your current culture and values are.

Discover Your Current Values

At some point during Scrum certification training, I like to do an exercise where I have dozens of value words written on Post-it notes. The words I use represent the five Scrum values, but I also include other words such as *complexity* and *analysis*. Before class, I place these notes on the classroom's walls.

I then ask the students to wander around the room and select the words they think are Scrum values. (There are multiple instances of the same word so they can be selected by more than one student.) Then I reveal the true core values and we discuss.

"What do you think commitment means?" I'll ask.

"To be dedicated, like in a relationship?" someone might say.

A good, close answer. Through further questioning and a little coaching, I help them come to the true meaning in regards to Scrum and gauge how closely current organizational behaviors mirror this value. Questioning helps to find the deeper meaning behind the answers. Questions include "What are you committed to in Scrum?" which is followed up by "And why is that important?" By asking these questions, the student can see the importance of the value on his own.

Why all this fuss? Because sometimes people wonder if Scrum values align with their company's values. This is a valid concern. I've said before that your organization's values have almost nothing to do with what's in writing and everything to do with the behavior—how you actually do things. You never know what a person values, but you can take a few guesses based on their behaviors. Going back to our couch potato friend in the last chapter, until he shifted his behavior, we would never guess that *health and fitness* was one of his values.

If your company has gone through the process of writing out your values, you may want to inspect them and have a serious look at whether the written values match your behavior. You don't want to become an Enron, do you?

But maybe you have never taken the time to discover the company's true values. Or maybe you jotted out ideal values quickly and have forgotten what they are. It's worth taking a moment to discover and refine them now.

Let's say we were at Enron and implementing Scrum. We would work with a division in Enron, so we would have the ideal mixed implementation: an executive sponsor along with pilot team members who are open and motivated about making this shift to an Agile framework. With the team seated, I'd go through the values exercise above and ask them what each value means.

Alice, an accounting executive, picks *respect*, a value shared by both Enron and Scrum.

"What does that mean?" I ask.

"Well, according to our values, that everyone is treated like they want to be treated. Ruthlessness, callousness, and arrogance don't belong," she answers. (Note: I find that when an executive committee or consultants are the source of the written values, most employees don't know what those values are, nor are they able to recite what they mean when asked. It is unlikely that true

Enron employees would have known the written values by heart.)

"Very good. Is that the behavior you see? Are people respectful here? Do they treat others as they would want to be treated?"

She hesitates and sheepishly looks to her peers. "I-I'm not sure."

The obvious answer is no. This is the uncomfortable part of a values audit—asking yourself and your people if the values you hope to embody are demonstrated by daily behaviors. One way to uncover your current values is to create a conduit, maybe an anonymous survey, that allows for candid answers.

I've seen leaders scoff at the Scrum values as if they're an automatic element of business. "Of course we value openness!" they say. "I want all our employees to be open."

But do the leaders exhibit a behavior that praises and supports openness? When they hold a meeting to launch an initiative and a manager raises valid doubts or concerns, is he rewarded for his view? Or is he explicitly or implicitly punished for being a "downer"? When an employee expresses issues with interoffice relationships, is the issue addressed or swept under the rug and she's told to "just do your best to get along"?

This gap analysis—looking at the gaps between your expressed or desired values/beliefs/culture and what is actual culture—is critical. The process requires a gut-wrenching ability to separate yourself from the situation, be open-minded, and honest. Only when leaders see that a change is needed can a shift occur. Psychologist Kurt Lewin called this stage of cultural change the "unfreezing" stage—the thawing of previously solid beliefs.[22] The next step is to actually make the change. That sounds daunting—changing the culture of an enterprise to launch Scrum. Let's look at how this is done.

Creating a Culture Bubble

Have you ever visited a biodome or maybe seen one in a documentary or news report? If you don't know, a biodome is a structure (usually a geodesic dome) where scientists create an ecosystem that's totally unique to the structure's surroundings. A famous one, Biosphere 2, operated by the University of Arizona, is located outside of Tucson in the scorching Sonoran Desert. Despite the arid external conditions, the facility features self-contained ecosystems such as a tropical rainforest complete with a towering canopy of trees and

22 Stephen Cummings, "Unfreezing Change as Three Steps: Rethinking Kurt Lewin's Legacy for Change Management," *human relations* 69, no. 1 (2016), 33–60, https://journals.sagepub.com /doi/pdf/10.1177/0018726715577707.

other flora and fauna needed to support the ecosystem.

Even a largely "arid" bureaucratic organization that's as agile as a dry twig can create a separate ecosystem—a unique culture—within a cultural bubble. We saw this at GoTelecom, where the division went so far as to hire its own contracted IT people. But this bubble is more than a shield protecting the team from project-mooching managers and politics; it creates a workspace—an ecosystem—in which behaviors in support of Agile and Scrum values are demonstrated, modeled, and lauded.

Having a strong sponsor and creating a separate culture can start the cultural shift for an entire organization. But even strong sponsors who welcome Agile frameworks can be slow to understand the difference. At one company I coached, we had a strong sponsor who had experience with Scrum. This leader—let's call him Jorge—created this protective bubble by separating his team of eager Scrum pilots from the rest of the company. However, he was slow to welcome the values. He thought he aligned well with the values of commitment, courage, focus, openness, respect, psychological safety, integrity, and trust. He may have accepted them at a logical level, just as I'm sure you do. Who doesn't welcome these values into the workplace?

However, Jorge's actions were quite different from his logical idea of values. An old-guard executive under a lot of pressure to produce results, Jorge was heavy-handed in his approach. When one team member wasn't producing "fast enough," he threatened to fire her. He even wanted to fire one of my coaches because he wasn't performing to Jorge's expectations. I needed to have a candid conversation with Jorge and give him some feedback.

"Do you see the importance of psychological safety?" I asked.

"Of course," he barked.

"What are its benefits?"

"It creates a space where team members feel they can contribute freely and produce faster and enthusiastically."

"Good." Now came the tough part. "Do you think employees feel safe to contribute and try things if there's *any* possibility their idea might not work and the Sprint doesn't produce the desired result?"

He was silent for a while. "No. No, I suppose not. You're saying my actions are killing creativity?"

I had to be tactful. "What I'm saying is creativity and risk-taking for the benefit of the team and the company could be stifled if the team feels like they could lose their job if something doesn't work."

He got the point and backed off, allowing the team to make missteps as they learned new behaviors.

Changing behaviors and aligning with values is easy to write in these pages. Years of cultural shift can be simply captured in a two-page case study showing you the virtual before and after pictures like those in a diet advertisement. As with ads, you have to pay attention to the small print. The shift to an agile mindset culture requires living the behaviors that embody the values consistently. Just like our couch potato friend had to put in the work, eat right, and go to the gym much more often than when he succumbed to the temptation of a cheesy pizza.

Peter Green led Adobe through an Agile transformation beginning in 2005. The transformation of his team is reflected in my own work. Here's what he has to say: "I have seen a pattern emerge at several organizations where I've worked . . . A team starts using Scrum. When they use it effectively, they start to think differently about the way they work. They build different social structures. They value different outcomes. They alter decision making structures. And the culture starts to change. We are rewarding different behavior, at least for that team. If they can stick with it long enough to solidify the new set of behaviors, the culture change lasts."[23]

When Salesforce made the shift to Agile, starting with their R & D division in 2006, they made sure the team leaders became champions of values alignment through behavior. They modeled the behaviors they wanted and adopted an "Educate without Enforcing" program. The leaders communicated the mindset of Agile and Scrum without rigidly enforcing those new behaviors.[24]

When steering your Titanic company away from a toxic-culture iceberg (or, at least, an iceberg culture not aligned with Scrum), it takes an enormous amount of energy and time to steer such an enormous vessel. The real Titanic wasn't able to make the turn, and, well, we all know what happened there.

But what if you put your team into a speedboat? Speedboats are fast, maneuverable, and fun. Sure they're missing a lido deck, but they can avoid the icebergs. That's what Green did with his Adobe team. Instead of trying to steer Adobe from a grassroots position, they figuratively jumped ship and learned the behaviors that steer the smaller craft. Salesforce modeled the behaviors that embodied their new values.

So let's now look at each of the values in greater detail.

---

23 Peter Green, "Scrum as an Agent of Change Part 2," Agile for All, September 2, 2015, https://agileforall.com/scrum-as-an-agent-of-culture-change-2/.

24 Arun Ramanna, "Salesforce Case Study," Scrum Alliance, February 4, 2019, https://www.scrum alliance.org/agilematters/articles/salesforce-case-study.

LIVING THE SCRUM VALUES

We briefly reviewed the five Scrum values in the previous chapter, defined them, and gave them a little context. Now we will explore how to reconcile any company values that seem to differ from Scrum's values, what living the values looks like, and how to ensure that you adhere to the values.

To review, the five values are commitment, courage, focus, openness, and respect. If your organization has clearly defined values, do you have to change them in order to adhere to Scrum's values? Not necessarily. Values are words or short phrases that represent beliefs and behaviors within the organization. And already your values may be more in alignment with Scrum's than you realize, thanks in part to the fluidity of language.

The good news for us is that modeling good behavior (culture) and the values desired can lead the shift toward a higher ideal. Lead with the values you wish your people to adopt, and you will climb the "slippery" slope into a stronger organization where Scrum will add tremendous value.

Scrum is the most highly utilized framework for working in the agile mindset. Of the companies adhering to the Agile Manifesto, 54 percent are using Scrum.[25] Values that must be reconsidered are those that do not align with the agile mindset.

For example, suppose you have a value called *excellence*, like Enron did. This sounds like a lovely value. A commitment to excellence is admirable. But suppose the meaning behind excellence, either inferred through example or explicitly defined, says something to the effect of "Never quit until excellence is achieved." Again, on the outset, this sounds wonderful. But can you see a potential pitfall?

Suppose you were creating a website to launch a new service that would set you apart from your competitors. Time was of the essence, so you could be first to market. Everything works: the links, the supporting databases, the opt-in system, and the shopping cart. However, the design is a little wonky. The menu's words aren't scaling right on mobile devices. Your web developer holds up release until *excellence* is achieved. Before you know it, your competitor hit the market first, and now you're playing catch-up.

What happened? A well-intentioned value grew into a debilitating and Agile-killing form of perfectionism. The value litmus test is to determine whether or not the value facilitates or potentially inhibits agility. When you look at your values, explore the various ways that, even if defined with

---

25 VersionOne CollabNet, *13th Annual State of Agile™ Report.*

a phrase, they could be misinterpreted and cost your company time, energy, and money—a lack of agility—because a person or team was trying to honor the values.

But what if your values are all different from the five Scrum values? I often find it humorous how some people have a visceral reaction to a display of the Ten Commandments because they disagree with religion. I respect all religious viewpoints, but what makes me laugh about this is that if you ask even the most anti-religious person how they feel about each of the commandments separately, they only have an issue with a couple. Even cultures who have never heard of the Bible generally have beliefs around showing love and being kind, and they are against things like theft and murder. So, yes, religions and cultures are different, but they tend to have similar ideologies for how people should behave.

It's no different in this situation. Your organization's values might look different from Scrum's at the outset, but they probably align—they have more in common than you think. Let's look at each, one at a time.

Commitment

This is a loaded word. We discussed how the team is committed to the Product Owner's vision and to each other, but what does that really look like?

If this value isn't on your list, the essence of it probably is. When we talk about commitment in Scrum, we're talking about giving the goal and the team your very best. This means that once the Product Goal is set and the team agrees how to do the work, you do the work to the best of your ability. I can't imagine a company that willfully disagrees with this concept. Even if commitment isn't on the list, its intent certainly is.

Can this value be misinterpreted? I think all values can. Certainly a team could be so committed to the original Product Goal that they ignore new information from the client or a change in the marketplace that makes that goal obsolete. You might believe you're practicing a value of Scrum, but in this particular case, you're ignoring a pillar: adaptation.

Done right, commitment is nothing more than being a fully participating team member and supporting the goals you've agreed on. If you disagree with the goal or don't believe the work can be done within the Sprint period, you need to bring up your concerns during planning. But once the concerns or objections are discussed, it is important to commit to the team's final decision, even if you still disagree.

Courage

You might be thinking your company already values courage even if it's not a written value. I wouldn't be so sure.

Yes, courage is always idolized as a worthy ideal, especially here in Colombia where *machismo* (a strong sense of masculine pride) still reigns strong in the culture. But does your company truly value it? I know you want to say yes.

Let's go back to Big OG. When the IT head addressed issues with upper management, it took courage for him to say what he wanted to achieve and ask for help in achieving it. Instead of honoring that courage, he was slapped down. I do not mean that upper management should agree to every request just because of the courage it takes to make it. What I am saying is the courage must be celebrated even if the idea isn't. In this case, because the IT head was discouraged, he didn't dare act courageously anymore.

What would it look like if courage were honored when it was part of a calculated risk? Author and speaker Dale Carnegie famously wrote about such a situation. Edward T. Bedford, one of John D. Rockefeller's partners, had made a courageous, calculated risk on a South American investment. Unfortunately, the investment soured. By the time he was able to liquidate, the firm had lost a million dollars (nearly $30 million in today's dollars). Sick over his mistake, he went to see Rockefeller. Carnegie writes, "John D. might have criticized; but he knew Bedford had done his best . . . So Rockefeller found something to praise; he congratulated Bedford because he had been able to save 60 percent of the money he had invested. 'That's splendid!' said Rockefeller. 'We don't always do as well as that upstairs.'"[26]

Imagine if all bosses valued and praised calculated risk-taking and appreciated the courage it requires?

Courage is valued, but I am not advocating for reckless courage. As with most risk decisions, I expect a fair amount of prudence. It would be bad, for example, if a surgeon decided to courageously try a new technique in the middle of a potentially life-altering surgery. There is a reason new procedures take years to gain approval within the medical community.

That said, a company desiring to be agile should affirm strategic courageous decisions when made for the good of all.

Lastly, it takes courage to make decisions that go against the status quo. This takes courage of a different sort—courage to do what's right, not what's easy.

---

26 Dale Carnegie, *How to Win Friends and Influence People* (New York: Simon & Schuster, 2009).

Focus

The term multitasking has lost some traction within the business world; however, far too many leaders and managers continue to give life to this mythical animal. Numerous articles and books have been written citing ample research and practical applications of single-tasking (Cal Newport's *Deep Work* and Gary Keller's *The One Thing* come to mind). Despite this, I still see job postings in search of people who are "great at multitasking." Sure. And I'd love to see a unicorn. For what it's worth, researchers have found that it takes an average of twenty-three minutes and fifteen seconds for our brains to refocus on a task after an interruption.[27] Put another way, an additional study determined that task switching can cost you 40 percent of your time.[28] If you have a staff of ten putting in a forty-hour week, that's eight thousand hours lost to task switching per year.

This idea of filling idle time to be "more productive" had good intentions. Workers who are idle are seen as costing money. They could help on other projects and tasks while waiting for their next assignment, right? But you wouldn't want your computer's hard drive operating at 100 percent usage all the time. The computer's function slows drastically, the time to complete a simple operation comes to an infuriating crawl, and if it continues unchecked, your hard drive is headed to an early grave. Why do we think humans are any different?

Focus, for our purposes, means single-tasking, but it has a larger meaning than just not reading your email while you're on the phone. In Scrum, focus means that everyone on the team is working together toward the same objective. There is no room for side projects or divided attention. An engineer on a development team shouldn't be "borrowed" by a department because they're behind (maybe that department should use Scrum?). The engineer is focused on one objective: completing the current Sprint with her team.

Nothing more.

All of her energy is centered on accomplishing the Sprint's goals, and if her work is done, she looks to how she can assist her teammates.

And, by the way, it's *not* a good idea to read your email while on the phone.

---

27 Kermit Pattison, "Worker, Interrupted: The Cost of Task Switching," Fast Company, July 28, 2008, https://www.fastcompany.com/944128/worker-interrupted-cost-task-switching.

28 American Psychological Association, "Multitasking: Switching Costs," March 20, 2006, https://www.apa.org/research/action/multitask.

Openness

Sometimes when I list this value in training, I see the participants squirm a little. Relax. Openness isn't discussing how you feel about your supervisor or addressing the unspoken grudge you've held against Mary. Based on the principle of transparency, openness means that all team members and stakeholders agree to be open about their work, what's been completed, and all issues or challenges they have in completing the work.

As we saw with the previous example with Jorge, many organizations believe they have a lock on this value. I'd invite you to take a closer look. As suggested, a couple of anonymous surveys or even comment boxes where employees feel safe to share honestly can be eye-opening. Ignoring the iceberg, or, worse, firing the lookout who's going on and on about it, will not make the issue go away.

When producing value quickly, there is no time to hide a challenge or work something out on your own. I fully understand the temptation to try to solve an issue by yourself. Under traditional models, it's often gratifying to show you've solved a problem. However, you might be wasting your time when you could have employed the full breadth of the team's knowledge and resources. Openness allows you to do that.

Openness is one of the values based on the pillar of transparency. Agile frameworks are not the only ones championing the need for transparency. Leaders in multiple industries utilizing various frameworks—like Ray Dalio, founder of the famous multi-billion-dollar investment firm Bridgewater Associates—have made the rallying cry for transparency and openness within work teams.

But openness isn't just about seeing issues—it's also about an awareness of the work being completed. While *The Scrum Guide* doesn't give detail on how to provide visibility, many teams construct a simple board with three columns: to do, in process, done. Sometimes they include "dependencies" as a fourth column—items that are dependent on contractors or other entities outside the Scrum team.

Whatever method a team chooses, the outcome is the same—the openness allows any teammate or stakeholder to see the progress. If the engineer has completed her work, she can look at the board for any open items that she can assist with (remember the value of T-shaped people?). Everyone works at different speeds, depending on both the scope of their work and their skill level. When the team is open, the team can work and solve bottlenecks and impediments together. Without openness, there is no opportunity to inspect the work, and growth is stifled because the ability to adapt is gone.

And finally, openness means being open to giving and receiving feedback. No one enjoys having their work criticized, but by being open to this feedback, you can greatly improve in knowledge and in skills. However, you must also be open to giving feedback. This is sometimes just as difficult as most people don't want to make others feel bad. It takes courage to do the right thing and listen to and offer feedback when necessary.

Respect

Unlike openness, I often do find respect somewhere in the midst of an organization's written core values. How consistently it is practiced is debatable, but the idea of respect is at least prevalent.

Here, there is little difference in meaning from what you're probably thinking. In 2020, *The Scrum Guide* said, "members respect each other to be capable, independent people." But how does this look when practiced in the real world? Leadership is key here. People will undoubtedly reflect modeled behavior.

Back at GoTelecom, the sponsor hand-selected a team of open-minded individuals from various disciplines. Because the sponsor, the division's vice president, held the team in high regard and showed respect for each member, he earned their respect and they in turn demonstrated respectfulness toward each other.

Respect shouldn't be confused with affection. You do not have to be friends with everyone on the team. You might not even like everyone. But it does mean acting with kindness and a professional decorum. Work will be criticized, and critical feedback given. But these instances are not personal and should never, ever be mean-spirited. Criticism and feedback are tools to improve the work and help the team member get better. The work done does not represent the individual who did the work.

Most of all, it's important to remember that each team member has different backgrounds, experiences, and skill sets. When respect is maintained, it allows each team member to feel good about the value they bring to the team without feeling better than anyone else.

Psychological Safety

As I said in the last chapter, psychological safety is not an official Scrum value, but it's the glue that holds the Scrum framework together. Without psychological safety, openness disappears, respect is lost, commitment wanes, and it's difficult for a team member to focus when she's worried about bureaucratic politics.

If you've been in the corporate world for any length of time, I'm sure you've experienced what it's like to not have the safety to take risks without fear of retribution or losing your job. It might have been an overbearing supervisor in a fast-food restaurant as a kid or more recently in your career. While psychological safety is a little difficult to define, it is easy to see where it is absent.

For instance, interdepartmental fighting is often sprung from politics in situations where a dearth of psychological safety exists. Suppose a project is late, losing money, and upsetting the client. When psychological safety is absent, it might play out like this: Somebody blames engineering for over-complicating the design. Engineering blames manufacturing for laziness and mistakes. Manufacturing and engineering both blame sales for overpromising. Sales blames everyone else. Does this sound familiar?

Now suppose that this is a Scrum product. The team consists of engineers, manufacturing, machining, and whatever other skill they need to complete the project. The first few Sprints are completed, and they have feedback. Things did not go well out of the gate. With psychological safety, items are discussed during the Sprint Retrospective. With commitment, courage, focus, openness, and respect, the team works together to determine what happened. Feedback is given, along with respectful criticism. With psychological safety, the team feels their employment is not in jeopardy, and they don't get defensive because they don't feel personally attacked.

Does this sound like a dream? It's happening every day in companies all over the world who are using Scrum. This level of psychological safety is possible.

Integrity and Trust

Two other values that are not in *The Scrum Guide* but that I feel are imperative are integrity and trust. In order to create change and empower others to make decisions, you need to act with integrity and a high level of trust. With these values in partnership with psychological safety, all other values thrive.

Integrity means doing the right thing even if no one is watching. If you say you're going to do something, then you should do it.

Trust is almost intertwined with integrity. When you act with integrity, I trust that you will do what you say you will do. If you fail, I trust that you did everything you possibly could. When teammates trust each other to have integrity, then a team can operate at a level that has to be seen to be believed. But while these two values are again agreed upon from an intellectual standpoint, it's critical to define what the behaviors of trust and integrity look like.

Let's take two, small fictional countries: Ricevia and Beefana. Companies from both countries work closely together, and it's not uncommon for teams to work together. Both cultures outwardly embrace the concepts of trust and integrity, but how they demonstrate these values is quite different.

A Beefananian believes integrity means that when you say you will do something, you will do it to the best of your ability and have it done when you said you would have it done. Ricevians, on the other hand, believe that integrity means something different. If you say you will do something, then it means you want to do it at that moment, but that it might not be done right away. Or it might not get done at all if things change.

As you can imagine, this leads to conflicts. A Ricevian said he would finish the design of a subassembly essential to complete a project. The Beefananian believed him. She thought that he would do what he said he would. But the project bored the Ricevian as he got into the details, so he put it aside and worked on a less critical part instead.

Your own native culture might influence you to see one country as right and the other as wrong. If only it were that simple. It's very complex. Until these mixed teams define what trust and integrity will mean within that team or organization, there will be a mixture of expectations and rules, and those kinds of conflicts can rip an organization to shreds. At least defining what you mean by integrity and trust helps you interpret the actions of others and may help avoid some tension.

Implementing the Values

As discussed, values are hard to change but chances are your organization's values either match or come close to Scrum's values. For organizations who, until now, had not uncovered their values clearly, the way forward might be difficult.

A values-driven organization measures everything they do against their values: the clients they work with, their marketing approach, and especially who they hire. If you have never identified your organization's values, I can almost guarantee you have people working for you who have the skills but are not a great fit for your culture. Maybe you knew they were "off" but couldn't put your finger on why.

It's the manager who consistently fails to give employee feedback and makes excuses for his failures. Or maybe it's the coder who constantly makes snarky remarks about others' work. When you have clearly defined values, you can seek people who already share those values and terminate those who don't.

Yes, in the worst-case scenario, you may have to let go of a few employees who are not willing to adopt your values. They might be the greatest coder, engineer, or accountant you've ever had, but they will be a hindrance to your progress. They're probably good people, but they're misaligned. This is a last resort. Obviously, if your company has one hundred thousand employees, you can't fire half of them just because of a values misalignment. But what you can do is find leaders throughout the company who are willing to be good examples of the behaviors you want modeled. Oh, and if you're a leader, that goes for you, too.

In agile organizations, you're not necessarily looking for superstar players. What matters is that those on the team are team players. Going back to poker, who would you enjoy playing with more—a great player who is a jerk each time he wins and is a poor sport the few times he loses (think Phil Hellmuth), or a player who laughs a lot, is eager to get better, and can give and take jokes (like Daniel Negreanu)? I suspect it's the latter. Your organization deserves no less.

Once you have identified your values, ensured they do not contradict Scrum values, and retained people who are values-aligned remaining, it's fairly simple to live the Scrum values. Simple, but not easy. How do you learn any new skill? Through consistent repetition and practice. That is how we learn values, too—through the actual practice of Scrum.

As we continue, we will see how values are demonstrated and adopted through the early days of Scrum implementation—from that very first Monday morning when you will have your first Sprint Planning.

CONCLUSION

The cards are shuffled and cut, your chips are neatly stacked in front of you, and you're eyeing that cheat sheet in the center of the table, hoping for a flush. You and your friends have agreed on the stakes (pennies and nickels), the goal (everyone has fun and learns a new game), and the values (no cheating!). You know what a good game and a bad game looks like, and you even understand a few strategies. The table is set.

But who's going to be the dealer? Is somebody looking up the rules in case of a dispute? And what do you do if your friend's dog won't stop licking your hand? In other words, you need to know who's going to play which role.

So, who is at your table and what role are you playing? Are you Steve Jobs or a sheepdog?

CHAPTER FIVE

The Players: Are You Steve Jobs or a Sheepdog?

Specialization is for insects.
—**Robert Heinlein**[29]

"It's not my job," he said.

I was dumfounded. This coder in a company I was training said that he couldn't help with the systems testing because it wasn't in his job description. But it was his job. Or at least it was now. This man was no longer working in his bureaucratic silo, cut off from the effects of his work. With his department implementing Scrum, his team needed him to help with everything from brainstorming to systems testing to resolving a tech problem the whole group was dealing with.

Yet this coder was still stuck in the old way of doing things—a way that involved him completing tasks A through D and moving on. He was now part of a team where end results mattered more than individual components, but he had not yet made the mental switch and was defining his work by an outdated description of what he was "supposed" to do. Our team had to coach and model new behaviors for this coder so he understood that his responsibility no longer stopped at writing and designing code but extended to include all the tasks that contributed to his team.

But it's not his fault. A Gallup study shows that only 34 percent of US workers say they are engaged in their work.[30] And though this number is slowly increasing, it reveals plenty of room for improvement. Too many workers go

---

29 Robert A. Heinlein, *Time Enough for Love: The Lives of Lazarus Long* (New York, NY: Penguin, 1987).

30 Jim Harter, "Employee Engagement on the Rise in the U.S.," Gallup, August 26, 2018, https://news.gallup.com/poll/241649/employee-engagement-rise.aspx.

to work, do their "job," and go home without any incentive or reason to care about how the quality of their work affects their coworkers, their department, the company as a whole, or the end customers. It's easy for leaders to say they *should* care about the end result, the company, and its customers, but the fact is that most workers are trained to not care. And that disengagement has little to do with the individual and a whole lot to do with having a sense of team.

Imagine a football team where the defensive midfielder thinks that his job is defense, to attack the opponents once they cross midfield. For the most part, he's not wrong. However, what happens when his team is losing by two goals late in the game? If he continues to play defense and never helps his own team's attackers, they'll lose for sure. In other words, the team's objective is to win. If the midfielder's objective is to protect his statistics to the exclusion of all else, then he's not a team player. Maybe he doesn't like his coach or captain. Or maybe he's hoping to be traded. Whatever the reason, it's clear that he's focused on a narrow definition of his job and not much else.

Compare that with a championship team like Germany who won the 2014 FIFA World Cup. Any championship level team in any sport comes on to the field with a high level of energy and passion. During a championship game, the stadium crackles with an almost tangible electricity. Two teams enter the stadium with the same objective. Is there any question why high-level competitions create the most sensational displays of athleticism? When you're part of a team and the stakes are clear, people tend to rise up to meet the challenge far more than they might have on their own.

But we're talking about Scrum, not sports, right? True. And I believe nothing demonstrates the power of a high-performing Scrum team like a championship-level sports team. Can that energy, passion, and drive translate from the ball field to the cubicle? I believe it can. It requires a values-driven culture, visionary and service-focused leaders, and a strong team cultivated through practice. In Scrum, every team member is valued.

That's one of the beautiful things about Scrum: the recognition that all team members are important to the project. But it is important for everyone to understand their role properly. Some of the roles in Scrum don't necessarily correlate perfectly with traditional concepts of project team roles. Having an overly enthusiastic goalkeeper trying to kick a goal on the other end of the field does not lead to a World Cup.

EVERYONE HAS A ROLE TO PLAY

If I mention Steve Jobs, what do you picture? Different people associate a variety of words with the man who forged Apple into the company it is today: cold, calculating, decisive, driven, passionate, among others. Whether your view is positive or negative, people tend to agree on one of his traits: he was visionary.

What if I mention a sheepdog? What words might come to mind? Unless you've had a bad experience with canines, most people use terms like affectionate, kind, and hardworking. And again, most people will agree that he serves his flock.

What kind of person would you want leading your company through a highly competitive and fast-changing market? Someone who embodies Steve Jobs or a sheepdog? Which would you want to work with to make sure the team feels safe, cared for, and supported?

What if I told you about a stellar soccer team who had strong—not star—players in every position? Which one would you remove from the field? None. Even if the goalie was average, he's still better than no goalie at all. Players on teams with star goalies might feel that they can relax and let her handle the bulk of the work. Other teams with a star forward might let him take the bulk of the effort and thus fall apart if he is injured. Strong teams without stars, however, all work together. When all are average to slightly above average, they have no choice but to bring their best to the game.

Michael Jordan who played for the Chicago Bulls was arguably the best basketball player of all time. Did he help his team? Without a doubt. Jordan was a high-scoring asset who led his team to six championships. Yet I wonder if he ever put his own performance above the team's performance. There were many games where Jordan scored over fifty points—a phenomenal feat—but the Bulls still lost. Maybe if he had focused on the team effort and passed the ball more, the team might have won.

The above examples might sound exaggerated. Surely the Bulls thrived due to Jordan, and no star forward would be left with all the work, right? Research tells us something different. Organizations with star cultures (top talent with high pay and unlimited resources), bureaucracy cultures, or autocracy cultures (purely transactional—money for work) were outperformed by a commitment culture, according to a 1994 Stanford research project.[31] A commitment culture is a company where the prevailing philosophy is one where

---

31 James Baron and Michael T. Hannan, "Organizational Blueprints for Success in High-Tech Start-Ups: Lessons from the Stanford Project on Emerging Companies," *California Management Review* 44, no. 3 (Spring 2002), 8–36.

the founder "[wants] to build the kind of company where people would only leave when they retire."[32]

The star and bureaucracy cultures lead to shortcomings. Stars are only ever concerned about their own achievements, sometimes at the expense of the team or the company. Meanwhile, in siloed bureaucracies, everyone is only concerned with their piece of the puzzle, whether it fits or not. People in these workplaces and in star cultures tend to pull the focus very tight—just on themselves and their own roles. With a team-based commitment culture, the focus zooms outward, allowing each individual team member to see their work in the context of the greater whole and to expand their horizons beyond one narrow task list. With commitment workplaces, each person has a job to do, but they also have the freedom and permission to step outside these borders, as needed, for the good of the team.

CREATING A SCRUM TEAM

Creating a cohesive working Scrum team takes time. Looking at the various implementation strategies, the mixed and bottom-up strategies work best for the formation of the team because you have almost automatic buy-in to the concept of Scrum. In other words, the team members have usually self-selected themselves and already possess the enthusiasm, open-mindedness, and positive attitude that make for good teamwork.

With the top-down strategy, however, you will have an executive who has decided to implement Scrum and, if there is a dearth of volunteers, may hand-select people to work on the team whether they want to or not. A strong leader could push the team past the point of resistance, but with an external motivator—the boss—forcing the change, does change really happen? No. Almost no long-term good comes from an authoritarian leadership style. As mentioned in the last chapter, Adobe adopted an "Educate without Enforcing" leadership philosophy. Leadership by example and modeling works best, and when the team experiences the benefits of using Scrum firsthand, any initial resistance they may have had usually dissipates.

I consulted an executive Scrum team once where all but one member was excited about Scrum. The reluctant executive showed up to the first day of training with his laptop. Maybe he was going to take notes, but I believe, based on his body language, that he had no intention to learn and every intention

---

32 Baron and Hannan, "Organizational Blueprints for Success in High-Tech Start-Ups," 12.

to work on other things. I'm not a high school teacher; I can't send unruly students to detention or the principal's office, so I'm limited in how I can engage listless students. Fortunately, his boss laid down the law on the first day of training.

"I don't want to see anyone doing something else on their laptops or cell phones," he said. That was the end of that.

If you've been a leader for any length of time, you know the struggles with creating strong teams and overcoming poor attitudes and resistance to change. You've probably experienced the problem of balancing overachieving workers who share loads with employees who are happy to let the overachiever carry the team. If we were all machines and one was working faster than another, it wouldn't be an issue—you compensate and plan accordingly. But we're not machines. We're creatures of complex behaviors and emotions. When teammates aren't working as hard, or another is working very hard, emotions creep in. Emotions like envy, animosity, resentment, and anger can lead to a breakdown of communications and behaviors that are not aligned with Scrum's values.

How do we overcome this pervasive issue and create a tight-knit team? I believe we can find the answer in the military.

Like special operations forces in most countries, Colombia's special forces are comprised of teams of elite soldiers who are highly trained and assigned critical tactical missions. The formation of a military team is not unlike the formation of a high performance Scrum team.

The team members enter the military like all other soldiers. In Colombia, there is compulsory military service required for all boys eighteen years of age. They enter basic training and all that entails. But if they enter special forces, the dynamic changes. There they train together, eat together, bunk together, shower together. Each day, they come to depend on each other more and more. They rehearse various mission scenarios over and over again until they're second nature, so they can rely on training during live operations.[33] While they specialize in various parts of the mission, they also cross-train to understand each other's function. If the radio specialist is incapacitated on a mission, another team member can step in.

Unlike what the movies portray, the commanding officers are committed to the well-being of their unit. If they're about to depart on a three-month mission and a soldier's mother is diagnosed with cancer, the soldier is given

---

33 Based on personal interviews with members of Colombian Special Forces who choose to remain unnamed.

leave and support. This serves two purposes. It allows the soldier to be where he's needed. Second, another member can take his place so there is complete focus on the mission. Had that soldier been compelled to go on the mission, his distracted thoughts could be detrimental to the team's safety.

The members of these special forces teams learn to depend fully on each other. The more confidence, trust, and empathy team members can have, the more effective they can be in completing missions.

5.1. High-Performance Commitment Model

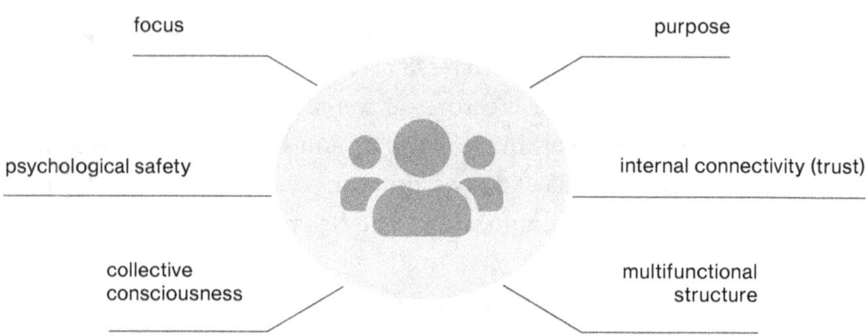

A high-functioning Scrum team is not much different—other than showering together, that is. Take a look at the High-Performance Commitment Model (HPCM) here. The terminology is the same as we covered in the values. And remember, values aren't just words you declare. You must live them as part of the culture you create in Scrum via your consistent behaviors. Only when you create an environment that embodies the actions and behaviors that model these values will you be able to cultivate a high-performing team.

It all begins with training.

First Part: Training

Training is the most important part of the process. Returning to the poker table, suppose you have seven players around the table. One learned to play poker from his grandfather and another from her mom. Maybe another learned through online gambling websites, and still another learned by watching tournaments on television. Everyone at the table has their own idea of how the game is played, which can lead to problems. The grandfather might have ignored a few types of hands for the sake of simplicity. Possibly the mom only played five-card stud, to the exclusion of all other games.

Assuming a team has had no formal Scrum training, this point is crucial. I may be biased; after all, that's what I do: I train teams and administer the certification. But training has been a crucial component to my own career. Each phase of my professional development involved formal classes and certifications. Some believe that such certifications are just nice things to have on your CV, and they're right. But these certifications are so much more than that. More than just gaining an intellectual understanding of Scrum, by training together, the trainees begin to learn about each other. They sprout the root of high-performance functionality when they learn and solve problems together. These are the team-building components similar to the Colombian military.

This is why I like training teams together. Even in instances where a team member has had training and certification, sitting in on another training only helps the team. By training together, the entire team learns and experiences Scrum together.

Second Part: Steve Jobs and a Sheepdog

Imagine if instead of tinkering in electronics, Steve Jobs was fascinated with animal husbandry and decided to raise sheep instead of making computers. No, this isn't the opening to a joke (though it could be—let me know if you come up with one). Let's further assume Steve's personality was fully intact, despite the different choice of vocation. Can you see him in the early days, lying in a field, his few sheep grazing nearby, while he dreams of a wool empire, Apple Woolwear?

As his flock grew, he'd need help managing the sheep. Dreaming of ways to revolutionize the wool-wearer's experience is one thing; getting a flock of a hundred sheep to move from pasture to pasture and into the barn for shearing is quite another.

That's where the sheepdog comes in. While Steve is dreaming, the sheepdog is there to manage the day-to-day movements, ensuring the sheep stay together, protecting them from predators, and making sure none are lost.

The roles they represent are equally as complementary.

Steve Jobs: The Visionary Product Owner

While many Product Owners are business leaders, they do not necessarily need to serve in an executive or any other positional leadership role within the organization. In fact, it's sometimes better if she isn't a leader, as I'll discuss a little later. But even if they are not a hierarchical leader, it is best if a Product Owner is imbued with some level of authority from the powers that be. In other words, a Product Owner should have the final word on all things pertaining to the Product Backlog and the work performed.

We outlined the Product Owner role in chapter 2, but the role is so much more than just a glorified list-maker. The Product Owner works with the client to determine what it is that they actually need. The Product Goal they create will be much more than just what the client says he or she needs. The Product Owner teases out the "why" behind asks and the larger intent behind a stated need.

Sometimes there's confusion regarding who the client is. The client is the person, organization, or group who will utilize the product the Scrum team creates. The client could be an internal company department, another company or companies, or retail consumers. Part of the Product Owner's job is to understand what the client needs and then prioritize those needs in the Product Backlog while also focusing on the long-term goal.

Steve Jobs's greatest skill, arguably, was his ability to see past what Apple's fans were asking for so his team could deliver the next evolution of what they needed. Many people couldn't understand why someone would need an iPad when he first introduced it in one of his famous unveilings, and yet this product and its copycats have become instrumental in an increasingly mobile society. Much like Steve Jobs's iPad, the Product Owner creates a Product Goal based on what the client doesn't yet know he needs.

Three things a Product Owner generally needs:

- **Understanding.** A solid understanding of the product, the market, and the client. She keeps her finger on the pulse of all three and is able to synthesize the data.

- **Authority.** Not necessarily positional power, but the power to decide what to do and in what order. If she doesn't have authority, then those with authority could divide the team's focus. Unfortunately, many Product Owners aren't given the authority they need to properly do their jobs. Instead, they have a Product Owner Proxy. The Product Owner handles all of the positional responsibilities, but she confirms final priorities with the boss. This adds to decision-making latency and betrays the team's effectiveness.

- **Time.** She needs time to synthesize all of the data about the market, the client, and the product. She also needs to have the time to be available to the team to guide them on these topics. In addition, she needs the freedom of time to continually refine the backlog.

When the team gathers for the first Sprint Planning with excitement and trepidation, the Product Owner has already established the first priorities of the backlog.

Together, the Product Owner and Developers negotiate how many items on the Product Backlog can be completed in the first Sprint. Since Scrum measures work in size and not time, the team determines how much work can completed within the Sprint's time box. The Scrum Master facilitates this negotiation to ensure that a balance is reached. On the one hand, the Scrum Master works to ensure the PO doesn't request too much work to be done. On the other hand, the Scrum Master shows the team they can achieve more than they might initially think they can. Some teams think they can move the world, while others might balk at the idea that they can be more productive than ever. The Scrum Master helps them overcome these hurdles and reach consensus.

This is where the Product Owner's job can get a bit tricky. If he's especially well-versed in the technical aspect of the product, he might try to tell the team *how* to complete the work. For the team to be effective and cohesive, he must let them figure out the work on their own.

Some think the Product Owner is only responsible for the Product Backlog. To some extent that's true, but she doesn't create a goal, populate the backlog, and then sit back, catching up on Netflix while the team works. The Product Owner's responsibilities continue throughout each Sprint. She will continue to refine the Product Backlog, work down the priority list to continually slice each requirement, and add details. She also continually works with the client, whether the client is a person who she can meet or talk to, or the client is a mass of consumers whose needs and feedback are available only through data analyses, focus groups, etc. She is present at the Sprint Review and Retrospective as well, making sure the team is focused on the priorities.

She sounds a little like Steve Jobs, right?

Sheepdog: The Scrum Master

The Scrum Master epitomizes a leader-by-coaching attitude. He has two main roles. One, ensure Scrum is followed correctly so that it doesn't morph into a Frankenscrum mutation. Two, serve the Product Owner and team by removing whatever impediments he can and doing everything possible to aid the team's learning and improvement process.

I feel that it's important to say here that, by comparing a Scrum Master to a sheepdog, I am not saying the Developers are mindless sheep. On the contrary, like the sheep of the real world, the Developers are those who produce the end product and are vitally important. I am not the first to use this comparison. In his book *Agile Project Management with Scrum*, Ken Schwaber writes, "Like sheep in an open field, individuals in a project tend to stray. The Scrum Master's job is to keep the flock together . . . I often compare a Scrum Master to a sheepdog, responsible for keeping the flock together and the wolves away."[34]

Like sheepdogs, Scrum Masters are leaders who ensure the team's well-being.

They verify that the team is moving in the same direction together, so their energies are focused on only one thing: the agreed-upon goal. And when other department heads or even company leadership attempt to disrupt the focused work, the Scrum Master keeps those distractions at bay so no time is wasted.

There are a number of leaders who have channeled the sheepdog-like qualities of a Scrum Master. Longtime Chicago Bulls and then Los Angeles Lakers coach Phil Jackson had a way of getting his teams to produce consistently at the highest levels while supporting each other. Darwin Smith, CEO of little-known but highly revered Kimberly-Clark Corporation (home of such brands as Kleenex and Huggies, among dozens of other paper-based goods), engineered the giant's turnaround with a philosophy of humility, believing that his job was to foster growth for his team and the company.

A Scrum Master leads the way while removing impediments and facilitating the team so it can travel faster. The Scrum Master receives extra training, as the name suggests. They are, in essence, a master of Scrum. They are the team's helper. The Scrum Master helps the Product Owner prepare for the next Sprint; he facilitates events like Sprint Planning and Sprint Retrospectives, making sure all events occur and that they stay inside the event's time box; and he helps the team remain committed and focused. In a sense, the Scrum Master is like a Scrum coach for the team, giving important feedback and guidance when necessary, and cheering them on at other times.

Mythbuster: *Scrum Masters can be removed from a veteran team or can serve multiple teams. False! The team velocity slows when a Scrum Master's duties are compromised.*

Because many organizations—especially those where Scrum is only partially implemented among one to three teams—think the Scrum Master only teaches Scrum, they often remove the Scrum Master from a team after they have matured. This is understandable. If a team has been using Scrum for a couple of years, is there anything else to learn? Well, there's always things to

---

34 Ken Schwaber, *Agile Project Management with Scrum* (Redmond, WA: Microsoft Press, 2004), 16.

learn—that's the nature of Scrum—but more than that, education is not the Scrum Master's only role. His main function is to increase the team's overall productivity—he helps the team go faster.

Another belief I see often is that a Scrum Master can "float" between various teams. This is possible but not advisable for the same reason. Focus is critical in Scrum. The Scrum Master helps to keep teams focused and to minimize distractions. How can he accomplish this if he himself is unfocused and distracted? In every case where a Scrum Master was removed or spread across multiple teams, the team's work slowed.

The Third Part: The Developers

With so much attention on the PO and SM, it would be inadvisable to exclude those who actually produce value. If the Product Owner is Steve Jobs and the Scrum Master is the coaching sheepdog, who are the Developers? They are the heart and soul of the work.

In some management circles, the traditional organizational hierarchy is flipped on its head. They view the C-level executives at the bottom and the wide labor level at the top. There is good reason for this. The philosophy is based on value. In their eyes, workers are the ones adding value and producing a product. All managers and higher-ups are nothing more than support for that process. They facilitate and manage transportation, procurement, benefits and training, and executive functions, all so the workers can produce the value that brings revenue in.

5.2. Inverted Hierarchy

Scrum embodies this spirit. The team members are those who produce the value and the actual work. We will define value in chapter 6, but for now, let's examine the Developers and how they work together.

As with the HPCM, the team begins forming in training. They are learning about Scrum as much as they are learning about how each other thinks, processes information, and asks questions, and are gaining glimpses into their personalities. The bonds are forming. Each Developer should add value in their own way. Together, they possess all the skills and experience necessary to bring any item on the backlog from concept to *done*.

So where do they begin?

Assuming they completed training, they might begin working together. Otherwise, they will start work during Sprint Planning. The Product Owner has set the goal of what they're trying to accomplish, and they've decided together with the Scrum Master's help that they can complete the first two priorities on the Product Backlog. They move these two items to the Sprint Backlog and begin to slice down the work further. At this point, both the Product Owner and Scrum Master leave, though some teams invite the Product Owner to assist. The Developers then decide *how* they will do the work. Read that again. It's important. In a world where people are used to being told *what* to do, the team decides for itself how it will accomplish its goal. It is self-directing.

This is where the magic really starts. When a competent team makes these decisions, they own the outcome. They agreed that the work could be done, and they decided how it would be done. If the Product Owner, knowing "best," tells them how to do the work, the team doesn't own the end result. If the project fails, it's not their fault: they can say, "I was only doing what I was told."

One of my friends back in Germany was working for a European luxury car manufacturer. He worked building brake assemblies for the final installation. But at some point during his tenure, the company had a major quality issue. Brake systems were failing or not meeting specifications, which led to problems. In an effort to solve the issue, the company brought in consultants who went around asking the assemblers about their jobs.

"What are you doing?" the consultants asked.

"What does it look like I'm doing? I'm making brake systems," would be the often snarky response.

The lack of ownership was clear. Every one of them thought they were doing a good job. They clocked in, built brake assemblies, and went home. In their little silo, they had no idea how little issues that might be viewed as "good enough" could cause issues for the car, the driver, or their passengers.

The company decided to take the team to headquarters and let them see the beautiful luxury car to which this particular brake assembly belonged. They dissected the car, and showed how everything fit together and what happened if things didn't work properly. "Without properly functioning brakes," they learned, "this beautiful work of art is useless and dangerous."

I don't know all of the details. Maybe they showed photos of proud car owners and their families; in those photos, they might have seen people who reminded them of their own friends and families.

Months later, the consultants took some performance measurements and crunched the numbers. The brake systems had vastly improved. Now when they asked workers what they did, they proudly answered, "I'm making brakes for the X model!"

They were no longer working a boring job making some parts for nice cars they'd never drive. Instead, they were making an important, lifesaving component for their customers—people like them, with friends and families they wanted to keep safe. They took ownership.

The team creates this sense of ownership as they tackle issues and work through challenges. When an iteration is inspected and fails, they collaborate to determine what went wrong and look for ways to make it better. Much like my team as we faced the insurmountable deficit of test cases at GoTelecom, the climate changes from tedium to electricity.

TEAMWORK IN ACTION

Once the Product Backlog is partially populated, the first Sprint Planning event has occurred, and the first Sprint is underway, the team begins to figure itself out. The Product Owner continues to slice the details, refine the Product Goal, and refine the stories on the board. The Scrum Master is busy helping to increase communication and collaboration and to tackle any issues or impediments beyond the team's purview. And the team is bringing their skills to each task and seeing how what they do impacts their teammates.

There are issues—maybe a heated conversation or two from frustration or lack of understanding. All change has its own inherent challenges. But instead of working in siloes, unaware or not caring about how their work impacts others, now everyone is in the same figurative boat as his teammates. Every untreated leak in the hull seals both his own as well as his teams' fate.

Like my friend making brakes, the coder at the beginning of the chapter, who thought it wasn't his job to address the issue with his work because it

was made to spec, soon changed his tune. He now saw that his work was giving his new coworker fits trying to correct it. He chose to make things right.
Because making code was no longer his job—making his team successful was.

YOUR SCRUM PLAYBOOK

Casting the roles is a critical component in creating a high-performance team.

PRODUCT OWNER (AKA STEVE JOBS)

- Is the team's visionary
- Synthesizes a vast array of knowledge about the client's needs, the product, and the market
- Creates, maintains, and refines the Product Backlog
- Understands all involved, has the authority to direct the team, and makes time for all of the above

Qualities of a Great Product Owner

- Has confidence
- Has a wide array of experience
- Does not blame others for own responsibilities
- Maintains a good network of people and research
- Focuses on values and behaviors, not "techniques"
- Is not afraid to share opinions
- Commits to the vision for success

SCRUM MASTER (AKA THE SHEEPDOG)

- Epitome of a coach
- Coaches, facilitates events, and helps the team achieve goals and improve
- Fully understands Agile and Scrum, and pursues ongoing education
- Demonstrates Scrum values through everyday behaviors
- Maintains the team's "bubble," protecting them from mismatched cultures and focus-stealing managers
- Ensures full transparency and commitment
- Works to remove team impediments

Qualities of a Great Scrum Master

- A great listener—hears deeper than what others are saying
- Ability to persuade others
- Has empathy for others
- Able to build a sense of community

- ▸ Loves helping others grow
- ▸ Takes ownership of responsibilities
- ▸ Works to mediate and maintain relationships during disagreements

Playing Your Hand

Now that you understand the players involved, it's time to assemble your team.

- ○ Choose your Product Owner.
- ○ Ask which people are interested in joining the team.
- ○ Let the team choose their Scrum Master.
- ○ Get everybody trained. Quality training is recommended. Remember, the idea is to cut your learning curve, so it's not about fast and cheap but about getting everybody on the same page and fired up.

CHAPTER SIX

The Rules of the Game

Learn the rules like a pro, so you can break them like an artist.

—Attributed to Pablo Picasso

A game without rules is pointless. If the dealer sets out cards for Texas hold 'em while some players arrange hands for gin rummy and others pair off for bridge, chaos will ensue.

Rules provide a framework that helps us understand what is expected—what a winning hand looks like, where we need to focus so we can work toward a win. The framework allows us to explore strategies and tactics, to work together with ease, and even to have fun along the way.

Whether you want to play ice hockey or Pot-Limit Omaha, understanding the rules begins with knowing the goal of the game. What does winning look like? In gin rummy, each player tries to be the first to gain a hundred points. The goal of hockey is to score more points than the other team in the time allowed. For a Scrum team, winning means creating value for the client—creating more value in less time, thanks to a fully empowered, motivated team.

THE GENESIS OF SCRUM

To understand the rules, it's helpful to have a sense of where Scrum originated. We've discussed the inspiration behind Scrum coming from the whitepaper titled "The New New Product Development Game." But much more than that paper and its rugby reference, Scrum's essence also borrows from the best of other philosophies with proven track records. Scrum was not born in a vacuum, but to paraphrase Isaac Newton, it stands on the shoulders of giants. Specifically, one giant called Toyota.

Lean

Scrum is based in part on "Lean," a business ideology developed out of Toyota's management philosophy. The Western world easily adopted the Toyota Production System (TPS), the side of Lean that looks at tools and processes, cuts waste, and maximizes profit. But TPS only offers perhaps 5 percent of the value of Toyota.[35]

The rest, 95 percent, comes from Toyota Product *Development* (TPD), which looks at a system holistically, at its vision, culture, and purpose. This part of the Toyota Way that concerns itself with people and philosophy and has often gone ignored in Western culture.

Lean's principles are derived from the Toyota Way and fall into four categories:

1. Long-term philosophy is more important than short-term profit.
2. The right processes will produce the right results.
3. You can add value in an organization by developing people and partners.
4. Continuously solving root problems drives organizational learning and continuous improvement.

This is where Scrum picks up, basing management decisions on long-term philosophy, even at the expense of short-term financial goals, working to develop the people in the workforce, naming a Scrum Master to carry the framework's principles and purpose throughout each project, and working by iteration so learning is constant. Toyota culture recognizes that good wages add value for a company, and that investing time and energy in suppliers develops a steady, reliable resource. Many of Toyota's suppliers, like Denso, have grown huge, nurtured by Toyota's growth. Toyota understood years ago that human values would drive corporate value.

The Three Enemies of Lean (and Scrum)

We cannot discuss Scrum's roots in Toyota's Lean culture without mentioning the three things that destroy Lean's existence. What Toyota refers to as the 3M model (not to be confused with the mega-corporation that supplies our favorite Scrum tool: Post-it notes!) consists of the following:

---

35 Takao Sakai, *The Secret Behind the Success of Toyota* (GPS Inc., 2018).

- ▸ Muda: Waste
- ▸ Mura: Unevenness
- ▸ Muri: Overburden

It's not headline-busting news that these three things hurt organizations. No C-level executive who desired to keep his job has ever said, "I think we need more waste, overburden, and unevenness." And yet, you've no doubt worked for companies where, from your unique perspective, the existence of at least one of the three—if not all three—was clearly evident.

Muda is pretty self-evident. It refers to the waste that comes from unproductive meetings, excess scrap material during production, or anything in general that doesn't add value. The elimination of this form of waste is built into the Scrum framework. The first Sprint will have more Muda than the second, and so on. With each increment and review, the team grows aware of how they can better work together in an efficient manner to nearly eliminate all waste.

The unevenness of Mura can happen when you have varying demand in production or have inconsistency in your approach. Look at a restaurant. During a Friday night dinner, they need a full complement of servers and kitchen staff, but if they had the same staffing for a Monday brunch, most of the people would be doing nothing. Most Scrum teams don't have the flexibility of a restaurant in regard to staffing. Scrum approached this enemy of Mura by creating teams that were multifunctional.

When you have the overburden of Muri, you have overload, overwhelm, and all the negative side effects that accompany them. With a machine station, it means you have backlogs that disrupt the workflow. With an individual, it results in absenteeism, sickness, and stress. When your computer's CPU or hard drive is constantly operating at 100 percent capacity, your computer slows to the speed of frozen sludge. And yet, many managers believe both a machine and worker should always be working and never have downtime. This doesn't make sense to me. In Scrum, the team determines the optimum workflow and, just like with the dynamic example above, can work efficiently to make sure overburden doesn't happen. (For more about Lean, consider reading the book *The Toyota Way*.)

THE ARTIFACTS OF SCRUM

What is value? It can be many things at many times. Air is free under most circumstances, but as a scuba diver who once ran out of it while twenty meters below sea level, I can tell you that sometimes air is priceless. But value isn't intrinsically connected to money. When Edison failed on iteration four thousand of the light bulb, he saw the value in learning what didn't work. Each product, no matter what it is, flows down a *value stream*, gathering value all the way. Coffee beans become more valuable as they are grown and picked, roasted, packaged, and finally brewed. Well-trained, experienced employees will add value even though they cost more in salary. In the growing process, value may be generated by fertile soil and sun. The more flavor gained in roasting, the more value. Even perceived value is important: slap a Starbucks label on that pound of coffee, and more customers will be interested. The value stream is dynamic: lately "shade-grown" coffee has been selling at a premium. Products change faster and more completely, and when a product solves a problem (or solves it faster), it is more valuable to the customer. In the past, you might publish a new atlas every ten years; now Google Maps updates continuously.

The three Scrum Artifacts exist to structure the work to be done in a way that ensures it continually adds value, provides transparency, and allows the team and stakeholders opportunity to inspect the work and adapt as necessary. Scrum is structured to usher a product through the value stream, maximizing value all the way. Let's take an example and follow it through the Scrum process. A group known as Wikispeed, on the US West Coast, is working to build a car that gets one hundred miles per gallon. They are open-sourcing the project, but for our purposes we'll assume we have a Scrum team in charge of developing such a car for a company called One Gallon.

Where do we begin? First, the Product Owner articulates the team's goal: to reduce the world's consumption of fossil energies, they must develop a safe, reliable car that uses only one gallon of gas per hundred miles. Quite a challenge, but an exciting one: such a car will cut its owner's gas budget by two-thirds, and if it works well enough, it will have an immense effect on the environment and on One Gallon's bottom line. From now on, each move, each decision, takes the team forward together toward the realization of that goal, slashing bureaucracy and creating value all the way.

Product Backlog

We briefly defined the Product Backlog in chapter 2, and we've discussed how it's created and maintained by the Product Owner. Now we'll dive deeper into how those items get on the Product Backlog. For those rushing into Scrum *techniques* with only a little understanding, the backlog can become more of a thoughtful to-do list of tasks instead of complete items that create value. This is more than semantics; it's the beginning of true Scrum.

Product Goal

The Product Goal is the long-term objective for the Scrum team. Like any good goal, the Product Goal is specific, measurable, and focused. In addition, this goal is strategic in that in does not necessarily represent the end goal—it can serve as a marker on the path to the ultimate destination. This goal rests in the Product Backlog, and the rest of the backlog will help define the items to accomplish the Product Goal.

STORY MAPPING

If you're familiar with *The Scrum Guide*, you won't find Story Mapping anywhere in its pages. Yet Story Mapping (created by Jeff Patton) is important to make sure you have covered all of the steps necessary to provide value to the customer. This allows the team to understand not only what they are designing, but why. The more completely they understand this, the more value they will create, and the less time they will spend on unnecessary efforts. So the team begins to map stories: developing the fullest possible understanding of the end users' needs based on a logical progression of steps.

> **Mythbuster:** *If you're familiar with The Scrum Guide, you won't find Story Mapping anywhere in its pages. Yet Story Mapping (created by Jeff Patton) is an important step. It ensures that you have covered all of the steps necessary to provide value to the customer.*

When planning a vacation, you may already perform a simplified version of this when creating a packing list. You may picture your morning routine and the products you use: various soaps, lotions, razor, toothbrush, etc. Then you might check the forecast and picture the items you would wear in that weather. Story Mapping is similar.

Story Mapping is accomplished in three main steps, which give you an idea of what goes into determining how the user is going to use the product. Each item has to be independent, negotiable, able to generate value, estimable, small enough, and, finally, testable.

6.1. Story Mapping

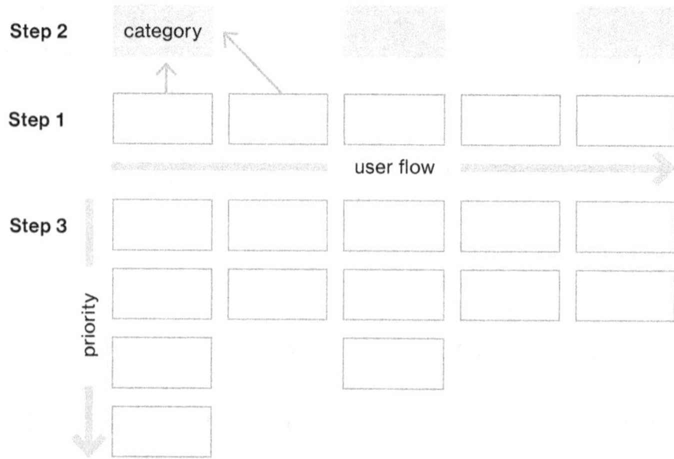

Step One: Sequence User Will Use the Product

In step one, working left to right on a piece of paper or a whiteboard with sticky notes, you map the sequence of how the user will use the product. For our car, the user will open the door, sit down, buckle a seat belt, start the engine, etc.

Step Two: Decide on Module

In step two, you decide all of the bigger steps that would need to happen. Let's look at item one, opening the door. What bigger parts do you need for that to work? Probably things like a door and a chassis to attach it to. Put these on top of the board above that first row. (I like to use a different-colored sticky note). So now you have a top row going left to right in one color of sticky notes, with items like "Door," "Chassis," and "Engine/Motor," and under that row is step 1, the story of how the user will use it. Under "door assembly," from left to right as shown in the example: unlock door, open door, close door.

These items in step two form the backbone of the Story Map, the high-level items the user will need to get value from our product.

Step Three: Add to the Backbone

The final major step—though we can get into far more detail than we are doing here—is to then populate the details under each module, top-down, from highest priority to lowest.

Each horizontal group, organized by priority, under each module will create a "slice" or represent a release of a product.

Ideally, in pure Scrum, we should be able to create a complete car in the first Sprint with everything needed to add value to the client and get feedback. If this is a start-up and our first Sprint car was not achieving one hundred miles per gallon, the seats were 3-D printed, etc., then the value would be the information we gathered from this first release. Unfortunately, cars are a tad more complex than this. For some especially complex products like cars and fighter jets, teams cheat pure Scrum a little—adapt it—in order to accomplish their goals. I'm not advocating a departure from pure Scrum here, and I'm especially not advocating for Frankenscrum or Stunted Scrum; I'm only suggesting that sometimes rules are broken. It's a good idea to master the rules, though, before you decide to break them.

I am advocating that you do your best to follow the pillars and values of Scrum. We could say that the first Sprint, for argument sake, is to produce a computer model that can be tested virtually. Or possibly our fictional car company is a new subsidiary of a traditional auto manufacturer, and we have an established base model to begin working with. With this point being firmly established, we can continue with our example.

What is the goal of Story Mapping? We want an ordered Product Backlog populated with Product Backlog Items (PBIs)—each item, ideally, would be a solution to a problem the client has. The steering wheel allows clients to turn right and left.

Some Scrum teams define PBIs as "User Stories," where each story defines the type of user, what the user wants, and what benefit she expects: "As a driver, I want to easily and quickly unlock the door." Or "As a driver, I want responsive steering." Personally, I'm not a fan of user stories. I feel too many people get too involved in the format of user stories, at the expense of everything else. But it's personal preference; as long as they accomplish the main task, get everything needed on the board! Like the travel packing list, putting yourself in the place of the user (or you on vacation) can help stimulate your memory so you cover every item possible.

The Product Owner works with the team to build a story map that considers what users will be searching for and how the team can deliver value by addressing these concerns. What items will be necessary in order for the team to build a car that users feel will save money and gas, and that will be as or more reliable as the car they drive now? Team members will have different opinions on each story, and each item: What is worth their time and One Gallon's investment? Which parts seem essential? Which may not merit the investment of time and resources? As the Product Owner negotiates these conversations, the Scrum Master facilitates the conversation, making sure the conversation centers on value and that the team doesn't commit to impossibilities or neglect essentials.

Now the Product Owner can prioritize the work items to create the Product Backlog. It's tempting to think of the backlog as a to-do list—but the items in the backlog are all *from the client's point of view.* The backlog is a bird's-eye view of the items necessary to create the greatest value for One Gallon and its customers. Like all things Scrum, the Product Backlog will change and change again, but this first effort will guide the Product Owner in visualizing the scope of the project and deciding on the work of the first Sprints.

PRIORITIZING

Prioritizing is perhaps the heart of Scrum. Every slice of work from the Story Map becomes a part of a Sprint, with the Product Owner continuously reprioritizing the backlog based upon Sprint Reviews, client feedback, and changing value. The Product Owner's goal as she prioritizes the backlog is to optimize value for the client. What is the next thing that will bring the most value for the client? To write this book, we started with an outline, then wrote each chapter in turn. But suppose we were delivering it a chapter at a time? Then we may decide that a real-world story in chapter 6 has the highest priority because it adds the most value. When we come to chapter 4, we will be sure that the reader knows the material in chapters 1–3 and so is ready to learn the chapter 4 material. But perhaps we learn that something we mentioned in chapter 3 needs further elaboration. Our Product Owner will reprioritize, perhaps calling for a rewrite of chapter 3, or suggesting that we address that item in more depth in a later chapter. We always prioritize according to value: if the reader won't be able to make any sense of chapter 4 without certain information, that information must be covered earlier. Value is not always counted in economic terms. It may be customer satisfaction, and it may be public interest.

The PO should optimize value for the long term. When a backlog item is "ready" to go into the Sprint, all of the criteria it depends on have been satisfied. A PBI is ready when it is fully actionable. In other words, the item's scope, requirements, and "story" have been completely defined by the Product Owner. If it has not, the Developers can refuse to add it to a Sprint. Suppose the next PBI is a Bolognese sauce (bear with me, pretend this is an Agile restaurant). The Developers (chefs and kitchen personnel) might look at the item and see that the exact requirements like quantity and level of quality (diner-fast or three-star-Michelin ready) are missing from the Product Owner's definition. This item is not "ready" for their Sprint.

But suppose it is ready. The staff knows what's required of them. They then decide how to make the sauce. When something is "done," it is fully useful to the client or, in this case, the customer at table seven. If we're making a Bolognese sauce, we'll need onions, but dropping an unpeeled onion into the pan will add no value to the sauce. Only when the onion had been peeled and chopped has it accrued enough value. If we're making our sauce as a team, we may need to discuss exactly what type of onion, how much onion, and how finely chopped our onion will need to be. The Product Owner may remind us that the customer at seven is Gordon Ramsay and somebody just dinged his car. So, while it's easier to chop the onion roughly, it will produce a more delicious sauce if we take the extra time to chop finely. We don't want to upset Chef Ramsay. He may also remind us that every single slice doesn't need to be exactly the same width—that we're wasting time when we indulge in that kind of perfectionism. No matter what ingredients we use or how we decide to process the sauce, it's not "done" until the sauce is hot and ready to eat.

REFINEMENT

The Product Owner prioritizes; she is continuously refining the backlog and, with it, the Product Goal. As she does that, she prepares for the next Sprints. The first items on the backlog are naturally more whole and more fully detailed.

As the team works its way through these items, they learn more, ask more questions, discover new impediments. The next tasks are larger and less detailed, but as the higher items are completed, the lower ones come into focus. Some of them fall away, and some change as the information from the earlier sprints informs the goal. Team members bring in new ideas, the client makes additional requests, and the market changes. If the product is a Bolognese sauce, the PO considers the customer's feedback that it was too tangy here; would a pinch of sugar change the acidity? If the product is a new type of car, the PO may have to deal with poor results from the crash testing and add PBIs related to improving the chassis's construction.

Refining is a continuous process informed by the changing needs of the client and the changing forces of the market. By working in short cycles, we are generating value in bursts that keep both the client and the team focused and motivated.

In a way, the "rules" of Scrum are simple. Led by the Product Owner, facilitated by the Scrum Master, the team takes stock of the necessary items, and then undertakes them in iterations known as Sprints. As each Sprint completes items from the Product Backlog, the backlog is refined and streamlined, so the remainder of the project is better understood and the next steps become clear.

As the Product Owner populates the Product Backlog, prioritizing the team's steps toward the goal, she is also deciding what the team *shouldn't* do—that is, what will constitute waste. For instance, many products require documentation that is never used. We did a project for the Colombian government, ordering the implemented technology for colleges. The project took two weeks, and we ordered everything necessary, confirmed that all was well, and sent the government a bill. Then they told us they had to have a detailed report before they could release payment. They'd never thought to mention it to us, but they needed an eight-hundred-page report in order to pay us. Producing the report took us twice as long as the actual project, and I doubt anyone ever made use of that document. It was a waste of time and money for us and for them. You can't fight City Hall, but you can be sure you say no to work that doesn't generate real value for the client.

The Scrum team will then decide how to define "done" for this product. "Done" must be specific to the project, but general enough to apply to all items in the backlog. What is "done" for this particular project? What criteria does each piece of our car need to meet? Perhaps it must be strong enough to meet crash criteria and light enough to save fuel, and it must also fit into the full interface.

Now that you have a goal and the Product Backlog, you know what you're aiming for, but you have to grasp the most effective way to get there. Sure, you can score a hockey goal by randomly zigzagging for an hour all over the ice, but it will wear out your players, frustrate the fans, increase your star's risk of injuries, and decrease your team's likelihood of winning the game.

ESTIMATING

If you're from traditional waterfall planning, forget everything you think you know about estimating. Gone are the days where you call various departments and stakeholders and pore over historical data to estimate the time involved in various tasks. Even estimating software with the duration of many tasks calculated via complex algorithms isn't without errors.

Look at your personal life. How often are you correct in estimating the time to paint a room, swap out a major appliance, or repair a broken hinge? The less experience you have with a particular project, the more likely you are to get the estimated time wrong. Add to that our inherent optimism that it won't "take that long," and you can see the problem. If we can underestimate painting a room, how can we accurately estimate bridges and oil wells? No wonder most projects are often over budget and late.

Scrum users rely on relative estimates of work instead of front-loaded time guesses. As detailed in *Agile Estimation and Planning* by Mike Cohn, planning time does not directly correlate with planning accuracy. There is a point of diminishing returns where more time spent planning yields no return in regard to the accuracy of the estimates planned.

In traditional planning, cost depends upon time. But how does time work, exactly? If you're a beginning runner, you may do five kilometers in half an hour. But if you slept badly, the weather is hot and humid, or your muscles ache, it will take longer. And your time may well improve month by month as your stamina and technique improve. On automobile assembly lines, managers' dreams of predictability could be achieved. Most projects today, from software rollouts to engineering projects to the design of new forms of transportation, are not very predictable. Excess planning time, time during which a multitalented group could otherwise be working on an iteration that pushes the project forward, is time wasted.

We can improve predictability in a different way. Humans can't make exact, absolute determinations through guessing. If you're in a room of thirty people, and I ask you to tell me each person's height within a couple of centimeters, you will fail. We *can* make comparisons, however. Take those same thirty people and line them up with the shortest on the left and the tallest on the right, set everyone else in between, and after switching up a few, you've got them in order and can make an estimate of their relative heights.

In a similar way, the team considers, compares, and **estimates** the amount of work, the uncertainty, and the complexity of each task. Each team member brings his or her expertise and a gut sense informed by that expertise. Considering all factors, the team can do a little bit of planning, enough to get started immediately. There are many estimation approaches available to the Agile community, but many like using Planning Poker®[36]. While not part of *The Scrum Guide*, Planning Poker has become a widely accepted and utilized technique. First coined by James Grenning in 2002,[37] it involves a deck of playing cards. It is through the act of playing this game that users can reach consensus on an estimate for each item.

Planning Poker is the method we will use to give you a tool you can use now (plus it has "Poker" in the title, which is good enough for me). Each player (user) receives a small deck of cards. These cards can be colorfully printed

---

36 "Planning Poker," after its inception, has since become a registered trademark of Mike Cohn and Mountain Goat Software (see https://www.mountaingoatsoftware.com). This mention should not be considered an endorsement of the software.

37 James Grenning, "Planning Poker or How to avoid analysis paralysis while release planning," SEWiki, April 2002, https://sewiki.iai.uni-bonn.de/_media/teaching/labs/xp/2005a/doc .planningpoker-v1.pdf.

decks you can purchase (look for "agile planning" or "story points" cards in your search), or you can use simple index cards. Instead of your usual card characters and numbers, each card has only a number on it. For our purposes, we will use the Fibonacci sequence, a sequence of whole numbers starting at zero, with the next number in the series equally the sum of the previous two. It looks like this: 0, 1, 2, 3, 5, 8, 13, 21, 34, 55, 89, etc.

Each number corresponds to a relative amount of work. In order to be relative, we need to determine a starting point—a reference point—that the team agrees with. I like to start with "2" or "3" as the baseline point since, if you come across an item that is smaller than you expected, you have two or three numbers you can assign.

If you were estimating items in your life, a simple item everyone does (hopefully) is brush your teeth. We might assign that a "2." Again, it's not the amount of *time* that's important here but rather the estimated amount of *work* we think an item will take. So, if brushing your teeth is "2," making dinner might be a "5," washing your car might be an "8," and mowing the lawn might be a "13," depending on the size of your lawn and the capability of your tools. Do you see what we're accomplishing? Just as with running five kilometers, we're not measuring the time but the distance (work). A world-class athlete can run five kilometers in thirteen minutes, and a coach potato might take an hour, but the distance remains the same. An accomplished chef might consider a single-family dinner a "3." Those discrepancies allow us to reach a more accurate picture.

But what happens when we introduce uncertainty to the mix? What if the couch potato has never run so much as down the block? How can he or she accurately represent the amount of work involved in a five-kilometer race? Even if our sedentary runner assumes it will be easy, they will want to estimate up to account for the uncertainty. He or she will further want to consider complexity. If the marathon is happening in the mountains or on a hill, measuring inclines and accounting for altitude is important.

Ideally, the estimation occurs during refinement. The Product Owner solicits the team's input in a time-boxed event. The Product Owner explains the details of the PBI, and each team member places a number card face down on the table that relates to the amount of points he or she thinks the item deserves. Let's say the One Gallon team agree that designing and 3-D printing a small assembly is a "3." One PBI discussed might be based on some feedback such as "Make steering more responsive." After every player plays a card from her deck, the cards are flipped over. If everyone guessed "8," great! You have reached perfect consensus and can move on to the next item. But consensus on the first try is rare.

What usually happens is you will have a number of 8s, maybe a couple of 5s, and then you might have an outlier or two. Sebastian played a "3" and Natalia played a "21." What's going on here? Are they inept or incompetent? Hardly. Instead, these outliers are often either misunderstanding the item, or sometimes they are seeing things from a unique perspective.

Those with extreme high or low numbers, compared with the average of the team, have an opportunity to discuss why they chose the number they did. This is done with openness and honesty—remember the importance of psychological safety? Lose that sense of safety here, and you may have team members who go along to get along, when they may actually see things differently—a perspective that may be critical to a product's success.

Maybe Sebastian explains that, from his perspective, all they need to do is tighten the tie-rod assembly and swap out the bearings with a different material (can you tell I'm not great with cars?). Meanwhile, Natalia agrees with Sebastian but explains that she thought reaching the goal would require a complete overhaul. The team listens to those who had very high or low numbers. Usually these anomalous numbers are the result of different assumptions about the item or the work involved and are often remedied with the PO offering clarification. Maybe Natalia is told a complete overhaul is not needed but Sebastian has a point—maybe his solution is one the team did not consider. After Sebastian and Natalia have their say and the PO re-explains the work, the team plays another hand.

The goal is to reach consensus. If everyone deals the same number, cherish this unicorn! If the numbers are close—5s and 8s—take an average. I recommend a maximum of three rounds of Planning Poker per item. If after three rounds, Sebastian continues to be stubborn with his 3 while everyone else is much higher, toss his number out and use the rounded average of the remaining estimates. Consensus doesn't mean everyone will agree 100 percent, only that each team member has had an opportunity to get buy-in to what work is required. Going back to the value of commitment, every team member demonstrates commitment by moving forward once a decision has been made, even if he disagrees with that decision.

Now you have points assigned to a number of PBIs. Due to the dynamic nature of Scrum, maybe not all of the PBIs have been fully refined enough for estimates. In any case, it's good that the team define points for at least the next two or three Sprints. That way, if they complete the items of the first Sprint early, they can begin working on the next PBI. We will see how these points play a role in understanding the work and increasing each Sprint's velocity.

The Sprint Backlog

The Sprint Backlog is created during Sprint Planning, which we will cover in a little bit. In many ways, the Sprint Backlog resembles the Product Backlog. The Sprint Backlog is comprised of the PBIs selected for the current Sprint but with added details down to individual tasks that must be completed for each. The Sprint Backlog must be made visible to all—usually by means of a large whiteboard where Post-its listing tasks can be arranged and rearranged, mapping out the work that needs to be done. This keeps the plan—today's plan and the longer-term plan—right out in front for everyone to see. It's a tool of transparency: every member of the team is aware of each other's work; tasks can be moved as necessary, and when something isn't working, it becomes very clear.

Once the work for the first Sprint is on the board, the team inspects and discusses, each member seeing the tasks he or she will be working on, and considering the order of the tasks. As a new task is defined, it's added to the Sprint Backlog.

SPRINT GOAL

Similar to the Product Goal being the singular objective of focus, the Sprint Goal is the singular aim of the Sprint. The Sprint Goal likewise helps the Developers to work together on the common end. And while the goal itself is fixed, the team has latitude in how to accomplish the goal.

The team decides on the Sprint Goal during the Sprint Planning process and the goal is subsequently added to the Sprint Backlog. Should the nature of the planned work change or in any way deviate from the planned approach, the team will consult with the Product Owner to discuss adapting the scope without changing the goal itself.

Increment

We've already discussed an Increment in chapter 2; however, since we're going over the Artifacts in detail, I'd be remiss if I didn't cover this one too, even briefly.

An Increment is the sum of all the Product Backlog items that are completed during a Sprint and the total value of completed items from the Sprints that came before. Yet, sometimes this concept still trips people up. If I asked you how many Increments you had after three Sprints and fifteen PBIs completed, what would you answer? If you said one, you're correct.

A football team might make seven individual goals during a game, but they still have only one score—in this case, the value of their score is seven. Put another way, you might build a small two-story house. Later you might add a third story, expand the kitchen, or create an addition off of the living room. After all this work, you still have only one house—there's just a greater sum of the work and value added.

The only requirements are that the value of the Increment at the end of each Sprint must agree with the team's definition of "done," the work can be inspected, and the work brings you closer to the end goal. Suppose the Sprint yields a product that's not releasable, that it only served as a lesson in what doesn't work. If it's not done, it cannot be part of the Increment. Since it's not done, it doesn't generate value, though it might come with valuable lessons.

THE FIVE SCRUM EVENTS

Event One: The Sprint

The team, along with the Product Owner and the Scrum Master, will have decided on the Time Box—the length of each Sprint, and the pulse of the project/team. Usually this is one to four weeks—a time short enough to facilitate a spurt of communal concentration on one task or group of tasks. The more uncertainty in a project, the shorter the Time Box will be, but each Sprint will be the same length. You could say that ice hockey proceeds in three twenty-minute Sprints, with the points scored in each one needing to add up to a winning score.

The Sprint is the one Time-Box event that contains within it the other four. The events below all occur within the Sprint. The Sprint's purpose is to produce a goal—an Increment adding value to an overall goal. Each Sprint goal is a kind of hypothesis. The first Sprint for One Gallon might produce a 3-D-printed prototype of the car as part of a PBI. Part of the hypothesis could be that it can achieve the 0.315 drag coefficient required for the car. The hypothesis is that such a drag coefficient can be attained. I want to point out that this is not good Scrum because the client can't use that prototype. It has added value to the project, but it's not a releasable Increment. It does, however, illustrate how Sprints can test hypotheses.

The rules of the Sprint are simple: once set, do not change the goal; quality may not be decreased; and any changes or clarifications of the Sprint scope must be negotiated with the Product Owner. Lastly, a Sprint may be cancelled, but only the Product Owner has the authority to do so and usually only under extraordinary circumstances (e.g., a major change in the customer's needs or a market disruption).

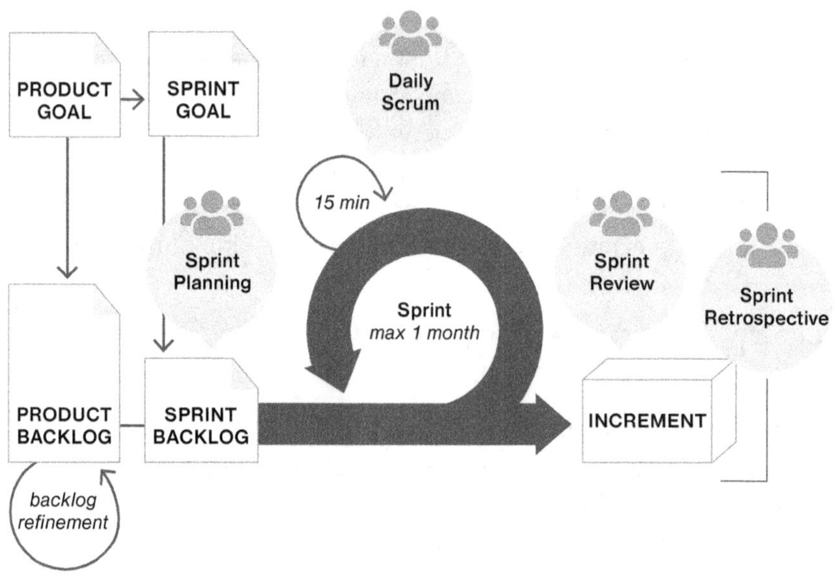

Event Two: Sprint Planning

There are three parts to Sprint Planning, each asking and answering a specific question. Part one asks, "Why?" Part two asks, "What?" And finally, part three asks, "How?"

The entire team is in the first two parts of the planning, looking at *why* the Sprint is valuable and examining *what* needs to be done. Because the team is cross-functional, the group is able to look at the work holistically, avoiding potential conflicts and quickly seeing around some obstacles. If the team was working in silos, in the traditional manner, the project would lose the power of communal focus—that chance that a design idea would immediately be supported by an engineer and a software developer, and more fully understood by public relations. There are lots of questions: are there other product backlog items that should be included? Are there ideas and tasks that seem to go naturally together? What other items add value for the client? The Product Owner is in attendance and responsible to clarify PBIs and answer questions. Is this too much work, and, if so, is there a different way to slice it?

The Scrum Master's role in Sprint Planning is, first, to assure it takes place. It's easy for Scrum novices to cut corners by assuming that the Product Owner is a "boss" and that there's no need for every member of the team to weigh in on each Sprint, but this small savings of time reduces buy-in and motivation and robs the team of its creative flow. Every single member of the team is responsible for using his or her expertise to help guide the process, and each one needs to have a voice in planning, accomplishing, and reviewing each sprint. A software developer may well see something a designer will miss. The Scrum Master also facilitates the Sprint Planning, holding the wisdom of Scrum theory and practice, and applying it as the discussion proceeds. He maintains the values and aspects of Scrum even when it may be tempting to overlook them, and demonstrates Scrum's virtues along the way. Lastly, the Scrum Master ensures that the planning takes place within the agreed-upon Time Box, a maximum of eight hours for a month-long Sprint, and four hours for a two-week Sprint for all three parts of Sprint Planning. This time is not split evenly between the parts.

Suppose our team negotiates that they can accomplish the first four PBIs on the list. The average points for each is as follows: 8, 15, 7, and 11 (remember, these are rounded averages based on the Fibonacci sequence). That's a total of 41 points. Later, we'll see how these points are used to calculate velocity.

In step three of Sprint Planning, subsidiary priorities and tasks are clarified. This is when the Developers discuss how they will do the work. Usually the Product Owner leaves at this point. Although she's not the boss, technically speaking, her presence can be intimidating. Also, if she has any technical expertise, she may be tempted to tell the developers how to do the work. Why is that bad? How likely are you to own bad results if a "boss" told you to do a task a certain way? However, when the team decides amongst themselves how to get the job(s) done, they are more likely to step up and adjust if their initial plans go awry.

Now while the subsidiary items are decided, the priority of the Product Backlog is not changed. If the Product Owner and team agree that the first four PBIs can be completed in the first Sprint, the Developers then decides how they are going to do the work of item one first and further define that item's tasks and priorities. Be clear on this: the team cannot decide to do PBI number four first—they must follow the order directed by the Product Owner. This is where commitment comes in.

The Sprint Backlog is populated during this event, its shape and the general arc of progress begin to become clear, but every day's work can lead to discoveries, as new impediments arise and new information becomes available.

Does this seem awfully loose? Shouldn't the team be costing out different plans, setting out the number of person hours required, deciding when one step ends and another begins? Ah, now you're seeing where Scrum excels in uncertainty. Admittedly, that level of uncertainty can feel both terrifying and freeing at the same time. We reign in the uncertainty a little during the next event.

Event Three: Daily Scrum

The team goes to work, coming together for fifteen minutes a day in front of the Sprint Backlog, an event known as the Daily Scrum. This event occurs at the same time and place *every day*. Frequently when I begin working with a client's team, somebody will roll their eyes a little and ask, "Does it have to be *every* day? Didn't we cover enough yesterday?" And while I think meetings are the bane of our existence too, I am a stickler for the Daily Scrum. One of Scrum's major assets is that it helps people communicate better, and better communication solves problems faster and more easily, creates more project buy-in, and charges a project with interpersonal energy that has an unquantifiably good effect on motivation. Face-to-face communication is by far the best, but sometimes a team is working from different branches in different cities so a good stable videoconference system is essential. You'll notice we don't call this a meeting, because it is a quick, regular, and *productive* event, focused on replanning the Sprint and synchronizing toward the Sprint goal, identifying impediments along the way. It's often best if the PO doesn't attend the Daily Scrum so the team can work on its own without any sense of a "boss" overseeing things. The Scrum Master is usually present at the first few Daily Scrums at least, to facilitate and teach as the team works through its challenges, and to see the impediments firsthand. The team always has the option to invite the Scrum Master if they wish.

The event is fairly simple. Each member checks in and together the Developers ensure they are aligned with the Sprint Goal, and secondly, they plan their next twenty-four hours.

Sometimes an impediment is quite simple—a laptop is on the blink. You go to the tech department and have it repaired or replaced. Sometimes it's complex and can even be something that's enshrined in the company's structure that would have to be resolved at a very high level beyond even the Scrum Master's power. I had one instance I touched on in chapter one where we had constant trouble connecting to Wi-Fi. Every little problem had to be referred to the tech help department and be addressed in order, although clearly the problem was systemic. It was slowing our work to a crawl, and we were always told, "Well, you have to follow the procedure." Finally, I invited one of the top executives to lunch, and the problem was solved. In its focus on impediments, the Scrum framework encourages innovation and cuts through bureaucracy. As we address problems and decide how to resolve them, we generate value beyond even what we've contracted to do.

Event Four: Sprint Review

The last portion of each Sprint—the feedback portion—is perhaps the most important: here the team shows its work to the client for review, hears the client's reactions, discusses what they've learned, and uses this information to focus and improve the product. Iteration by iteration, the product grows and evolves until the work is finished—worthy of Chef Ramsay's kiss or an investor's buy-in.

In this case, we get feedback during the Sprint Review, which is when the team shows what we have done to the stakeholders. What gains did we make? What did we learn that will change the project going forward? The team sits down with the client to go over the product of the Sprint—in this case, the prototype of their car. We show what we have done and get feedback from the client. I've sometimes had to convince a client that it was important for him to be in the planning and review sessions. We need to confirm that the client's priorities haven't changed or, if they have, to adjust our own prioritization.

This prototype gives everyone something essential to inspect and consider; it will generate many ideas, and, in doing so, it proves successful. We are at the beginning of the project, where our uncertainty is very high, but the cost of change is negligible. By finding essential overall changes now, we have saved money and time. Our next iteration, and, in fact the whole project, will be informed by this feedback. During the review, the Product Owner tracks the progress the team has made toward accomplishing its mission. Each Sprint serves as a launchpad for the next, and the project backlog is completed item by item, sprint by sprint.

Getting back to our points. Let's say the team easily accomplished the four PBIs as we saw in Sprint Planning. They achieved 41 points of value and began working on PBI number five. If they have achieved 41 points in their Sprint, their current velocity is 41. Next, they'll look at what they can do more.

Event Five: Sprint Retrospective

Finally, we have the Sprint Retrospective. This is the team's chance to analyze the process, with the Product Owner acting simply as another team member. How did the team work together? What really yielded value? What held the team back? The Scrum Master facilitates this event as well as giving his own comments. This is where you have to be open, and work to give credit and analyze your own performance and consider how to improve it. How well did you uphold the scrum values, and where did you see friction? I've worked in so many different cultures, and there can be difficulties between people from a culture that values timeliness and honoring promises, and those from a culture where promises are considered more of a social nicety and less of a commitment. It's the kind of thing different people can talk out with good-will and adapt to. This may sound difficult, but in fact it's one way to grow as you work, to make a real bond with your colleagues, and to deliver the most value for the client.

Scrum is about learning and improving. Each Sprint hopes to improve on the last. There's no such thing as a perfect Scrum process, and the beginning of a Scrum project always feels a bit chaotic and uncertain. In fact, this is where any project starts, and while reams of data and planning may make people *feel* more secure, this is no more than a feeling. Security lies in thinking on your feet, working with a team you trust, coming in to work every day with a sense of agency and excitement.

We pay a lot of attention to assure that we do the retrospective on every single Sprint, and that we talk about what went well and find the tools to help ourselves improve. When you don't do the retrospective, you can have problems that, unaddressed, can turn into nightmares for the team. The retrospective is the team's opportunity to discuss what went right and what could be better. Maybe there are five suggestions for how to improve the next Sprint. In that case, implement only one. If you went to the doctor with an ailment and were prescribed five medications alleviating the ailment, which one did the trick? You're not sure. By implementing only one solution, you are able to gauge the impact of that change and make further distinctions in the next retrospective.

What if the team says nothing needs improving? Nonsense! There's always room for improvement—you're just not looking hard enough.

LOOKING FORWARD TO THE NEXT SPRINT

A full Sprint—a full iteration—has been accomplished, in all its stages. The Sprint produced a rough prototype, resolved some issues, and raised some new ones, but most importantly it produced value. Now it's time to begin a new one. But the outcome of the sprint is not just the sum of the tasks completed: it is the knowledge gained from those tasks, which informs all of the work to come. Throughout the Sprint, the Product Owner, with the team's help, is refining the Product Goal and prioritizing the Sprint Backlog and the Product Backlog.

For our example, let's say they completed all PBIs—all 41 points—in the first Sprint and, because they finished those items early, completed an additional

PBI worth seven points for a total of 48 points. Should they now aim higher for the next Sprint? If you're a manager, who will become a Product Owner, you might be thinking, "Yeah, let's set a stretch goal! Let's shoot for 60 points!" Resist the temptation. The history of Scrum philosophy believes in setting a target based on the average velocity of the last three Sprints. Let's say each had a target velocity of 41 points, but each of the first three Sprints finished early, yielding 49, 55, and 50 points. The forth Sprint's target will be 48 points. The value of the work, just like the five kilometers for our runner, remains the same. What changes as our team learns and progresses is that they get faster. They get used to working together, they understand each other's individual working styles, and they increase their productivity as their focus narrows to only the goal at hand.

In the next chapter, we'll look at some case studies, full of the grit and surprise of real life—the kinds of challenges Scrum was developed to use to best advantage.

YOUR SCRUM PLAYBOOK

- ▸ Scrum practices focus on actions that take us closer to the goal and "done."
- ▸ Scrum has three Artifacts: the Product Backlog, Sprint Backlog, and Increments.

CREATING A PRODUCT BACKLOG

- ▸ Story Mapping identifies user needs in story form. Each item has to be independent, negotiable, able to generate value, estimable, small enough, and, finally, testable.
- ▸ Three Steps of creating a story map.
  - Create the user's sequence with the product from left to right with Post-its or another medium.
  - Create the larger steps—modules of the backbone—within which the above items will be included.
  - Populate the details required under each module, working top-down.
- ▸ The Story Map is used to generate a **Product Backlog** of necessary items to achieve the Product Goal.
- ▸ Items in the backlog are estimated, prioritized, and then sliced into Product Backlog Items.
- ▸ Estimating is accomplished a number of ways, Planning Poker being one of the more popular methods along with numbers following the Fibonacci sequence.
- ▸ The length of Sprints and definition of "done" are decided on before the first Sprint and are continually refined.
- ▸ The **Sprint Backlog** created by the Developers breaks the Product Backlog down further into a Sprint Goal and tasks, and makes the work visible by posting the items in a central location.

THE FIVE SCRUM EVENTS ARE:

- ▸ **The Sprint:** a Time Box event in which all other events occur. Maximum length for the Sprint is four weeks. A Sprint can be cancelled by the Product Owner, but goals and quality measurements cannot be changed.
- ▸ **Sprint Planning:** a three-part event. In the first part, the entire team

clarifies why the Sprint is valuable, then in part two they present and decide what PBIs will be worked on. The PO and Developers negotiate, and the Scrum Master mediates. In part three, the Developers decide how they will do the work and further break down the PBIs into smaller items and tasks. For four-week Sprints, the Time Box for this event is eight hours and then shorter for smaller Sprints.

- A fifteen-minute **Daily Scrum** brings all Developers together at the same time and place to ensure they are aligned with the Sprint Goal, and secondly, they plan their next twenty-four hours.
- Throughout the process, the Product Owner is continually Prioritizing and Refining the Product Backlog.
- When the Sprint is finished, a **Sprint Review** brings the team and client together to inspect the results, discuss, and consider what is needed next.
- Finally, the team holds a **Sprint Retrospective**, considering what worked, what didn't, and what needs to be changed going forward.

Playing Your Hand

You now have a solid idea of how to create a Story Map, Prioritize it, Refine the Product Backlog, and estimate PBIs.

Here are your action items:

- ◯ Create a Product Backlog using the techniques discussed in this chapter.
- ◯ Together with the team, estimate story points for roughly enough PBIs to cover two or three Sprints.
- ◯ Decide your Sprint Length and define "Done."
- ◯ Select a date for your first Sprint and hold your Sprint Planning.

CHAPTER SEVEN

Place Your Bets: Defining and Delivering Value

Price is what you pay. Value is what you get.
–Warren Buffet[38]

Drew had done the unthinkable. An MIT student who had taken a year off to work with an emerging test prep start-up, he had planned to utilize a four-plus-hour bus ride from Boston to New York as an opportunity to get some much needed work done. He boarded the bus and removed his laptop from its case, and that's when he realized a critical error in his planning: he had left his USB thumb drive, or flash drive, at home. That meant he couldn't do any of the work he had planned. Four precious hours wasted. Out of that frustration, Drew birthed a brilliant idea to start working on a new project; something that could make the necessity of thumb drives obsolete. But would it have value? Would people actually want to use it?

Scrum is about creating and adding value as quickly as possible. We discussed value in the last chapter. In this chapter, I will further define value, show how value changes over time, and examine how to test your theories to determine if the value you perceive is true in the client's eyes. Ideas are a dime a dozen, the old adage goes, and many good ideas are pursued with time, energy, and money, yet they produce poor results (does anyone remember beta tapes?). We've all seen businesses come and go quickly. While there are numerous reasons for failure, a common one is uncertainty about value added to the customer. Another common error is lack of understanding about how that value is changing and adapting to the changes happening all around us all the time.

---

38 Zack Friedman, "Here Are 10 Genius Quotes from Warren Buffett," *Forbes*, October 4, 2018, https://www.forbes.com/sites/zackfriedman/2018/10/04/warren-buffett-best-quotes /#220ca6d94261.

VALUE WITHOUT CONTEXT ISN'T VALUABLE

Imagine you're playing a game of poker and your hand includes an ace, king, queen, jack, and a ten, all diamonds. That is a valuable hand. But if you fold it up and walk away without playing that hand, those cards are just pieces of paper. So, too, in Scrum. Value refers to what you can offer to customers. Your collection of parts or services adds value only when it is offered as a product or service that customers can use. Even the best car will not have much value to a driver if a wheel is missing. *The Scrum Guide* doesn't define value because value is best determined by your context. You will have to carefully consider what value means to your team and organization.

The story doesn't end there. Value is a word often tossed around without much thought. We say we value our lives, our families, our careers, but don't quantify that value. Nobody says, "I increased my family's value 3 percent last quarter." But value does change over time.

The first laptop had a five-inch screen, had no battery, and very little computing power, but it retailed at $1,795 in 1981 dollars! If I made a duplicate machine now, I couldn't give it away. We understand that value changes in our daily lives. Your car depreciates the moment you drive it off the dealer's lot; that box of cereal with ripped cardboard or a floor model refrigerator with a small dent sell well below their typical retail. Why? Because their perceived value has changed. Not the actual value. That cereal still tastes as good, the refrigerator still keeps my food cold, and that laptop still performs as well as it did its first day. They haven't changed; we've changed.

Suppose you had one hundred dollars in your pocket and I offered you a glass of tap water in exchange. You'd laugh at me. However, if I found you in the middle of the Sahara after you had spent a day wandering aimlessly in the sweltering sun, and I made you the same offer, you'd quickly accept without argument. The perceived value of the water changed. In the first scenario, water was abundant. You could walk into any corner store and purchase a bottle for two bucks or fill a glass from the tap for nearly nothing. In the second, the water was scarce and lifesaving.

We understand this at an instinctual level. But when we are in the business of providing a product or service, for some reason this understanding diminishes. Determining value in real-world, everyday situations is often much more difficult. "But Scrum is client-focused," you might say. "Shouldn't we ask the client what they value?" If only it were that easy. Many times the client says they want one thing when, in fact, they need something else entirely.

Henry Ford made automobile ownership accessible to middle-class families. Today, many of us believe that owning a car is a need—a necessity for survival in many cases. We place a lot of value on the car, but we once managed fine with just horses. Cruise ship designer John McNeese said, "There is a problem trying to figure out what people want by canvassing them. I mean, if Henry Ford canvassed people on whether or not he should build a motor car, they'd probably tell him what they really wanted was a faster horse."[39] If you visited Manhattan's Time Square in 1905, you would have found far more horse-drawn carriages than automobiles. Back then, the perceived value and expense of owning a car versus a horse was stark. Cars didn't travel much faster, broke down often, and were dirty, loud, and expensive. Today it's difficult to imagine life without cars.

Let's look at another instance of perceived value. Go ask a carpenter or handyperson if she needs a drill. No doubt she'll say yes. But if I argued that she didn't need a drill, she might get heated. However, she doesn't *need* a drill; she needs the ability to make holes of various depths and diameters in wood, plastic, and metal. Each purpose requires a different size and type of drill bit to accomplish the task. If I asked her what could add value to her ability to make holes, she might say a drill that can change bits quickly. But remember, the actual value is not in the drill but in the ability to make holes. What if instead we gave her a lightsaber-like tool that offered a multitude of diameter settings and could easily make clean holes of various depths in any material? Assuming it was around a similar price point as the drill, the electric drill would become obsolete. We supplied the real need of the customer and not just what she wanted.

When implementing Scrum, delivering value faster is the name of the game. Now we need to look at how to determine value when even the client doesn't know.

OUTCOME VS. OUTPUT

When scrambling in your first Sprints (and in every Sprint), it's easy to focus so much on speed and productivity that you lose focus of the value you're creating—*why* you're producing in the first place. When you become fixated on a metric or quantity (output), you miss the opportunity to deliver value (outcome). Creating more Blackberries faster in a world of smartphones is a recipe for disaster.

This is like my friend making brake systems for the luxury cars. Prior to

---

39 Greg Miller, "Creating Cruise Ships with an Eye on Next Generation," *The Cruise Industry News Quarterly* 9, no. 37 (Summer 1999), 67.

the consultant's intervention, he and his colleagues were focused only on output—making as many brake systems as they could within their workweek. When they got a glimpse of the bigger picture and saw why things needed to be within specification for both safety and functionality, their focus returned to outcome: producing braking systems that exceeded quality standards so they could help keep their customers safe.

When implementing Scrum, the Product Backlog Items (PBIs) should represent items that, once done, provide value. When the Product Owner is synthesizing all the data, he has to determine if the slice they are producing provides value to the client and meets his needs better than even the client might have conceptualized—an automobile instead of a faster horse.

Determining whether you're focused on output or outcomes is just a matter of questioning your intentions. Why do you need what you are producing? Back when I was still setting up and training project management offices, I had one large client for whom we had created nine new processes. The client requested that my team create a graphics-rich presentation on the nine processes so it could be provided in a handout to the executive team that would be attending the final presentation. Each process was complex, and each overview required many graphics and pages to explain. My associate who was putting it together expressed frustration when, after two full days of working on it, he had only completed about 20 percent of the handout.

I realized we might be focused on output and not outcome, so I called the client to ask what the outcome was.

"What do you really need for this presentation?" I asked.

"I want the executives to understand the nine processes."

That I knew. Now I needed to clarify. "Do you need an in-depth overview of each of the nine processes?"

"No, nothing that complex. I think a broad overview of the nine and how they work together would be enough."

Had I not clarified the client's expectations and determined what he really needed, we would have continued wasting time (and needlessly killing trees).

CREATING VALUE WHEN THE CUSTOMER CAN'T DEFINE IT

Let's revisit our poor thumb-drive-less friend, Drew, whom we met at the beginning of this chapter. At the time, in 2007, when he began writing the first lines of code during his bus trip, the internet already had alternatives to carrying around a flash drive everywhere. There were a number of cloud-based file-sharing apps, but only the most tech-savvy people were using them. They had clunky user designs and a complicated app interface, they were difficult to use, and they were unreliable, with many users reporting hours of work lost to errors.

Drew soon calculated that coding an app that met all of his ideas—it was easy for non-tech people to install and use, it had a clean design, and had enough security and file backup so no users would lose work—would take hundreds or thousands of hours. If he could make such an app, he thought, it could be a lucrative business, but even if he had a team of engineers working for free, they could spend thousands of hours and produce an end product that nobody but a select few computer engineers and academics might use. In other words, they could be wasting their time. There was no obvious need to replace the "trusty" flash drive. How could he get client feedback and determine how a product that didn't even exist provided value?

Drew is hardly alone in this conundrum. For example, let's look at a group of students who faced a similar dilemma. I took some project management classes at Stanford University, one of which was taught by Silicon Valley icon and angel investor Steve Blank. He shared a story with the class about how he offered a class of entrepreneurial students a uniquely special competition: Blank was willing to invest start-up capital in a rock-solid business proposal presented by any of the students. Talk about extra credit! Of course, if none of the ideas were worthy of investment, nobody got any money.

One group of students proposed a truly unique idea: they wanted to build a drone and use that drone to take agricultural photos so farmers could get a birds-eye view of their fields and plan accordingly. This was back before aerial drones were available to consumers. As I recall, the business model was to perfect a drone that was capable of taking aerial photographs and selling this as a service to agricultural professionals. They believed that it would take a million dollars to build a working prototype.

Blank said to them, "An interesting idea, but you haven't proved the business model works."

"We need to build a drone to prove the business model works," a student replied.

This doesn't sound like a relative low cost of change, does it? Not even billionaires like risking a million dollars on an unproven business model.

Blank said he thought for a moment before making them an offer. "I'll invest $400 for you to prove your hypothesis."

Many start-ups make the mistake of building something they think a customer base wants only to see their dreams die as they present their completed prototype or fully developed product to a less-than-welcome market. Oh, but if only start-ups made this tragic mistake. New Coke, the Ford Edsel, RCA Videodisc, Blockbuster, and Blackberry, among numerous other products and companies, demonstrate the chronic issues of not understanding either what the customer needs or how value in the market is changing. Blockbuster, for instance, was once that glistening beacon of water in the desert for avid movie enthusiasts but became an expensive bottle of tap water in a well-hydrated world when they failed to adapt to the market and their client's needs (i.e., the emergence of Netflix and streaming video).

Value Changes Over Time

The biggest issue I continue to have with traditional, waterfall project management is its dedication to planning months or years ahead of an actual product. Even if your data and estimates are 100 percent accurate on day one of the Gantt chart, the chances of everything—the client's needs, the market, prices, etc.—remaining static during the project are as likely as the resurgence of dinosaurs.

By building value in each Sprint, as the Increment grows, you are receiving feedback. Throwing ten darts at a dart board all at once based on how you think they will fly will likely yield worse results than if you throw one at a time, making minor corrections with each throw based on the feedback (i.e., seeing how close to your target the darts are landing).

When my new dive watch that was supposed to tell me how much air I had left didn't work (and, yes, I tested it on dry land before I got in the water), I had no reliable feedback to tell me if I had enough air. Experienced divers like me consume less air than new divers, so my solution was to stick close to them. When they ran low and surfaced, I could surface, too. The only casualty would be missing ten or fifteen minutes of diving.

But when the dive leader began exploring a shipwreck, I couldn't resist the option. The new divers weren't rated for shipwrecks, so they remained outside. I followed the diver leader an additional ten meters as we entered the wreck. I let my curiosity get the best of me. You see, the deeper you go, the faster you consume air. I followed the leader out of the wreck, and we rejoined the group. I turned back to the wreck to take a few outside photos and didn't notice that the team was slowly making their ascent. By the time I turned back around to see where everyone was, it was almost too late.

I was out of air.

What's worse is that I was too deep to surface quickly. If I bolted to the surface, I might get the bends (decompression sickness)—a potentially fatal syndrome. My only chance was to swim after the dive master and grab his "octopus," a second regulator used for such emergencies. I felt my lungs burning like they were about to burst as I desperately swam toward him before he faded into the blue fog of the ocean. I made it, barely. Not only did I risk my life by not having the feedback I needed, but I had to sheepishly explain my error in judgment to the dive leader.

My value of air changed from low value in the first few minutes of the dive, where I lost my feedback (watch), to high value, where I would have gladly given a year's salary to be able to use the dive leader's air.

Just as my value changed, what a client values changes over time.

PRODUCT, NOT PROJECT

As a former dyed-in-the-wool project manager, I know how hard it is to give up those precious, colorful charts and reams of beautifully outlined documentation. How can you complete a project if you haven't fully estimated its size and scope in advance? It's difficult giving up the "knowns" (even if they're imaginary) in favor of living on the edge of what feels like chaos. Here's the distinction: where a project exists for the sake of making a thing, a product in Scrum exists for what it will accomplish. This is more than semantics. A project is set in stone with changes coming with high resistance and at great cost, and with most if not all of the deliverables coming at or near the end. A product is fluid, flexible, and adaptive—it starts with the idea of a faster horse and ends with a Ford Model T instead.

Another key distinguishing feature is how each one—a project and product—are concluded. When a project management team concludes a project, they typically hand it off to another team for maintenance. Most products introduced to the world need support, upgrades, spare parts, or some other form of maintenance. The problem is, the new team has to learn everything the project team already knows, so the work doesn't really end here. The resulting knowledge gap between the project and maintenance team is expensive—it takes time and money for them to learn.

On the other hand, when a Scrum team develops a product, that product is continually maintained by the same team that created it—what a concept! Instead of a steep learning curve and lack of ownership by the new team, the product team continues to support, build, and improve the product without having to reinvent the proverbial wheel. Scrum teams understand that the work only ends when the product itself is removed from the market.

Projects certainly have their place, but I argue that that place is constantly shrinking. We've discussed its nature and where it exists best in the Cynefin framework—where there is little that is unknown, the relative cost of change is high, and uncertainty is low. Are you making a ship that you've constructed dozens of times with hardly any changes? Sure, a project view should work fine.

The difficulty exists when switching from project-thinking to Scrum's product-thinking. The whole point of a project is to make a thing: a ship, a car, a software package. The point of a product is to create and deliver value. It's a subtle but important difference. Remember Frankenscrum? When a dubious manager or other department requires documentation, charts, or progress reports, or when an overzealous and undertrained leader jumps into Scrum, it often looks like this: a Product Backlog whose items are just tasks from a work breakdown structure—each one dependent on previous items.

For GoTelecom, the PBIs for their digital conversion were things like change data plans, pay bill, and view data usage. With a traditional work breakdown structure in project-thinking, the accounting, graphics, API, databases, etc., would all be interdependent. You can't radically change one without affecting other systems and requiring a massive redesign. But with Scrum and vertical slicing, each item is a complete, functioning product that adds value when added to the website. When the team decides to add a phone purchase option, that module can then be used in the existing backend website development as long as its interface with all other systems matches what was predetermined. It's literally plug-and-play.

If you've been working in traditional projects for any length of time, the transition to product-thinking might be a difficult one. However, as you see the results of what you're working for every two to four weeks and getting regular feedback, I almost guarantee that you're going to be glad you embraced the new mindset.

PRODUCT GOAL: STARTING WITH THE BIG PICTURE

Defining and delivering value begins with looking at the big picture. When the Product Owner looks at all the data, she can begin connecting the dots and synthesizing the information. This data is ideally collected through conversations with the customer(s). She can additionally utilize data from various data analyses and reports, or a combination of all the sources available. She then contrasts that information with her understanding of the product and the process—she creates the Product Goal—the ideal picture for how the product adds value to the client. This Product Goal might possibly meet their need in a way that even *they* didn't imagine. You don't *need* a big goal to create PBIs and begin a Sprint like we did at the end of the last chapter. Laying the groundwork can be intuitive. However, by clarifying what it is you want to accomplish, it makes the path forward clearer.

The Product Goal doesn't have to be as grand as that of an iPad or getting a human to Mars; it can be as simple as creating an electric toothbrush kids will actually want to use—or whatever. In other words, the product doesn't need to be cool or sexy in order to create a Product Goal that motivates the team. Most people want to work hard and know that their hard work created something someone else appreciates. The very act of progress, even on a product as mundane as a ballpoint pen, can be exciting when a team is willing to explore possibilities together.

For our fictional company, One Gallon, the Product Goal is simple: develop a safe, reliable car that uses only one gallon of gas per hundred miles. Is there a demand for such a vehicle? Probably, as long as it can be produced in such a way that the market price doesn't eclipse the gas savings completely. So there's a need, whether the customer knows it or not. In addition, we would look at ways to make the car more attractive than its eco-friendly competition, the electric car.

The goal is broken down into the Product Backlog—each item a section of value, as we showed in the last example. But we are human—even those of us using Scrum. Work has its own inherent frustrations. When impediments get in the way, or a solution to a technical issue seems momentarily insurmountable, we have a tendency to get discouraged. We focus on the obstacle instead of the goal. This is partly how our Product Owner uses the Product Goal to keep the team inspired. During each slice and increment of work at One Gallon, as the team struggles with ways to make the chassis modular so it can easily interface with each individual component, come under the maximum weight requirement, and supply the needed structure for a good ride while passing crash tests, the Product Owner reminds them of what they're working toward. Think of what kept Frodo and Samwise moving toward Mount Doom and their most likely deaths in the *Lord of the Rings* trilogy. It wasn't the adventure or being heroes anymore. They were focused on the fact that, if they failed, their beloved Shire, their homeland, would be lost forever.

A strong vision for why the Scrum team exists can keep a team moving quickly and willing to put in the hard work necessary to overcome frustrating challenges. They're not just making brake assemblies, but they're making critical components to save lives. Drew wanted to not only code another app but also revolutionize how people access their important digital files. When

I worked with a mining company, their goal wasn't just drilling for gas but also harvesting fuel so they could make their own electricity and add excess to Colombia's electrical supply for a small profit.

Focus on the enormity of the task and the occassional drudgery of getting there is a sure way to dishearten a team. The speed and often fun of collaborating together will still allow a team to produce value quickly, but I can't underscore enough that the best world-class teams are excited about what they are accomplishing. Nobody, no matter how high the pay and how cheerful the work environment, wants to dig holes that are only going to be filled in. There must be a higher purpose to our work. That's the Product Goal, and that goal is represented in the Product Backlog.

We've already covered this in great detail. The trick is creating a Product Goal compelling enough that it helps motivate the Scrum team into action. For "sexy" products, sometimes the ideal outcome is motivating enough. But for more mundane products and companies, the task of motivation is a little more detailed. The rest of the chapter will show how this is accomplished.

SAVING TIME AND MONEY BEFORE THE FIRST SPRINT

There are literally hundreds of possible reasons why you're reading this book right now. There are various motivations regarding why you want to learn about and implement Scrum into your organization or workplace. Maybe you're looking to change the process on one product line from traditional to Agile, or possibly, like GoTelecom, you're transforming an existing product or creating a new one from scratch.

Some leaders may want to climb the mountain so quickly they want to dive into the first Sprint, produce value, and get feedback. This is Scrum, without question. But when considering the definition of "done," and the vision of your goal for the product, does it always make sense to build something of real value before getting feedback? If you were a homebuilder constructing a home for a client, does it make sense to build even the frame of a house before getting the owner's feedback? No. You want the simplest, most cost-effective way to solicit feedback before you even begin. You want to create a minimum viable product (MVP), a term coined by Eric Reis in his book *The Lean Startup*. The MVP is a product that secures feedback from the client for minimum investment as quickly as possible. The concept is not pure Scrum, and you will not find it in *The Scrum Guide*, but this lean concept is wholeheartedly Agile and aligned to the principles.

When Drew realized the enormous amount of time required to make his idea of eliminating thumb drives a reality, he saw the problem with this potential opportunity. The question he needed to answer first was this: would that investment be worth it? As an MIT student on a work break, he wasn't exactly flush with cash to throw around on a high-stakes gamble. He might have been able to secure initial seed money from Boston's tech-savvy venture capitalists, but as an engineer and not an entrepreneur, that task seemed dubious. Before the idea of crowdfunding became a mainstay, Drew found an alternative to test his idea on his meager budget: he'd make a simple video. The video was full of crude, stop-action animation that showed all the potential ways his app could benefit the user. It was a simple way to keep all digital content updated, safe, secure, and accessible even from your new iPhone. The video highlighted the problem (inaccessibility to files and lack of security), and the name of his proposed solution: Dropbox.

Since this chapter is about bets, I'm willing to wager a fair amount that you have used or are currently using Dropbox or one of its major competitors. In case you've been living in a box (get it?), Drew Houston's idea worked. With only a basic working prototype of Dropbox at that point, he was able to gauge interest to determine if he should invest more time and money into Dropbox. In order for Dropbox to work on multiple platforms and handle multi-gig transfers with full security and without crashing, his prototype still needed hundreds of hours of development.

The video was animated, and he recorded the audio in one take. The first day his video garnered five thousand people willing to exchange their email for a chance to beta test Dropbox. The next day, the total was up to seventy-five thousand.[40] With that support, Drew was able to continue working, find a much-needed cofounder, secure capital, and quit his day job. He succeeded in testing his theory and created the first secure, reliable cross-platform cloud storage and file-sharing service along with a cofounder and investors.

Zappos.com performed a similar experiment. Before they became the famous Z brand, its founders launched a simple website called shoesite.com (this was back when registering a dot-com address was as easy as naming your cat). Instead of creating a complex database, establishing relationships with shoe companies, and establishing supply lines, the founders took pictures of shoes at the local shoe store, posted them, and created a simple shopping cart with the promise of free shipping. Zero employees, overhead, and stock, and

---

40 "How Dropbox Became the Startup Steve Jobs Wished to Own," Mixergy, December 21, 2011, https://mixergy.com/interviews/drew-houston-dropbox-interview/.

very little time invested. When an order came in, they purchased the pair from the store and shipped them. Not exactly a money-maker, right? It wasn't supposed to be . . . at first.

By creating a simple site and utilizing existing stores' inventories, Zappos tested their concept with very little out-of-pocket investment. Let's say they lost ten dollars per transaction and established a customer base of one hundred. They were out $1,000 by the end of the experiment and learned that there was enough interest to officially launch. What if they created the partnerships, supply lines, employees, databases—the whole enchilada—and it failed? They'd probably still be paying off that debt today, if they didn't have to declare bankruptcy.

Now let's consider a million-dollar idea and go back to our Stanford student team who wanted to build a drone to help farmers. The students had no idea how only $400 would allow them to test the value of a product, which, in their minds, required a million-dollar prototype. Professor (venture capitalist) Steve Blank pointed them in a distinct direction. His advice to the students was simple: buy a good quality GoPro-style camera and convince a crop duster to let you ride along as you take multiple pictures of their fields.

It must have been a lightbulb moment for them because they didn't waste any time. With eager dreams of riches and all the enthusiasm of a child at Christmas, they did exactly what Steve suggested. They photographed the fields belonging to multiple farmers and presented them with their photos.

According to Steve's telling of the story, the farmers' responses were unanimously as enthusiastic. "What the hell do I need those for?" was the average response.

Not one farmer was interested in the offering. Whether the photographs would be useful and they didn't understand, or they already had more than enough information from other sources, I'll never know. All I do know is that Steve painted a picture for me in class that day: save a million dollars and bet $400 instead.

I imagine those students were heartbroken. They thought they had a stupendous idea only to be told they had a stupid idea. But I don't view it that way. Instead of going broke or bankrupt and wasting a year of their lives, they got a quick answer as cheaply as possible. I'd look at it as if someone just wiped out a million-dollar debt and gave me an additional year to my lifetime. I'd be ecstatic. You can do this too.

EXPERIMENT CANVAS: HYPOTHESIS, EXPERIMENT, ANALYSIS

As a child, I loved science. I know not all reading this share my enthusiasm. Nevertheless, you probably passed your science class and have at least an inkling of an idea of the scientific method: ask a question, do research, formulate a hypothesis (an idea of what works), test the idea with experiments, observe results and analyze, formulate conclusions, and repeat as much as necessary.

Achieving goals, succeeding in business, and building great products require the same process. Each of our three examples above performed those steps in some fashion, whether intentionally or not. When done intentionally, you can save yourself major headaches and losses by getting feedback as quickly and as cheaply as possible. This is the essence of the MVP and also the minimum marketable product (MMP), which we will not cover here. The two are sometimes confused. The only difference is that the MMP is concerned with an end product, which can be purchased by the consumer, while an MVP's value may only lie in the feedback it provides, like with the farm drone idea or the Dropbox video.

Before we get too deeply into the waters of hypothesizing and experimenting, I'd like to make one point clear: not every product requires this process. If you are producing a new release of an existing product based on user feedback, creating an MVP would not be the best use of your time because you already have a solid, working hypothesis. This process is best used to test new ideas for emerging products and businesses, like with our company One Gallon. Let's take a look at how it might work.

When considering the Product Goal of One Gallon, we need to determine, as quickly as possible, whether we can produce a car that meets its one-hundred-mile-per-gallon goal, has a broad enough consumer appeal, and can be sold at a price point attractive to the end user and provide enough profit to sustain the company.

One Gallon's team would start with an experiment canvas. Again, this is not "true" by-the-book Scrum, but it's widely utilized and complies with Agile principles. Just as with the scientific method, we start by asking questions. You see a customer need or have an idea for a product or service that could meet a need and add value. Instead of rushing forward, question your assumptions. What if you're wrong and farmers don't have a need for aerial photos? What if the marketplace isn't clamoring for a sustainable car with near-zero carbon emissions? Maybe you've already made a feature, release, or new product that failed. Start there. What mistakes were made? Now, it's easy to defend the idea and blame the market, economics, politics, or other change outside of your control. Even in those circumstances, you can own your share of the responsibility by acknowledging you could have better read those situations or accumulated more analysis regarding how it could have impacted you.

7.1. Experiment Canvas

1. PROBLEM / OPPORTUNITY	2. CUSTOMER SEGMENTS	3. POSSIBLE SOLUTION
Existing solutions / alternatives?	Early adopters?	What makes it costly?
4. UNCERTAINTIES / RISKS	**5. EXPERIMENTS**	**6. SUCCESS CRITERIA**
Which is riskiest/least certain?	Lowest cost viable experiment? *(survey, lo-fi mock, hi-fi mock, fake, concierge, prototype, MVP, A/B test)*	What does success look like? *(objective / quantifiable)*

Step One: Identify the Problem

The Experiment Canvas can start with a blank sheet that looks like the above diagram. This diagram is based on a process created by my friend, trainer and coach Brad Swanson,[41] who was inspired by Ash Maurya's Lean Canvas.[42] To start, we first identify a problem in the marketplace. Many problems are opportunities lying in wait. Using the example of having a base car with which to start One Gallon, the problem might be stated like this: "There are no green vehicles that offer flexibility comparable to the traditional automobile."

---

41 Brad Swanson, "Validate It Before You Build It!: The Experiment Canvas" (Global Scrum Gathering, Minneapolis, 2018), https://www.scrumalliance.org/ScrumRedesignDEVSite /media/ScrumAllianceMedia/Global%20Scrum%20Gatherings/2018%20Minneapolis /Presentations/Brad-Swanson-swansonb_validate-it-before-you-build-it.pdf.

42 Ash Maurya, *Running Lean: Iterate from Plan A to a Plan That Works* (Sebastopol, CA: O'Reilly, 2012), 6.

We may then list possible potential existing solutions and alternatives like the Tesla and Prius. This may sound like a SWOT (strengths, weaknesses, opportunities, and threats) analysis, but it's not. For Dropbox, the problem was inability to access and update critical computer files. Alternative solutions were highly technical and unreliable software that worked most of the time but crashed with large data transfers, lost data, and were about as secure as an igloo bank. There seemed to be an opportunity for an app that could solve all these problems and reliably give customers access to their most important files.

Step Two: Customer Segments

Next, we would look at the customer segments we are targeting or who would stand to benefit from our solution (idea). For One Gallon, it may be upwardly mobile, earth-conscious consumers as well as corporations who provide fleet cars to their employees. For Dropbox, the customer segment was broader as practically anyone with more than one device could benefit, but most specifically for an SaaS (software as a service) model, Drew and his team may have eyed IT professionals, business managers, and executives who travel and need ready access to important files, presentations, and documentation they might otherwise leave at home, the office, or stuck next to an in-flight magazine in the plane's storage pouch. The more specific you can make the customer segment(s), the better able you are to test your eventual hypothesis.

Step Three: Possible Solutions

In the third step the team would brainstorm possible solutions. For One Gallon, they may consider strictly battery-powered vehicles, combination battery and solar, as well as a hybrid. Possible solutions for Dropbox, despite the initial idea, may have been an app that connects all your devices like a cloud-based network, or as simple as a thumb-drive that was automatically synced, reliable, and kept in your wallet, or some other solution.

I won't put a number on possible solutions, but I will say to write down the craziest solutions you can think of if for no other reason than to stimulate your thinking. Maybe fuel-efficient hot-air balloons for One Gallon. Yes, we know that's not feasible, but then someone else thinks, "Well, why not a car that runs on a gas like hydrogen through fuel cells?" Ah, not a bad idea and worth considering.

Step Four: Assess the Business Risks and Uncertainties

So now you've stated an idea, considered the market as well as many other possible solutions to solve those market problems. Now we need to decide what risks are involved. The idea is not to find every risk/uncertainty you can think of, but what is the business risk? One Gallon risks include the technology being too expensive for enough drivers to purchase, or not being able to meet performance standards that will appeal to a mass market. A car that goes from zero to sixty miles per hour in over two minutes is not going to impress too many people no matter how economical it is. Or maybe the hydrogen idea is not quite safe enough and refueling stations are too sparse to support a marketable product.

For Zappos, the obvious risk was whether or not people would feel comfortable buying shoes—an intimate experience—online where they couldn't walk around in them or look at how they appear in those weird, angled mirrors. How would they handle returns for poor-fitting shoes, address the differences in size by manufacture, and guarantee satisfaction while still making a profit?

One Dropbox risk, among others, was that the market was too narrow. Only certain IT professionals and C-level executives might be interested; too few to keep the company sustainable. Other inherent risks were the level of digital security they could provide. Without adequate protections, one major hack could end their company before it really started.

Most likely when you are considering all the factors with your product, there will be several risks. As you look at the ones you've written down, decide which of those is the biggest risk or which is most uncertain. Where the biggest risks exist is where we formulate our hypothesis and brainstorm a solution(s) that will minimize that risk. In other words, you now have a basis for your hypothesis.

Step Five: Brainstorm Experiments

With a hypothesis formulated, you need to decide how you're going to test that hypothesis. Ask what experiments you perform to test it. Then further deduce which of the experiments is the fastest and cheapest way. Maybe it could be as simple as a video like Dropbox did, or substituting a piece of complicated technology that's not yet in existence (like the farm drone) with an adequate facsimile (GoPro and crop duster) just to see if the theory is viable.

Some quick examples include a 3-D-printed mockup, a minimum viable feature (MVF—the simplest possible feature of your product to test), a clay model, market research, a "launch" presentation, or taking advanced orders, among others. The internet has added many avenues to quickly and cheaply experiment, and new options seem to be emerging almost daily, like crowd-funding websites, "fake door" one-page websites to solicit interest, or A/B testing with cheap social media advertisements to determine which of two (or many) features people are clicking on to see. If it's an idea for a complete store, many websites offer plug-and-play technology so little development is required (low cost) in order to test your hypothesis. I guess Zappos could have been tested even more cheaply these days.

Step Six: Determine Criteria for Success

Suppose that all of your wildest dreams come true and the initial offering seems to garner interest for your product. How do you determine success? Much like the definition of "done," you need to determine what criteria or benchmarks achieved will make the experiment a success.

If Alexander Graham Bell only needed to hear one second of a conversation or Edison only needed to produce a soft glow from his lightbulb, neither would have been commercially successful. Instead, the phone had to be clear enough to carry a full conversation, and the lightbulb had to be at least as bright as a candle and last for a certain length of time before burning out. For your product, success criteria might be to get five thousand sign-ups from a Facebook ad, achieve at least one thousand preorders, or something similar. It's whatever makes sense for your company, product, market, or combination thereof.

A successful test for One Gallon might be to have five hundred viewers of our introductory video securing their vehicle with refundable deposits. When determining success criteria, think about the bare minimum metrics that would indicate worth in developing the full version.

7.2. Example of Experiment Canvas

1. PROBLEM / OPPORTUNITY	2. CUSTOMER SEGMENTS	3. POSSIBLE SOLUTION
Using cars for transportation produces a lot of CO2 emission	Environmental conscious people that need a car and would buy an economically friendlier car if had a street permission and doesn't cost more than a regular car	Car that runs 100miles with 1 gallon of gasoline, street permission, affordable
Existing solutions / alternatives?	**Early adopters?**	**What makes it costly?** Crash testing the car to get street permission can destroy several prototypes before it fulfills requirements.
4. UNCERTAINTIES / RISKS	5. EXPERIMENTS	6. SUCCESS CRITERIA
Car has to be light and has low wind resistance to spend less than a gallon of gasoline on 100miles. The requires light materials and certain design both which can negatively affect crash test results.	Create a CAD computer model that fulfills wind resistance and weight criteria and crash test it on the computer	Computer model fulfills crash test requirements, doesn't weigh more than 600kg and a drag coefficient of not more than 0.22Cd
Which is riskiest/least certain? Can you build a lightweight car that still fulfills crash test requirements	**Lowest cost viable experiment?** *(survey, lo-fi mock, hi-fi mock, fake, concierge, prototype, MVP, A/B test)*	**What does success look like?** *(objective / quantifiable)*

VALUE IS SUBJECTIVE

Until you discover where the value is, Scrum is of little value to you. You can drill wells all day in areas void of gas, create thousands of lines of code for a beautiful app nobody thinks they need, set up an online shopping experience for an item people would rather purchase in person, or waste a million dollars on a prototype that won't make one dollar.

We've seen how it's important to determine value and to keep a fishing line in the water to detect the nibbles of a changing landscape. Breeding faster horses and easier movie rentals won't work when Ford and Netflix come along.

But more than just value, we saw how through the process of creating an Experiment Canvas, you can begin to formulate the basis for an experiment and begin experimenting to determine where the value truly lies. Only when Ford improved upon the motor car did all but the rich, early adopters take notice of its advantages over the horse and buggy. Only when Drew Houston created his crude video did people understand how *valuable* having access to important files was.

Once you have the results from your experimentation, you know where the value lies and you now must make a decision. Not some willy-nilly flip of the coin, but a hard, committed decision. It may be reversible or nonreversible. From that decision you will get more feedback and learn what's working and what's not working, and how to read the information that you might otherwise miss. That's what we'll cover next.

YOUR SCRUM PLAYBOOK

Deciphering value, noting how it changes over time, and how to begin experimentation to test theories of value and create an MVP are not necessarily pure Scrum, but these determinations will help you save significant time and energy and possibly avoid costly errors in judgment (like you, Blackberry).

VALUE

- Is what a client really needs to solve a problem, whether she knows it or not.
- *Outcome* is not the same as *Output*. Know why the client needs what she needs.
- Is subjective depending on the circumstances and changes over time— tap water in a restaurant vs. a bottle in the Sahara.
- Is not produced by a project. It is determined based on constant feedback from the stakeholders with each iteration—it's getting the darts closer to your target.
- Can be hypothesized and tested.
- Is incorporated into the Product Goal.
- Creates, maintains, and refines the Product Backlog.

SIX STEPS OF THE EXPERIMENT CANVAS

1. Clearly identify the problem/opportunity and any possible solutions already in existence.
2. List customer segments who would benefit from a solution.
3. List possible solutions to the problem that will add value to the customer and identify what, if anything, makes the solution costly.
4. Identify the inherent uncertainties and business risks with experimenting: market could change, customers may switch to a competitor's product, you might miss the timing, etc. Decide which is the riskiest and/or most uncertain.
5. Brainstorm possible experiments that can determine the value and risks. Choose the best experiment that is a) relatively low in cost, b) produced quickly, and c) viable enough to give you true results.
6. Make a list in advance of what a successful experiment will show (e.g., a certain percentage of engagement based on ad impressions).

Playing Your Hand

- ○ If you haven't already done so, determine both the intrinsic and perceived value your product offers clients.
- ○ Help your Product Owner synthesize a Product Goal based on that value, using as many sources as possible.
- ○ If your product is based on an untested or unproven hypothesis, work through the experiment canvas to determine the quickest, easiest, and cheapest experiment to test your hypothesis.
- ○ *Even if you have a proven product*, it may be beneficial for your team to go through the experiment canvas to question any new assumptions.

CHAPTER EIGHT

Plays, Bluffs, and Tells: Decisions, Feedback, and Learning

Decisions without actions are pointless. Actions without decisions are reckless.

— John Boyd[43]

It might seem hard to believe these days, but there was a time before GPS devices and smartphones—a time when people relied on paper maps or printed directions to drive to unknown locations. If you decided to take a trip somewhere, you would need to gather information (maps), make a decision (which route?), interpret if you were going the correct way (observation and feedback), and learn from and respond to that feedback: either you were on track and no changes were necessary, or you had to recalculate your route (without a snarky computer highlighting your mistake by saying, "Recalculating").

Once you selected a destination, you needed to take time and plan out your route in advance. No matter how much planning you did, however, there was always a risk of getting lost. Once lost, how quickly you found your way depended on how quickly you noticed that you were lost. That assessment depended on feedback such as landmarks, street signs, bodies of water, route numbers, or town names.

Maybe you knew the next turn should have been a kilometer down the road, and that there were no lakes on your intended route, but when you

---

43 "Using Decision Management to Avoid Pointless and Reckless," JT on EDM, August 11, 2015, http://jtonedm.com/2015/08/11/using-decision-management-to-avoid-pointless -and-reckless/.

observed a marina, that's when you had a mismatch to your assumptions. This new information meant you were on the wrong road, and you were then able to reorient yourself. Learning that you made a mistake, you would then decide on a course correction (or if you were humble enough, ask a stranger for directions).

Today, we have voices coming from Google Maps or a Waze app with instant feedback regarding mistakes. Any decision that leads to a wrong turn is almost always reversible at some point. Even if you're in a sparse section of Florida and have to drive over thirty miles to the next exit, you can turn around. It's inconvenient, but no major damage is done. But if that wrong turn caused you to miss your flight, the kiss at your friend's wedding, or witnessing the birth of your child, it may have been a costly mistake.

It's no different in projects or organizations. The faster you can make decisions, get feedback, and learn from the results—positive or negative—the faster you can make changes. We've already discussed how Scrum is ideal in complex and uncertain products and processes. Now we'll discuss how making quick decisions, acting, getting feedback, learning, connecting the dots, and questioning your assumptions allows you to serve your clients, be more responsible to the market, pivot past competition, and actually add to the value you're creating.

TYPES OF DECISIONS

Champion poker player and decision strategist Annie Duke has said, "A bet . . . is . . . a decision about an uncertain future."[44] But just like there are different kinds of bets, there are two major kinds of decisions, each considering the factors of what and how. Let's explore these decisions and the best ways to make them.

A poker player has many decisions to make during a game: when to fold, when to check, when to bet, when to raise, when to hold, and whether to play loose or tight. Many players make these decisions based on their gut instinct—mental models—that they've subconsciously honed through many games. Some professionals rely on a system or a complex set of algorithms to determine or influence their decisions. But what does that player do when something extraordinary happens? Another player makes a bet that makes no sense to you given the community cards showing and what you have in

44 Annie Duke, *Thinking in Bets: Making Smarter Decisions When You Don't Have All the Facts* (New York: Portfolio/Penguin: 2018), 3.

your hand. You still need to make a decision. Sometimes the safest thing to do is fold.

Folding is not a great option for a business, so decisions need to be made yearly, quarterly, and daily to ensure the business remains viable. There are major decisions such as creating a new division, committing to a new product line, buying out a competitor, entering into a partnership, and smaller decisions such as choosing which item to work on next, which color to select for the user interface, which new team member to hire.

Decision making is as much a business operation as it is an individual operation. We all make decisions both consciously and unconsciously daily. Which route to drive to work when we hear there's a major accident on the highway, what to have for lunch, or how to phrase that email so the recipient doesn't take your intentions the wrong way. Some decisions are so minor they're practically automatic (the decision to swat a biting mosquito) and others so major you delay making them at all (starting a business). More than just determined by size, decisions also come in two varieties: **reversible** and **irreversible**. Let's define these two types of decisions.

A reversible decision is just like it sounds: a decision that is easily reversed once made. We make reversible decisions all the time like writing a few lines of code to see if the approach will solve a problem, cutting a piece of wood a little too long just in case, buying paint samples to see which will look best on our wall.

An irreversible decision is a decision that, once made, is either impossible to reverse or costly either in time or money (or both) to reverse. Irreversible decisions are ones like investing in a new, custom coding compilation and testing system; cutting a piece of wood too short; building a wall. Each of these are reversible but with time and money costs. The decision to swat the mosquito, on the other hand, is impossible to reverse—you can't revive the flattened creature.

For each of these two types of decisions, there exists two subsets: *what* and *how* decisions. These decide *what* work you will do and, once that's decided, *how* you will do the work. For instance, the Product Owner makes the *what* decisions when she prioritizes the backlog. The Developers decide *how* to do the work without changing the priority.

Whether your decision is reversible like buying a sweater, or irreversible like choosing which location to lease for the next five years, both *what* and *how* will need to be considered for each. What sweater will you buy? How will you pay for the one you choose? And what location suits all of your requirements? How will you coordinate the logistics involved in relocating? If the sweater doesn't work out, you can return it a few days later. However, once a lease agreement is signed, you can't back out without contractual penalties or the possible logistical nightmare involved in relocating *again*.

For example, let's say a one-car family gets a $10,000 bonus, and they've whittled their spending options down two choices: purchase a new car, or take a memorable family vacation. (For the money-conscious readers who might be freaking out here, let's assume they're already debt-free and have fully funded their retirement and education accounts.) The family will have to evaluate these two options. Where do they get the most value for their money? The car would help them be more mobile, cut dependency on others when the other car was used by another family member or in the shop, and give the household more flexibility with planning. On the other hand, a vacation could create a unique family experience, a lasting memory, and a bond between family members. Which is the better bet?

The car is a long-term solution to an inconvenience. The vacation: a short-term getaway that yields a life-long memory plus time to bond and expand their worldview. If they purchase the car and it doesn't meet their needs like they wanted it to, they can always sell it for a small loss. Once the vacation is taken, though, the money is gone forever, even if it was the worst vacation they could have ever imagined. You can't sell a used vacation. If I'm wrong, please let me know as soon as possible.

For each of these decisions, we also have elements of *what* and *how*. What vacation destination is best, and how will you plan your trip? What (which) car meets your needs, and how will you take delivery?

So how do we tell the difference between the types of decisions and who should make them? Should you take a long time to make a decision—like signing a lease agreement—or make it quickly, like with buying sweater? And in Scrum, who makes these types of decisions? I'm glad you asked!

Reversible Decisions

How great would life be if you could have an unlimited number of decisions without any of the consequences of poor ones? When playing a game with my friends as a child, sometimes I'd mess up and simply demand a do-over: the opportunity to make another attempt without losing anything. Imagine a world of limitless do-overs. Do you want to invest all of your money in Bitcoin or attempt a solo crossing of Antarctica? Go ahead! You can always request a do-over. Except life doesn't work that way. Regulators or high-level hackers could devalue Bitcoin overnight, and you only have one life and chance to cross Antarctica without succumbing to hypothermia, exhaustion, or starvation. Fail at either, and you die financially or literally.

While many decisions like those above are not to be trifled with, many other decisions *can* be made and unmade if they turn out to be wrong. When you found out the sweater looked hideous in daylight, you were able to return it, having lost only a little time—and possibly dignity.

A reversible decision is any decision that, once made, is easy to undo with little to no time or money lost. It's making the wrong turn and rerouting a few minutes later. Like a swinging door, you can enter and return with little effort. According to the popular Farnum Street blog, Jeff Bezos viewed his launch of Amazon as a reversible decision. "Bezos used this heuristic [asking himself if the decision was reversible or irreversible] to make the decision to found Amazon. He recognized that if Amazon failed, he could return to his prior job. He would still have learned a lot and would not regret trying."[45]

When making decisions, it's usually easy to intuit whether the decision is reversible or not. But if you're not sure, what would happen if you began and realized it's not working? Could you take another path without wasting too much time or money? If the answer to these questions is yes, then it is a reversible decision.

For our family deciding what to do with their newfound wealth, the car is a reversible decision. What type of car and how they choose to utilize it are decisions to be considered once they decide against a vacation, and are decisions that should be made with care. Deciding on a sporty convertible and driving it off the lot would be a mistake once they realize they barely have room for their kids in the backseat and virtually no trunk space to speak of. A large SUV (used, at this price point) might not work for their needs either, if they live in a city and rarely, if ever, have more than four people in the car.

But even after these considerations, they may purchase the right vehicle for their needs only to find they are longing for the vacation. They've made a mistake. The car still has most of its value, and for only a little hassle of having purchased and now negotiated a sale price, they are able to recoup most of their money. The car was a reversible decision.

For your Scrum team, reversible decisions could be small attempts to solve a problem or, during Sprint Planning, determine the work to complete the first PBI. But during the Daily Scrum the next day, the team could realize they're having challenges. The task they determined to be third needs to be completed

---

45 "Go Fast and Break Things: The Difference Between Reversible and Irreversible Decisions," Farnam Street, April 29, 2018, https://fs.blog/2018/04/reversible-irreversible-decisions/.

second so they have a better understanding of the next step. They can regroup and reverse their decision. They learned how to handle this particular task next time it arises and, by taking action, were able to learn from the results (an important aspect we will cover more deeply at the end of this chapter).

Irreversible Decisions

Now that you know what a reversible decision is, how do you determine what an irreversible decision is? Is there a point of no return? There is. Which is why it's ideal to keep your options open for as long as possible. At some point a decision usually has to be made. Whether that decision is reversible is determined by the situation and circumstances.

Irreversible decisions are decisions that, once made, require full commitment. If a reversible decision is a door that swings both ways, an irreversible decision is one that locks behind you once closed. There may be another way to return to that room, but it's not going to be easy or cheap.

THE VALUE OF OPTIONS

With irreversible decisions, it's good to keep your options open for as long as possible. If a decision is a bet against an uncertain future, then I want to place that bet on as close to a sure thing as I can. I mean, if you could guarantee a win by playing both sides, wouldn't you?

In the stock markets, there are options known as puts and calls, which allow you to reserve the option to buy or sell a stock at a certain price point without risking your full investment. It's very complicated. I should know. I had a sadistic professor that made me memorize the Black-Scholes formula that calculates the value of options.

Instead of stocks, let's discuss roulette—real betting. Imagine that you have a hundred dollars to wager. You can bet on black or red. But instead of betting a little bit, you spend ten dollars on an option to bet on red, and invest another ten dollars in the option to bet on black. In other words, the red option allows you to bet your money if the ball lands on red. The black option allows the bet if it lands on black. At the start of the spin, you're out twenty bucks. The wheel whirs, the ball bounces around and finally settles in 26-black. You discard your option for red and use your option for black and bet the rest of your money on black—a result that's already happened. You can't lose!

Casinos don't allow put and call options for obvious reasons: they'd go broke. And, if you're not familiar with stock markets, I'd hate to burst your bubble, but you can't bet both ways there either—the calculations will most likely make this a zero-sum game (but calculating options is still better than risking your full investment). But with decisions, especially irreversible decisions, you can have options. They might not be a sure thing, but by waiting for as long as possible before making an irreversible decision, you can see where the ball might likely drop.

Toyota faced this enormous choice when they began creating the Prius. They knew they were going to be the leaders in energy-efficient cars, but they had a myriad of options like I just outlined above for One Gallon. At one point, they were seriously considering electric and fuel cells before they realized the support for these types of cars didn't exist to their satisfaction. They kept their options open for the drive train while working on all other design options up until they had to make a decision. Eventually they committed to the hybrid—one that offered the benefits of electric power while providing their customers the long-distance travel option they wanted. Given the success of the Prius model, it seems they made a solid decision.[46]

Our family's car purchase doesn't require a full commitment. Yes, they have to choose a car and register it and sign a title, but at any point they can sell it or decide to trade it in for another. When your team decides to work on a PBI and get stymied, they can change *how* they planned the work.

What if our example family decides on the vacation, for instance? This is an irreversible decision. Once the vacation is paid for, the money is gone and the car is no longer a possibility. After they go on vacation, take their flights, stay in the hotel, eat the food, use the rental car, and see the sights, that money is gone. The only decision they may be able to reverse was the one to buy a souvenir because you can either return it or sell it on online.

For our fictional One Gallon company, early on—before they decided on their name—they may have looked at various options for their concept car that would achieve their vision for a green, environmentally friendly vehicle. They might have considered electric vehicles, fuel cells, solar power, and wind power (maybe car-sailing will become a thing). Once they chose the extremely fuel-efficient model, however, they were locked in. Sure, they could have tried fuel cell technology for six months only to discover the technology is not yet at the level they need it to be. Meanwhile, a competitor working with hybrids leapfrogs their progress. So they switch and attempt to play catch-up. Was it reversible? That depends. If switching is costly and results

---

46 Jeffrey K. Liker, *The Toyota Way: 14 Management Principles from the World's Greatest Manufacturer* (New York: McGraw-Hill, 2003).

in enormous amounts of wasted time, effort, and money, then, no, it's not reversible. A decision to switch from one technology to a completely different technology is costly. Make the wrong choice on a decision of this magnitude and you could bankrupt the company. Kodak made a commitment to keep a large part of their resources in film while attempting to conquer digital. This irreversible decision to diversify led to their demise while their competitors at Fuji fully embraced digital technology.[47]

DECISION LATENCY:
WHEN TO MAKE DECISIONS

We have so many parables and sayings around doing things too quickly that I think ideas like "Look before you leap," "Haste makes waste," or "Fools rush in" can lead to excessive caution. Like many adages, there is an element of wisdom. Taken too far, though, it becomes bad advice, because as we all know, "He who hesitates is lost." (Our ability to create conflicting advice goes way back.)

There is an inherent danger hidden under the guise of caution. Studies show that those who don't decide quickly are doomed to failure. Along with the Internet of Things (IoT) and the resulting interconnected world, new phrases are populating our modern vernacular—like Facebook's "Move fast and break things" mantra. But you can move *too* fast, break *too many* things, and end up in a hole you can't get out of. Let's see if we can figure out which is the *baby* and which is the *bathwater*.

Decision latency is just a fancy way to say "decision speed." This is what happens when we let engineers make up terms. Decision latency is the measurement of time between the need for a decision arising and the time the decision is made. Latency comes from the Latin root *latentem*, meaning hidden or lurking. It has a shared root with *lethargic*. The longer a team or organization takes to make a decision—high latency—the more lethargic you get. The shorter the latency period, the more likely the project will succeed. We've all been frustrated by governments or committees pushing off hard decisions offering only excuses instead. Yet industry magazines gawk over young, gutsy entrepreneurs who saw opportunities and capitalized on them by deciding quickly. The studies show that fast decisions will more likely lead to success. Take too long . . . well, do you remember the '90s western classic *The Quick and the Dead*?

---

47 Oliver Kmia, "Why Kodak Died and Fujifilm Thrived: A Tale of Two Film Companies," PetaPixel, October 19, 2018, https://petapixel.com/2018/10/19/why-kodak-died-and-fujifilm-thrived -a-tale-of-two-film-companies/.

The Quick

The Standish Group, an independent international IT research advisory firm, has been studying software projects for twenty years. Perhaps their most important finding is this: teams that make decisions in under an hour have a success rate of 58 percent. The Standish Group defines Decision Latency Theory as this: "The value of the interval is greater than the quality of the decision." In other words, the slower the decision is made, the worse the results. To improve performance, you must make reversible decisions faster.[48]

This doesn't mean that you have to decide on a market strategy, a major building project, or other major decisions within a solitary workday. That would be foolish. However, many decisions mercilessly languish in committees and get stacked on executives' desks not because of bureaucracy and fear but in the name of caution and prudence.

The Dead

But what if you take longer than five hours? What if your internal bureaucratic processes require a lot of sign-offs and—egad!—meetings before a final decision is delivered regarding even minor changes? According to the same Standish Group study, teams that take over five hours per decision have a success rate of only 18 percent. Did you catch that? There is over a 300 percent better chance of success for teams that make decisions quickly![49]

Does this mean that if your decision takes five hours and two minutes, it's going to fail? Of course not. However, this data offers a strong indicator that making decisions as fast as possible is the better way to go.

ACTUALLY MAKING DECISIONS

We've talked at length about the different types of decisions, including irreversible, reversible, *what* decisions, and *how* decisions, and we've discussed how *fortune favors the bold* when discussing decision latency (to throw yet another proverb into the mix). So who is making all of these decisions, and which decisions should be made quickly? Good questions! Depending on the decision type and context, there is a time to make a decision unilaterally, make a decision as a team, or make a decision quickly, and there are also

---

48 James Johnson, *Decision Latency Theory: It's All about the Interval* (The Standish Group, 2018).

49 Ibid.

times when you want to keep your options open and only make a decision at the last possible moment.

Lowest Possible Level

All decisions should be made at the lowest level possible. Within the Scrum framework and even with larger organizations using Scrum@Scale, the hierarchy is relatively shallow—only a few levels—when compared with traditional bureaucratic organizations. The team is aligned with the company's vision and culture; you should trust they will want to make the best decision possible.

Reversible decisions, especially those surrounding the issue of *how* to perform the work, should be made quickly. Most decisions around the work to be done, or experimenting to solve an issue or complete a task within a Sprint, do not need a lot of consideration. The more easily reversed the decision, the faster it should be made.

As entrepreneur and speaker Taylor Pearson puts it, "Compare how you feel about Zappos customer service, where employees are allowed to use their judgement to get the best outcome for the customers, with United Airlines, which forces everyone to follow rigid guidelines with no flexibility."[50] Zappos customer service is continually lauded within the business industry, while United Airlines recently finished last in J. D. Power's customer satisfaction results.[51]

You're probably not as concerned with customer service. The lowest-level decision power extends well beyond the realm of service. The more decision-making power you have invested in the lowest level, the faster and more cheaply decisions can be made. While there are pretty heady studies done on this, let's just walk through a thought exercise.

Let's suppose a team member needs a new $200 office chair because hers broke. She goes to her boss and is told to file a requisition. The paperwork takes ten minutes for her to find and complete. Her boss then reads over the requisition, signs it, makes a copy, and forwards to purchasing. Purchasing has a question about why the chair broke. Some emails are exchanged, and then they place an order. How much of the time that could have been spent working on productive goals was occupied by meaningless back-and-forth?

---

50 Taylor Pearson, *OODA: How to Turn Uncertainty Into Opportunity*, accessed November 11, 2019, https://taylorpearson.me/ooda-loop/.

51 Lauren Zumbach, "United Last on J. D. Power Customer Satisfaction Survey, but the Airline Is Improving," *Chicago Tribune*, May 29, 2019, https://www.chicagotribune.com/business /ct-biz-united-airlines-ranked-last-jd-power-20190529-story.html.

How much money was wasted? The reason these layers of bureaucracy were installed in the first place was most likely an attempt to minimize waste and maintain accountability. And while a level of checks and balances is healthy, removing lower-level people's decision-making power removes time effectiveness and only accomplishes two things, in my opinion. One, it tells them that the company doesn't believe they are competent enough to make intelligent decisions and learn from their mistakes. Two, it tells the worker that, in the end, they're not responsible if the choice was poor. Somebody else signed off on it, so it's not their problem but management's.

If our sample family buys a car, the decision will most likely be made by the parents. In some families, depending on their family dynamic, such decisions are sometimes made by one person.

But in business, sometimes a team member might be a bit out of their league, or they're new to the team and aren't as adept in product knowledge. There's no reason the team member can't ask a fellow team member, the Product Owner, or even the Scrum Master for assistance in making a decision. Consulting, though, is different from consensus, as we will see.

Consensus: When to Make Decisions as a Team

While any decision can be made by any individual at any time—assuming they have the authority—this doesn't mean it's necessarily the right thing to do. Some kings of old would decide to go to war, marry a particular woman, or behead an alleged enemy with little to no regard to their counsel. Those kings were usually ousted by their subjects through a coup or rebellion. And that's why you shouldn't behave like an arrogant king.

Of the two main types of decisions, irreversible decisions should be made by consensus whenever possible. Even when the path is clear, some decisions warrant team input. While your head probably won't end up on a pike if you don't get consensus, the opportunity for the team to have buy-in and be committed to the final decision is invaluable. Factoring in the needs and wishes of every stakeholder, whether these are family members or departments in a business, can help clarify the action needed.

To be clear, consensus means that every team member has had a right to express his or her beliefs or doubts and voice any issues they may have with the decision. Consensus to move forward doesn't require every team member to heartily extend their fist in the huddle and chant "Victory or death!" again, harkening back to our old tyrant king. It requires every doubt to be considered and, once heard, for that doubt to be addressed in the decision-making process.

Let's go back to our family. They've chosen the irreversible vacation. The parents have always wanted to visit East Asia but have a special affinity for Mongolia. The kids agree with the idea of a more exotic country, but they prefer to be near an ocean. The parents—the leaders—consider their kids' need to be near water and look for a consensus. They may eventually decide on Hong Kong, which meets all their interests.

To reach consensus, leaders must consider the intent behind the disagreement, consider its validity, and look for ways to address it. However, the point is not to reach 100 percent agreement. That may never happen, and even attempting to get to 99 percent could take far too much time. Even the framers of the United States Constitution were happy with just a two-thirds majority vote for all future amendments.

Taking the time to listen and consider all points of view allows everyone to buy into the decision and work together to make the decision successful. With a nonreversible decision, you want to keep your options open, keep gathering information. Of course, speed is still important—the world is changing, the children are growing, the family vacation cannot be put off for years. If the family were planning a vacation before the eldest goes to college in the autumn, they have a deadline to book it before all their options are gone. They may decide they have until June 15 to decide so they can travel by July 15—well in advance of packing for a dorm. Similarly, your division might want to launch a new video gaming console. The decision must be made before a certain date if you wish to launch it before the busy Christmas season.

With some types of decisions, a deadline is necessary, but that doesn't mean all options need to be decided upfront. Deciding in January for a South African trip in August doesn't mean that all the *hows* need to be decided in January as well. This allows you to keep some options open. Which flights to take, what hotels to book, and what sights to see can all have later deadlines, keeping options open for deals or incentives that can keep costs down.

I may sound contradictory here, but sometimes you want to avoid making a decision for as long as possible to keep your options open. For instance, suppose you decided to buy a house in 2007 and realized that the biggest home you could afford at the time was a cramped, two-bedroom condominium. If you didn't absolutely have to buy a house that year, you could wait. After the housing market crash, your same budget could afford a larger single-family home. Had you made a decision in under five hours for something as life-changing and irreversible as this home purchase, you would have regretted the result.

Sometimes you reach a decision on the next action to take only. That's fine. Just like a thousand-mile road trip can be planned in advance, there are numerous options for reaching your destination. For the first hundred miles, your option might be limited to one particular highway. But after that stretch, you may have three options. You could select one of those options now, but things like traffic, floods, and construction could arise before you reach the point where you must decide. My point is, decide quickly with reversible decisions, but keep your options open for as long as you are able to on irreversible decision (but sometimes you will have a deadline). But when a decision must be made—especially an irreversible one—hear out the team, consider and address their valid input, and then act.

Sprint Planning gives us a taste of this type of irreversible decision consensus. Once the Sprint is planned, it's an irreversible decision. Only during extraordinary circumstances is a Sprint changed, and, even then, only changes authorized by the Product Owner can be implemented. So part of Sprint Planning is a team event working toward consensus regarding *what* should be worked on. The Product Owner might prioritize one PBI over another and make a mistake, refine it, and make adjustments to the next PBI as the team works through Sprints. During Sprint Planning, *how* decisions—as in "how many PBIs should we work on?"—are a team decision, with the team having final say.

This simple matrix shows ways of making reversible versus irreversible decisions.

8.1. Decision Matrix

THE VALUE OF LEARNING

You learn from feedback. The faster you can make and act on a decision, the faster you can learn. And it's only in seeing what happens—the feedback from our decisions and actions—where we learn. By seeing poor results as just that—results—instead of failures, we can adjust. Like throwing darts, it's only from our first release that we can make adjustments based on how close to the bullseye our first dart landed. A dart-throwing coach can only make adjustments to our technique *after* we have thrown it. In the next attempt, we aim a little higher and release the dart sooner, and hold our elbow higher based on our result and the coach's input. For One Gallon's chassis, it's in fabricating our first chassis and getting the feedback that it doesn't pass the physical crash test—information that can help us further refine the computer crash-test model we used to help plan our design.

If Scrum is about adding more value faster, then learning through feedback is the turbocharger in the process. When a team works together for dozens of Sprints, they begin to see patterns (something we will cover more in chapter 10). Instead of only one result a year, they have twenty-five.

This is why making decisions and taking action quickly is critical. But how can an average difference of only a few hours of decision latency make such an immense difference? An educated, experienced Scrum team through quick decision-making and feedback can begin seeing what may appear to be separate issues as a whole. By making decisions and taking action over and over, they have developed their instincts and can act on them almost instantly. It has become second nature. And those actions, informed by years of observation, are likely to be successful. The fastest team wins. If you change faster, the other person can't keep up. The result: you win.

The human brain is a whiz at making mental models—finding patterns— so we can make sense of new situations quickly based on similar past scenarios. Our ancestors learned to run from the rustling in the brush regardless of whether the rustler was a hungry lion or a feeble goat. By running away, our ancestor survived either way. That instinct to make a quick assessment survived as a result. Using mental models serve us well in most, but not all, circumstances (like if we're starving and could have really used that feeble goat). As we will see, sometimes we have to question our instincts even when all seems perfectly logical.

But your learning is only as good as the quality of your feedback. If you have poor feedback, you can still learn, but not as well as you might have. For instance, back when I was still a college student, I loved playing chess. I was pretty good at it but not nearly as good as nationally ranked chess masters. Out of my desire to play better, I decided to create my own chess-playing computer program. I admired my finished creation and began playing the computer. And it worked! Well … sometimes it did. I'd play and then the computer would make a move, like surrendering its king. Even if you've never played chess, you can probably guess that's the worst move you can make. I eventually gave up on my pet project. I wanted to be a better player, but the computer's programming was limited to my own skillset. The feedback I was getting was not helpful because the machine couldn't learn the game any better than I did.

Spikes, and When to Use Them

Learning is an important part of the decision-making process. The cow who doesn't learn from her decision to continually walk into the electrified fence will continue to suffer. But sometimes learning isn't required just from decisions. Sometimes we have to learn more about a Product Backlog Item before we even begin estimating it. When are we supposed to do that?

That's when we run what is called a Spike, a solution to address learning during a Sprint. Invented by software engineer Kent Beck, a Spike is used when you have no idea how to estimate a Product Backlog Item. Let's say you're running a Scrum team in a brick-and-mortar business with the old reliable systems of customer purchase orders, fulfillment, and billing. But now your team is taking on the product of a digital system. You want your customers to be able to place purchase orders and pay for them through a web portal. One of the PBIs is "Create Payment Module," which you all determined should allow the client to pay their bill digitally through bank draft, PayPal, or a number of credit cards. But there's a problem: no one on the team has ever created a payment module. When it comes time to estimate the Story Points, via Planning Poker, the points are all over the place. The team confesses that they really don't know what it takes to create a payment module. If you can't estimate a PBI like the payment module, it can't make it into the Sprint. Only items that have been estimated should be in a Sprint.

For this example, a Spike would be used. Some say a Spike is a Scrum Pattern (we'll look at patterns in chapter 10), but I disagree. If anything, it is more of a Product Backlog refinement tool. Spikes give you the opportunity to explore and learn about an unknown PBI. Remember, the whole purpose of a Sprint is to produce a deliverable item that has value for the client. Learning, while valuable to the team, is not valuable to the client. A Spike allows the opportunity to learn during a Sprint.

To use a Spike, you take the payment module PBI and split it into two PBIs.

The first would be called "Spike payment module," the second just "payment module." You then add this new PBI called "Spike payment module" to a Sprint.

What you are doing during the Spike is research—learning—about what is involved in a payment module. If you're like me, you could spend countless hours researching something like this, especially if you find the topic fascinating. To avoid that, we dedicate a set time box like four hours or half a day for the team to learn all they can about what is involved with payment modules. The team would add the Spike to a Sprint during Sprint Planning. Then, in the other part of Sprint Planning, the Developers would decide *how* to do the work of the Spike—the learning. They may decide to spend time on PayPal's education pages, collate other sources on Google, and possibly reach out to their network to gather leads. The goal of the Spike isn't to learn everything the team can about the item, only to learn enough to estimate the number of Story Points it will take.

When the Spike is completed, the team can then estimate the PBI "payment" module during their next estimation using their newly acquired understanding. Spikes are useful whenever you encounter an item where the work involved is largely unknown. I've heard of people who use Scrum in their personal lives, using a Spike to learn about a project they've never attempted before, like reseeding a lawn.

OODA LOOPS: THE BREAKFAST OF CHAMPIONS

Colonel John Boyd, an Air Force fighter pilot in Korea and instructor at the Air Force's Fighter Weapons School, had a standing bet that he could out-maneuver any opposing pilot in forty seconds. How could this be? Learning, adapting, and deciding—*fast*. Boyd maintained that as a pilot flew mission after mission and learned from each one, he trained himself to recognize and respond to the maneuvers of other pilots almost instinctually. The pilot who learns the fastest, adjusts the fastest, and responds the fastest, wins the battle. Boyd became known as "Forty-Second Boyd" and "Genghis John," and his ideas endure today, not only in the Air Force but throughout the business world.[52]

Boyd invented a framework he called the OODA Loop. OODA is an acronym for "observe, orient, decide, and act." A fighter pilot observes his opponent, recognizes his maneuvers, and makes his decision: he can guess what

---

52 Robert Coram, *Boyd: The Fighter Pilot Who Changed the Art of War* (New York: Hatchett Book Group, 2002).

position will be most advantageous for him, and he will take it immediately and shoot. The pilot is not going to stop and look up historic air battles, he's not going to radio a superior and ask for suggestions or radio his squadron to have a quick meeting. These actions would only slow him down and weaken his position. He's going to follow his training and instincts, take a position, and strike.

OODA doesn't just work in the (un)friendly skies. In the boardroom and in any business, the competition can be just as fierce as an aerial battle and requires some fast decision-making. Boyd learned to make OODA part of muscle memory, so he could react seamlessly. Learning to observe, orient, decide, and act before you get into a heated negotiation means you're ready to become the "forty-second CEO."

Observe

Observing sounds easy. We observe the passage of time, people at the market, a squirrel collecting food. But observing is more than just looking at results; it's about seeing with a specific intent. A footballer might see his teammate waving his arms for a pass, but he also observes an opponent closing in on his position; meanwhile, another teammate is running downfield away from his guard. The footballer is observing everything he can. For fighter pilots, observing means having a situational awareness not only of the enemy fighter, but his airspeed, altitude, heading, enemy ground fire, distance from the base or ship, and what weapons are left in his arsenal. Even minding the sun's position in the sky could be advantageous in an attack pattern. And you thought driving a stick shift was tricky!

Once you are able to take in all of this information, it's easy to shift into action. Much like our cave-dwelling ancestor running from the rustling brush, our brain uses the shortcut of mental models to choose a preset action. But mental models can be flawed, and instead of running from death, we're instead running from a meal. During key decisions, it could be the decision to assume the housing market is going to continue making us money in 2007 because it's been on a steady incline for the previous five years. We must question our assumptions and orient ourselves to all the information.

Orient

Most people miss this, so I implore you to pay attention. This is where you connect the dots and synthesize all of the information you have. It's important to look for mismatches to how you think. Avoid *confirmation bias*, which Tufts University professor Raymond Nickerson defined as anything that "connotes the seeking or interpreting of evidence in ways that are partial to existing beliefs, expectations, or a hypothesis in hand."[53]

However, it's so tempting to see situations and look at data as we wish it to be. We have many "filters" through which we view our world. Those filters—how we interpret and make sense of our reality—are colored by various influences such as genetics, previous experiences, and cultural traditions (including work cultures). When it comes to making good decisions for Scrum, your organization, and even your personal life, you must intentionally analyze and synthesize new information and question your assumptions. In other words, don't be a zombie.

There's a popular tale that sounds far-fetched, but it demonstrates how easily we use even contradictory information to confirm our preconceived conclusions. A man developed a mental illness one day where he believed that he had died and risen as a zombie. His wife tried to convince him he was alive, but to no avail. She solicited the help of his mother and their minister, but every challenge they offered to him was easily shot down. She then made an emergency appointment with a psychologist. The psychologist approached the man's logical side.

"So you say you're a zombie?" the psychologist asked.

"I *know* I am a zombie," the man said plainly.

"Well, then, I have a question: do zombies bleed?" The psychologist leaned in, gauging the man's reaction.

"Of course we don't. We're dead."

The psychologist smiled, took out a pin from his drawer, and pricked the man's finger. The man's face revealed astonishment as he watched the crimson bead trickle down. "What do you say now?" the psychologist asked smugly.

"Well, I'll be!" the man said, after a moment of silence. "Zombies do bleed!"[54]

You will probably never think you're a walking member of the undead, but confirmation bias exists in the boardroom as much as the psychologist's study. Once you learn something, it's difficult to unlearn and think a different way.

For instance, an insurance company could have difficulty retaining customers.

53 Raymond S. Nickerson, "Confirmation Bias: A Ubiquitous Phenomenon in Many Guises," *Review of General Psychology* 2, no. 2 (1998), 175–220, http://psy2.ucsd.edu/~mckenzie/nickersonConfirmationBias.pdf.

54 Robert Fritz, *The Path of Least Resistance: Learning to Become the Creative Force in Our Own Life* (New York: Fawcett Columbine, 1989), 140.

Maybe there's a financial collapse, and they conclude that customers can no longer afford the insurance premiums. This makes perfect sense, which is why such thinking is dangerously insidious. Once the economy recovers, they might continue to see the same rate of lapsing policies and continue to conclude it's an affordability issue. So they advertise cheaper rates, cut corners, and sacrifice agents' commissions with little effect. This company, convinced by data that at one time may have been true, might continue down this path at its own detriment until someone questions the bias: what if the policies are lapsing for other reasons?

Questioning an assumption is a great way to detect biases. The executives, now with a bit of doubt, hire a firm to survey their recent lapsed customers. Instead of affordability being the primary drive for the decline, it might turn out that customers felt ignored by agents, or the company didn't educate them about the need for insurance, so, when deciding between insurance and a cable TV package, entertainment won.

Data alone can't tell the whole picture, though. Numbers don't lie, but analysts do. I don't mean analysts are maliciously creating falsehoods, but even data analysis can be influenced by our mental models.

In May 1997, Russian chess grandmaster Garry Kasparov sat down to an unusual chess game—the first of six in their match—in New York. His opponent was an IBM supercomputer known as Deep Blue. A lot was riding on the game. Kasparov was not just a world champion but had also stated publicly that he would never lose to a machine. Kasparov had won their previous match, over a year before. In game one of the rematch, however, Deep Blue made a surprising move. The computer sacrificed one of its pieces. Kasparov stared intently at the board. Some masters watching the game thought it was part of a sophisticated long-term strategy. After all, Deep Blue was a computer. It didn't make mistakes or fall prey to the type of human emotions or quibbles that can affect a game. Kasparov analyzed and pondered before making his next move. He was certain Deep Blue's move was so "human" that a deeper level of intelligence was at work.

Eventually, Kasparov made his countermove and went on to win that first game, but ultimately he lost the rematch. Years later, one of the designers of the supercomputer admitted that the move wasn't some sophisticated "for computers only" chess move. It was actually a glitch in the program. A bug caused the computer to select a completely random move.

Many speculated that the bug upset Kasparov because it didn't make sense, a notion he refutes in his book *Deep Thinking*, conceding that he had made an error in the rematch and underestimated Deep Blue's strategy, which had been specifically tuned to Kasparov's style and match history.[55]

It's a question of two tales. The notion of being rattled isn't out of the question for many people. I know people who have grown frustrated in other games against computers, assuming that the machine didn't play fairly.

What happens if we don't orient ourselves and check our biases? We could continue throwing money and time at a problem that doesn't exist, as with the insurance company, or lose a chess game because a computer move doesn't make sense, as with Kasparov.

When we question our assumptions—even those proven right a hundred times before—we may prove ourselves right yet again, but we may also realize that we're not as dead as we thought.

Decide

This is when you've considered many of the options (maybe not all), and it's time to decide. While we want to make decisions fast, some decisions you will want to wait until the last possible moment to make.

By this point you've observed and oriented and checked yourself for any blind spots (confirmation bias) and assessed the field. For fighter pilots and sports heroes, the decision is made in split seconds. An American Football quarterback observes the field and any rushers, checks his receivers, and intuitively analyzes the coverage patterns of the defense, then within a second he throws the ball either to someone or out of bounds if no option looks good.

The Standish Group—the same organization that studies decision latency—even wrote an analysis of Tom Brady of the New England Patriots where, in 1.9 seconds, he was able to take the ball from his center, find a receiver, and throw the football. The receiver caught the ball and ran ten yards downfield in another 1.1 seconds. Only three seconds. Had Brady held the ball for another half-second, he could have thrown it to his tight end forty yards down the field, except at the same time that the tight end got open, Brady was already on the ground, tackled by a defensive lineman. Had Brady held the ball the additional half second, the play would have lost yardage instead of giving the Patriots a significant first down.[56]

In baseball it's been said the best batters decide whether or not they're

---

55 Garry Kasparov, *Deep Thinking: Where Machine Intelligence Ends and Human Creativity Begins* (New York: Hachette Book Group, 2017), 176–80.

56 Johnson, *Decision Latency Theory*, 1.

going to swing before the pitcher has even released the ball. We have more than seconds, but that doesn't mean we can take all day.

Act

There's a lame old joke that goes like this: Three frogs are sitting on a log. One decides to jump off. How many are left? The answer is three. The frog only *decided* to jump off. Until it takes action, nothing has changed. There are a myriad of reasons why so many otherwise good managers delay making decisions and taking appropriate action. In my opinion, the delay in taking action boils down to fear. Fear of loss of money, respect, position; fear of pain from failure; or just the fear of being fired. If you've cultivated a culture that gives space for psychological safety, then your team will feel more empowered to take calculated risks and see what happens.

The key is to move through OODA smoothly as well as quickly. When faced with a situation in business, observe and take measure of your situation like a fighter pilot, orient (connect the dots, question your assumptions and biases), decide, and act. Like Boyd, practice this loop until you automatically engage each time there's a decision to be made. Maybe you won't be placing bets like he did, but you will get past the paralysis that stops so much of leadership.

DECISIONS, OODA, LEARNING, AND SCRUM

I've said it before: Scrum helps you add value faster. While some who start using Scrum do so for the culture and productivity or even to have happier employees (don't get me started on Hippie Scrum), in the end it works because Scrum's culture, combined with its methods, allow a team to make ever-faster decisions.

Decisions that languish in executive committees or are procrastinated on—kicked into an ever-distant future—only harm your team and organization. But decisions made are not necessarily decisions acted upon. The decision to hire someone is not the same as sitting down with her, negotiating the salary, and getting the employment paperwork completed. Instead, "Create employment ad" sits on someone's to-do list while busy-work fills their calendar.

You've learned how to stop that cycle of bureaucratic lethargy. With the simple tools and frameworks herein, you now know how to tell the difference between types of decisions, make them quickly as an individual or gain consensus as a team, enact the decisions, question your assumption, orient, learn, and make another decision based on the feedback. While OODA Loops aren't Scrum, its decision-making framework is like Scrum's close cousin.

Enough learning. It's time to make some decisions.

YOUR SCRUM PLAYBOOK

Making good decisions quickly depends on a number of factors and your ability to incorporate them in the process. Knowing what kind of decision is being made and who should be involved is only the start of the process. Engaging with feedback, learning what you need to know, and developing the mental models needed to go through a solid decision-making process quickly can make all the difference between quality actions that move you forward and poor choices that lead you nowhere.

DECISION-MAKING FACTORS

- Is the decision an individual or consensus decision?
- Reversible decisions can be backtracked without losing much in time or money, such as buying a car and deciding later not to keep it.
- Irreversible decisions require full commitment, such as going on vacation—once the money is spent, it's gone.
- Decisions should be made at the lowest level as much as possible, particularly regarding reversible decisions.
- Irreversible decisions should be made by consensus to encourage full team buy-in and to consider all valid concerns.
- Sprints goals are irreversible decisions made by consensus.
- All decisions have two sub-sets:
  - What is going to be done (during a sprint, for example)
  - How it is going to be accomplished (reversible decisions made by individual as much as possible)
- Feedback is the turbocharger of decision-making, as it's where learning takes place and builds our mental models for faster future decision-making.
- A Spike is a time block of targeted learning about a topic, which allows for better planning and decision-making (how to add a payment module to a website).
- OODA Loop: observe, orient, decide, and act

Playing Your Hand

- ○ Observe what is happening and what needs to change to accomplish a goal.
- ○ Orient yourself to the problem.
  - — Question your assumptions.
  - — Watch for mismatches.
  - — Beware of confirmation bias.
- ○ Decide on a course of action.
  - — Make it quick but reasonable.
  - — For irreversible decisions, wait as long as is feasible to lock down options, but have a deadline.
- ○ Take action.
  - — Failure to act typically boils down to some fear. Find the fear and address it.

CHAPTER NINE

Obstacles and Measures: How to Tell if You're Winning the Game

I fear not the man who has practiced 10,000 kicks once, but I fear the man who has practiced one kick 10,000 times.

—Bruce Lee[57]

Hopefully you go to the doctor regularly to make sure that, even though you feel fine, there isn't any insidious disease lurking beneath your otherwise healthy exterior. During the checkup, the doctor looks at your vitals and takes a variety of metrics, including height, weight, body mass, and blood tests to check your cholesterol and triglyceride levels. The results come in: you're obese and your blood pressure, triglycerides, and cholesterol are all high. The prognosis isn't good unless you start making drastic changes to your activity levels and diet.

A week later, you're having lunch with a friend and order some fried food with lots of sour cream. Concerned, your friend speaks up: "I'm not sure that's the healthiest choice."

You chuckle. "I'm healthy. After all, I go to the doctor every year."

This sounds absurd, doesn't it—thinking you're healthy because you see your doctor regularly? Unless you look at the feedback from your doctor and make changes to get those levels under control, you'll never be healthy.

While it seems inane to think simply seeing your doctor will make you

---

57 Abishek Kumar, *The Life and Times of Bruce Lee* (New Delhi: Prabhat Books, 2008).

healthy without taking any of the recommended actions, I often meet people who think their organization is agile because "we use Scrum." I did say that Scrum is one way to be Agile—like vanilla is one flavor of ice cream and by far the most popular—but Scrum doesn't make you Agile. Scrum shows you where you're not Agile yet. As you implement Scrum, there will be issues. But instead of seeing these issues as problems or headaches, welcome them because, like the high blood pressure and cholesterol, they're telling you a story. Ignore the story, and your attempts to become Agile will lead you to an early grave.

Impediments are nothing more than indicators that tell you where you are not yet Agile or where you could become more Agile. They are to be expected—especially as you begin your Scrum implementation. Other managers will try to "borrow" their former staff, the PMO may request reports, or another department may inform you that your support request was denied until you submit a budget request and await approval. Impediments like these can make you want to rip your hair out at times, but they're part of the learning process.

In this chapter we will cover some common impediments and solutions. Are these the only impediments and solutions? No. In the beginning, these serve as a guide. As you grow in your learning and mastery of Scrum, you will be able to intuit best practices for unique situations.

By this point, you might already be playing the game, getting your team trained, and possibly planning or performing your first Sprint. Or maybe you want to read the entire book and think about it (not really in the spirit of Scrum—the learning is in the doing, but to each their own). Kidding aside, you've learned a lot and (hopefully) have taken action on what you've learned.

Let's recap briefly what you should understand at this point: You've learned the values of Scrum and how to shift the culture through Scrum implementation; culture is behavior, and behavior is changed through doing. You've learned how to create an independent and protective "bubble" in which to form your team. You've learned about the roles, events, and artifacts and how to assemble your team as well as your implementation strategy. Your Product Owner now knows how to create a Product Backlog through Story Mapping, including cutting, refining, and synthesizing a Product Goal. And you've learned about the events crucial to Scrum, such as Sprint Planning, Daily Scrums, Sprint Review, and the Sprint Retrospective.

Maybe you are a real dive-in type who's already had a number of Daily Scrums. On the board, your team has begun listing issues—impediments—that the Scrum Master needs to work on possibly with the sponsor's help. Using the OODA loop framework, maybe the SM has been able to orient himself around the impediments and look for mismatches to her mental models.

SHU-HA-RI: THE JAPANESE PHILOSOPHY OF MASTERY

If you're one of those people who read a book cover through appendixes, you might have noticed my mention of *shu-ha-ri* as a Japanese martial arts concept and wondered what this was doing in a book about business systems. The term has its roots in ancient Japanese culture and is used to define the learning path from beginner to mastery. In an interview, aikido master Endo Seishiro Shihan defined the term this way:

It is known that, when we learn or train in something, we pass through the stages of *shu*, *ha*, and *ri*. These stages are explained as follows. In *shu*, we repeat the forms and discipline ourselves so that our bodies absorb the forms that our forebearers created. We remain faithful to the forms with no deviation. Next, in the stage of *ha*, once we have disciplined ourselves to acquire the forms and movements, we make innovations. In this process the forms may be broken and discarded. Finally, in *ri*, we completely depart from the forms, open the door to creative technique, and arrive in a place where we act in accordance with what our heart/mind desires, unhindered while not overstepping laws.[58]

Alistair Cockburn introduced the idea to the Agile community in his book *Agile Software Development*.[59] The three words translated from Japanese roughly translate to mean *hold, break, leave*. In *shu*, we first we learn the foundations and "hold" to the original principles laid before us. In martial arts, these are the blocks, punches, kicks, and basic holds. During the *ha* state, we've achieved a solid understanding of the basics and have demonstrated solid technical application of what we've learned. We can "hold" to the core fundamentals in various situations and begin experimenting with new ways to use what we've learned. In the final *ri* state, we've attained mastery. We not only know the rules and fundamentals, but we can depart from them, adapt, or even introduce other concepts that blend well with what we know.

Growing up, I was a big fan of Bruce Lee, though I don't know many boys from my generation who weren't. The typical storyline in his movies were not unlike American westerns. A small community tries to eke out a life when

---

58 "An Interview with Endo Seishiro Shihan by Aiki News," trans. Daniel Nishina and Akiya Hideo, *Dou*, no. 144 (Spring 2005), Internet Archive, accessed January 8, 2020, https://web.archive.org/web/20110610205348/http://homepage3.nifty.com/aikido_sakudojo/Shihan_Interview_Dou144-e.html.

59 Alistair Cockburn, *Agile Software Development: The Cooperative Game* (Upper Saddle River, NJ: Addison-Wesley, 2006).

an evil bully (drug lord, gang leader, or political tyrant) enters the picture demanding retribution and respect. Eventually Bruce Lee's character becomes the community's equalizer by first vanquishing the villain's henchmen and eventually the villain himself.

Bruce Lee's journey from kid to martial arts legend is a perfect example of the *shu-ha-ri* concept. When Bruce Lee was still very young, his father taught him the basics of, t'ai chi ch'üan, a Wu style of martial arts. Not long after, he began learning wing chun from the legendary Yip Man (made popular by the 2008 film *Ip Man*). Lee continued his training through Yip's students along the years, eventually mastering wing chun. Later, after moving to Seattle, he opened a school called Lee Jun Fan Gung Fu. This evolved into the Bruce Lee philosophy of fighting called jeet kune do. It was largely based on the wing chun he had become proficient in, yet it still varied and borrowed from other philosophies.[60]

Lee had started with Yip Man as a *shu*-state student. Man taught him to hold to the fundamentals of the style. After he mastered the basics, he was able to break some of the rules and experiment with other styles, including dance and boxing. This eventually led him to develop his own philosophy or, in essence, *leave* the style of his childhood by taking the solid fundamentals and building on them with other approaches that complemented them.

This is the core of *shu-ha-ri*. The impediments you encounter help you to learn and hone your understanding and mastery. Understand the rules in *The Scrum Guide* and put forth herein, and after you've achieved mastery, then, and only then, can you effectively make changes and experiment without destroying the Agile heart of Scrum.

IMPEDIMENTS: IDENTIFYING AND SOLVING THE MOST COMMON

There are an endless number of impediments, but what is an impediment? An impediment is anything that can derail or "impede" a team's velocity and progress toward its goal. Unchecked and unresolved, impediments can wear down a team's motivation. They can be as simple as the fictional TPS (total project status) coversheet highlighted in the hit movie *Office Space*, where our hero Peter has a boss who is constantly reminding him to fill out this useless piece of paperwork. Impediments can also be as complicated as our technical

---

60 Bruce Thomas, *Bruce Lee: Fighting Spirit: A Biography* (Berkeley: Frog Books, 1994).

problem with Software Giant in chapter one, when the company failed to address our service tickets in a reasonable timeframe.

While possible impediments are seemingly infinite, there are a number of common impediments you should be aware of: bad Scrum, lack of focus, little or no psychological safety, distributed teams, architecture, manual testing, delivery, and bureaucracy.

As we learned from the OODA Loop in chapter 8, we're really good at the observe, decide, act portions of the loop. What's really difficult to do is see beyond what your mental models and biases are telling you is true. To solve impediments, sometimes you must "orient" yourself, question your assumptions, and look deeper, so you can connect the dots. Let's say you felt ill with a fever, chills, aches, and extreme exhaustion. You might take a drug like Tylenol for the fever, chills, and aches, and drink tons of coffee to overcome the exhaustion. In other words, you could examine and treat the symptoms individually. You might feel some relief, except the coffee, a diuretic, is dehydrating you. This isn't good when you have the flu, the symptoms of which you may have missed.

If you were able to look at all the symptoms and question the common source as the flu, you might have gone to your doctor or clinic to receive a Tamiflu treatment, which would have reduced your suffering from two weeks to only a few days.

Making an Impediment List

Part of the Scrum Master's work is to identify and remove impediments. Some impediments raised during the Daily Scrum are trivial. Others are more substantial, pointing to something more like an organizational "flu," and require the Scrum Master to raise these impediments to people within the organization with the authority to erase or minimize them.

For this reason, many teams have created an impediment list. Like it sounds, it's a list of impediments raised by the team that require action from outside the team to remove, like my issue with Software Giant.

Keeping this list, usually near the Sprint's list of priorities in full view of the team and stakeholders, is invaluable. Have you ever been in one of those seemingly pointless meetings and raised an issue with a teammate or manager who promised she'd "look into that"? Most likely you have. What happened? With the best of intentions, the matter might have been looked into, found to be more involved, and moved to someone's to-do list. Or worse. The item was jotted in a notebook, never to be seen by human eyes again. This type of behavior, good or forgetful, leads to workplace cynicism and disengagement.

By keeping the impediment list in the forefront, it shows the team that it hasn't been forgotten.

The Scrum Master maintains this list and, much like the Product Owner refines the Product Backlog, orders the impediment list by priority, with the most critical impediments receiving top billing. The list should never be empty. I agree with the Published Patterns team when they say, "An empty Impediment List means that you aren't looking hard enough for ways to improve."[61]

Because we've already used the doctor and flu metaphors in describing Scrum's Agile health as well as seeing the proverbial symptoms of impediments as a potential for larger, flu-like issues, we will be looking at each of these common impediments in the following format:

- ▸ What the impediment is
- ▸ Why it's an impediment
- ▸ Symptoms of the impediment
- ▸ Cure: how a Scrum Master or sponsor can address this common impediment—actions

Let's dive in.

Impediment One: Bad Scrum

WHAT BAD SCRUM IS

The worst impediment is rushing into Scrum's techniques without building on its pillars and values. You can place a rudder, a sail, and keel on your car, but it still won't float. Bad Scrum is partial Scrum, Frankenscrum. It's taking a work breakdown structure that has critical paths and multiple dependencies for each deliverable and calling it a Product Backlog, or delivering value to the client every six months but holding daily meetings. Bad Scrum shows up in many forms, and each is a monster.

WHY BAD SCRUM IS AN IMPEDIMENT

Jumping into Scrum while using only some of the techniques is a recipe for failure. Some may point to my Bruce Lee example and show how he combined his elements of jeet kune do with other styles including kenpo, tae kwon do,

---

61 Jeff Sutherland, James O. Coplien, and the Scrum Patterns Group, *A Scrum Book: The Spirit of the Game*, ed. Adaobi Obi Tulton (Raleigh, NC: Pragmatic Bookshelf, 2019), 196.

and even boxing. That's true. And there are people applying Scrum to industries and businesses where pure Scrum is difficult. However, these are experts with years of experience, and they are staying true to the Agile mindset as they make these changes.

Bad Scrum (Frankenscrum or Stunted Scrum) is using only a few parts of Scrum and mixing it with parts that are anti-Agile. It's like a mixed martial arts (MMA) fighter entering a championship match with training in only one fighting style (boxing, let's say), a little ballet, but without any cardiovascular conditioning. His match will end . . . quickly—especially after his plié. A true MMA champion masters various styles and conditions his body. Like a well-rounded MMA fighter, true Scrum uses the 3-5-3 structure (three roles, five events, and three artifacts) and embraces the rules put forth in *The Scrum Guide*.

However, true to the concept of *shu-ha-ri*, once you've mastered not only the practice but the understanding of things, then you can add and experiment as you master. Like Bruce Lee did with wing chun, you're staying true to the core, and changes become intuitive. But this happens *only* after you have mastered the principles *and* techniques—the whole of Scrum, including a shift in mindset and culture.

SYMPTOMS OF BAD SCRUM

When bad Scrum begins appearing, the symptoms can include the need for reports, team members tasked with estimate duties, a Product Owner acting like a project manager, a PBI that has no value, and Sprints that don't produce a testable product. Bad Scrum can show up more subtly in other impediments such as lack of focus and bureaucracy (which we will cover).

Ultimately, the best test for Bad Scrum is any action or process that flies in the face of the fundamental rules of Scrum laid out in *The Scrum Guide*. I've illustrated incidents of not-so-good Scrum in our One Gallon example. These are simulations of real-world adjustments that are sometimes made. The point is to make room for the variance and then return to true Scrum as quickly as possible.

CURE FOR BAD SCRUM

Identify the source of the bad Scrum. It could be a Product Owner returning to what she knows when the pressure is on, or an upper-level manager interfering with his own agenda. Or sometimes the result is other impediments the team doesn't know how to address, so they go back to the "old way of doing things" in order to solve the problem instead of relying on the team and the process to solve it.

The most common cause of bad Scrum is lack of solid training. Is training absolutely necessary? No. However, receiving solid, fundamental training can solve many implementation headaches.

When bad Scrum is encountered, remove the source or provide additional training. The Scrum Master is the coach to ensure the framework is followed. But even a Scrum Master can be wrong. No team member is above reproach. Like a nefarious weed, bad Scrum can soon choke all agility out of your team. Target it before it gains root.

Impediment Two: Lack of Focus

WHAT LACK OF FOCUS IS

Focus is a core value of Scrum, and a lack of it goes far beyond the after-lunch malaise that strikes every workplace. A lack of focus is when any work is done that does not further the Sprint's goal or is not concentrated on one outcome. That definition might sound rigid, and it is. Of course things will come up. Coworkers will email jokes or small requests for favors, and sometimes you need to go up and talk to another worker about a "problem," when really you're taking a mental break and looking for a distraction. These are fine when limited. A true lack of focus is far more devastating because it often shows up in the form of work, either in the form of multitasking on a dozen tasks at once or busy-work that doesn't move the Sprint forward.

WHY LACK OF FOCUS IS AN IMPEDIMENT

Remember the concept of "opportunity cost" from economics class? A dollar spent can't be spent on anything else. It's the same with time. Time spent on a priority, task, or distraction can't be spent elsewhere. If you have two weeks to complete a hundred story points, each minute spent on any task that doesn't help that goal is an opportunity lost. You don't get those minutes back.

Again, this isn't to say that every minute has to be spent with the intensity of a draconian office. Far from it. In Scrum, the happiness and engagement of the team is vitally important. Only each item that doesn't help the goal undercuts the team's effectiveness overall. This includes any attempts at multitasking that only dissipate focus. Earl Philip Stanhope once wrote this advice to his son: "There is time enough for everything in the course of the day if you do one thing at once, but there is not time enough in the year if you will do two things at once."[62]

---

62 Henry B. Wheatley, "Letter-Writers," in vol. 10 of *The Cambridge History of English Literature*, ed. by A. W. Ward and A. R. Waller (Cambridge: Cambridge University Press, 1913), 258.

Like the good earl said in the quote, lack of focus yields poor results. The more tasks or projects a team member works on simultaneously, the more diluted their efforts become. We've already highlighted the studies showing the cost of task switching. But even if you are able to easily switch tasks, there's more lost than just the time spent on the new task; you lose the ability to focus or learn, and you increase your stress levels at the same time.[63] [64]

SYMPTOMS OF LACK OF FOCUS

The symptoms of lack of focus can be multiple instances in the Daily Scrum of team members starting several tasks but not completing them. Look at your whiteboard. If few Post-its are being moved from the In Progress column to the Done column, you may have a focus issue. At the same time, if you are moving too many too fast into the In Progress column, you will also experience lack of focus as each team member is trying to focus on multiple tasks.

With new teams, these symptoms can stem from their old supervisors asking for favors in addressing one "little" thing, or an overeager team trying to focus on multiple tasks at once. These items could be symptoms of bad Scrum, too, if this multitasking comes from dependencies between PBIs. While this sometimes does happen—PBIs have some dependency—it should be minimal at best. If it occurs frequently, your issue is more than just lack of focus.

CURE FOR LACK OF FOCUS

The best way to cure a lack of focus is to have clearly defined priorities from the Product Owner. If the first five PBIs are to be completed this Sprint, the Developers should begin working on the first PBI exclusively as soon as Sprint Planning is finished. The team has decided *how* they will do the work by that point and their focus should be squarely fixed on Product Backlog Item one.

But when interruptions in focus come from outside the Scrum Team, that's where the Scrum Master acts to minimize the outside influence. Specifically he needs to have conversations with those interrupting the work and set some boundaries.

---

63 Cynthia Kubu and Andre Machado, "Why Multitasking Is Bad for You," *TIME*, April 20, 2017, https://time.com/4737286/multitasking-mental-health-stress-texting-depression/.

64 Gloria Mark, Daniela Gudith, and Ulrich Klocke, "The Cost of Interrupted Work: More Speed and Stress," *Proceedings of the SIGCHI Conference on Human Factors in Computing Systems* (April 2008), 107–10, https://www.ics.uci.edu/~gmark/chi08-mark.pdf.

Impediment Three: Lack of Psychological Safety

WHAT LACK OF PSYCHOLOGICAL SAFETY IS

We've discussed this value and its effect on workplace behavior. With a strong sense of safety comes an energetic and engaged team, a willingness to take healthy risks, and an immeasurable element of positive energy, where you can just feel the team enjoys the work they're doing. Like a light in a windowless room, you don't have to be an organizational psychologist to know whether psychological safety exists or not. It's visceral—no words are necessary.

WHY LACK OF PSYCHOLOGICAL SAFETY IS AN IMPEDIMENT

In order for a team to thrive, it needs to feel safe and like it's making a contribution. When an issue arises, the team needs to feel like they can point out the issue without being attacked, singled out, or criticized. It's particularly important during Sprint Retrospectives—when you're reviewing how you work as a team.

Without psychological safety, you'll see a breakdown or complete lack of communication, feedback, and learning.

SYMPTOMS OF LACK OF PSYCHOLOGICAL SAFETY

When it's missing, the symptoms of psychological safety can be passive: high absenteeism, less contribution and interactions within the team, decline in the team's velocity, fewer objections or flag-raising at events such as Sprint Planning and refining, team turnover, and less or nonexistent risk-taking—no one will take a chance on a reversible decision.

Symptoms can appear in more aggressive ways as well. Frequent arguing, name-calling, or aggressive behaviors such as threats of physical violence, whether explicit or implied, can occur.

The symptoms can be blatant or subtle, but they can be felt. If the team's behavior seems to be toxic, apathetic, or both, you've got bigger problems beside a lack of productivity.

CURE FOR LACK OF PSYCHOLOGICAL SAFETY

Overcoming an instance of missing psychological safety is a long road. When it's missing, there are hurts and fears. Depending on the dearth of safety, it can be like infidelity in a marriage, where achieving a level of safety will require a lot of hard work and consistent effort. Whether the reason for the lack of safety is a feeling of being criticized or diminished, the Scrum Master needs to address the "elephant" in the room. If it's a problem-employee or -employees, then the situation may need to involve the team responsible for Human Resources. A team member may need to be fired. This sounds awful, but remember that the best way to ensure a Scrum-positive culture is to hire people who reflect the values you want.

Scrum is about teams being able to self-organize. When toxicity or fear exist at any level, this ability declines. Hopefully the culprit is not aware of the damage he is doing with his actions. In one company, we had a sponsor who threatened to fire anyone who he felt wasn't living up to his ideals. He had no idea how this threat was impacting the team's performance until the Scrum Master and I confronted him with the issue.

This cure isn't easy, but it's doable.

Impediment Four: Distributed Teams

WHAT A DISTRIBUTED TEAM IS

I encountered this impediment when I was consulting with mining giant Drummond Company. I had helped set up their PMO years before I embraced Scrum. When my contact Alberto Garcia—then a division vice president (now Country Manager for Drummond Energy)—read about Scrum, he thought it could help his gas-mining division. He was happy to hear that I was now teaching Scrum.

We quickly assessed some of the issues within his team: lack of collaboration and communication. With a team spread between a main office, an office in another city, and workers in the mining fields, it was clear to see why.

But teams don't have to be dozens of kilometers apart to be distributed. They can be on separate floors or even in different corners of the same floor. The closer a team can work together, the better they communicate.

WHY DISTRIBUTED TEAMS IS AN IMPEDIMENT

Scrum relies on fast feedback and communication. Anything that interferes with communication is a detriment, and I'll share more on how in the next chapter with the Collocated Teams Pattern. For now, know that the farther team members—or people in general—are separated from each other, the less likely they are to talk to each other. The closer people are, the more frequently they talk.

SYMPTOMS OF DISTRIBUTED TEAMS

When a Scrum team is separated by cubicles or kilometers, they're not going to think to mention critical items or ask if there have been changes. Your Daily

Scrum—assuming you are able to hold it—reveals a lack of knowledge, people not being on the same page, or wrong assumptions about what's being worked on.

Other symptoms can include impediments being missed because there's no central board, tasks being tackled by two people simultaneously unbeknownst to the other, and just a slowed velocity. Instead of speed, things feel like they're moving in slow motion.

CURE FOR DISTRIBUTED TEAMS

The best solution is to have the team share one office. If you have multiple offices, redistribute the employees so each Scrum Team can share the same office. This is not always possible, but it is ideal if you can. The second solution—though not preferable and second to having a collocated team—is having robust, broadband videoconferencing and other online communication tools that can capture all forms of human communication including body language and other nonverbal cues. Some research is emerging that shows collocation is preferable whenever possible, especially when it comes to virtual teams, who are more prone to conflict and feeling less satisfied with their work.[65]

At the time of this writing, we are seeing the possibility of a global pandemic, which could make distributed teams inevitable. In a fully remote or virtual office, one of the most important aspects of communication is lost: those accidental conversations around the water cooler that can spark ideas and serendipitously solve problems. I'm hopeful that new technologies will emerge to foster this type of communication for distributed teams.

Impediment Five: Architecture – Lacking Structure from Which to Manage Scrum

WHAT ARCHITECTURE IS

While this impediment might evoke visions of open office spaces with table tennis, natural light, and visually pleasing workspaces, we don't mean that type of architecture. Nor, if you're a software developer, are we talking about the blocks of your coding . . . at least, not entirely.

Architecture has to do with the product itself. To move away from the traditional project management thinking, we need to slice a product in such a

---

65 Shikha Gera, "Virtual Teams versus Face to Face Teams: A Review of Literature," *IOSR Journal of Business and Management* 11, no. 2 (May–June 2013), 1–4, http://www.iosrjournals .org/iosr-jbm/papers/Vol11-issue2/A01120104.pdf.

way that each PBI adds value. To accomplish this, we need to eliminate dependencies as much as possible. This is accomplished through modular design. Instead of overlap and unified design, each component can be updated independent of all other components.

Saab accomplished this with their fighter jet JAS 39E Saab Gripen. Where the typical fighter jet is a tangle of interdependent systems, the Scrum teams at Saab created a modular architecture for the jet, with each team owning one or several modules. This allowed each component to be updated with a new release without having to change any other system. If the radar team were able to increase acquired target colors (or something like that), they could change out the old radar system. They just had to keep the overall dimensions, connections, and instrumental interfaces the same as the old jet. In other words, they only had to match the radar's interfaces. They didn't have to concern themselves with what other teams did with their modules. In fact, Paolo Sammicheli shares a story in his book *Scrum for Hardware* about how the engineers were testing the new radar system before the new jet was ready. They seat-belted the radar unit into the spare seat of the older two-seater model so they could get the necessary recordings.[66] Doesn't that sound like our Stanford students snapping pictures with their GoPro in a crop duster? Ah, the fast-paced fun of Scrum!

WHY ARCHITECTURE IS AN IMPEDIMENT

Whenever any item on a Product Backlog can't stand by itself independently, be improved upon separate from the whole, and updated as necessary without having to change other parts, you will have issues.

Scrum teams deliver value every Sprint. If what they're working on—whether it's a jet engine or a block of code for payment processing—relies on other teams' deliverables, you no longer have Scrum. You have a tangled web of interdependencies—a house of cards—that succeeds or fails as a whole. At best, you have Bad Scrum, and at worst, you are just suffering through traditional project management.

SYMPTOMS OF ARCHITECTURE ISSUES

Architecture issues involve a lot of "waiting fors" on the whiteboard. If any team member is waiting for something other than information, you probably have a bad architecture symptom. If a team is waiting to see how their part will interact

---

66 Paolo Sammicheli, *Scrum for Hardware* (Leanpub, 2019), 147.

with another, or the delivery of a subassembly, then architecture is your culprit.

Another symptom is the inability to address clients' feedback because creating a new release for a particular feature would require updating many others. Imagine if your significant other wanted to update the refrigerator but to accomplish that would require a new electrical circuit and modifications to the existing counters and cabinets. You would have a major problem. It's no different with product architecture.

CURE FOR BAD ARCHITECTURE

To remedy this impediment may require the entire team to rethink the product design itself. For legacy software—software that's developed over a long period building on accumulated experience—this may mean starting over from scratch. If possible, it's best to start with modular design. Going back to the One Gallon example, our team would have created interfaces for each module on the car. Any engine would work as long as it fits in the designated space, connects to the drivetrain interface, and provides the right electrical feedback for our dashboard monitor interface. This idea at its simplest is not unlike Lego blocks. No matter which color or build set you use, all the pieces still work together.

You would only order a refrigerator that has the same electrical requirements and is the same dimensions as the old one—in other words, it matches the interfaces you already have in your kitchen.

Impediment Six: Manual Testing

WHAT MANUAL TESTING IS

If anyone has to manually inspect each product and all its other features with each new release, you have manual testing. It may not necessarily be an issue depending on your industry, but it has the potential to wreak havoc.

This is almost exclusively a software impediment. I say "almost" because I have not experienced every hardware issue in Scrum. I just have not yet encountered an issue with manual testing in hardware. Manual testing is exactly what it sounds like. A person or team of people has to manually test or inspect each new item. If you are creating a website's backend with various databases, input fields, search modules, etc., then with each new test case, you will need to test the test case that preceded it to ensure the new code hasn't interfered with or disabled any previous item.

WHY MANUAL TESTING IS AN IMPEDIMENT

Each Sprint grows the Increment. If you have a large website with hundreds of individual items—that translates into a lot of testing. With each new test case, you need to test the ones before it. In effect, as your product grows, instead of your team getting faster, it slows down.

For instance, we had two hundred test cases with the Ecuadorian telecom—my birth into Scrum. Our client was manually testing each one. It looked like this: test case one—one test. Test case two—test one and two. Test case three—test one, two, and three. You can begin to see the issue. With each new test case, their testing department was growing more and more backlogged.

SYMPTOMS OF MANUAL TESTING

The symptoms with manual testing are obvious. Instead of growing in velocity, your team is growing lethargic. If you have one person whose expertise is quality assurance, they are overloaded while others are idle. Or all the team members are testing, and no other progress is being made. This will come up in the Daily Scrums either explicitly or implicitly through frustration, annoyance, or feelings of futility. The whiteboard will show no progress since "In Progress" grows with tasks that involve testing.

CURE FOR MANUAL TESTING

The cure is straightforward: automate testing. Software developers can purchase or develop systems bots to automatically test each piece. Instead of a quality person checking test cases one, two, three, etc., with each new release, the testing bots can test them all automatically.

Impediment Seven: Manual Delivery

WHAT MANUAL DELIVERY IS

This is another common impediment for software developers. If you own any major brand of software like an operating system, you know the occasional pain of waiting while the software updates. Some offer you an option to wait; others don't. This is an example of delivery. They are known as either push deliveries or pull deliveries. Push deliveries are like push notifications on your computer. They show up and sometimes, depending on the developer, install whether or not you want them to.

Both of these types of deliveries can be automatic or manual. You wouldn't know one way or another since the choice is up to the developer. Some developers, especially smaller app developers, release these updates manually. This means somebody manually approves and moves the software from testing to production so clients can receive it.

One bank I worked with relatively recently would develop each application in a closed test environment before rolling it out to a production server, where it could do what the code was designed to do. They would have to manually check parameters to ensure that what worked in the test environment worked in the production environment.

WHY MANUAL DELIVERY IS AN IMPEDIMENT

Just as with manual testing, manual delivery requires time and focus to move the code from testing to production. If your Scrum team is optimized but still reliant on a team member or a separate department for manual releases, then that department can experience bottlenecks. Instead, the process of release should be automated by bot software set to check the parameters you determine.

SYMPTOMS OF MANUAL DELIVERY

Left unchecked, the symptoms of bottlenecks with one team member or an external department can lead to your organization finishing second to the competition. One bank I know had made major strides in leaping over their competition by completing a digital bank account option well before their competition. But then their hard work sat in a queue with the testing and release department, which had a three-month backlog. Three months later, by the time they were finally ready to release their digital offerings, their competitor had already released theirs. Instead of being first to the market, they were now playing catch-up, looking like they were copying their competitor's products.

CURE FOR MANUAL DELIVERY

Ditch the release department and automate your deliveries. Whether your client is an internal department or division, or the end user is thousands of software engineers, establish a platform that allows the releases to be accessed and delivered automatically upon request.

Impediment Eight: Bureaucracy

WHAT BUREAUCRACY IS

You don't need me to tell you what bureaucracy is and the issues with it. If you're a citizen of any democratized and developed country, even partially developed, you know what a pain it can be. Bureaucracy is a monster created by stakeholders needing—or, more accurately, thinking they need—tons of data, metrics, documentation, and multiple layers of approval in order to maintain control.

WHY BUREAUCRACY IS AN IMPEDIMENT

Scrum is speed. In an Agile world, Scrum is Olympic gold-medal runner Usain Bolt, and bureaucracy is blocks of concrete chained to his feet. Imagine Usain competing in the hundred-meter dash and having to report his progress to his coach every twenty-five meters. In true bureaucratic fashion, his coach would then demand to know why Usain finished last.

As we've explored, the implementation of Scrum requires fast observations, feedback, and responses. Constant adjustments and refinements are made sometimes the same day new information comes in. The Standish Group has demonstrated the suffering inflicted by slow decision-making caused in part by layers of approval.

If you are creating a Scrum pilot team in a large company, you may be requested to provide Gantt charts and project reports, budgets, estimates, and sales forecasts from the PMO and other departments. Every minute spent answering pointless emails, completing reports that no one is going to read, or a myriad of other nonproductive work is a minute less spent pursuing your goal.

SYMPTOMS OF BUREAUCRACY

The symptoms of bureaucracy are prevalent: team members getting stuck in their email inbox, paperwork, or getting calls from other managers (maybe because the Product Owner is ignoring them) are signs that the bureaucracy's tentacles are winding their way into your bubble.

It would be great if we could sever all influence from the bureaucracy outside the bubble. You can create an airlock of sorts, however, to protect your team from the organization's bureaucratic beast while still encouraging your team to stay in close communication with clients, end users, and other teams as needed.

CURE FOR BUREAUCRACY

Creating the protective bubble is the cure. Minimize the bureaucracy's influence by talking to department heads and managers requesting any kind of report of documentation.

If you have a strong Scrum sponsor, their pull in the organization will be a tremendous asset in circumventing the "powers that be." Sometimes you will have to adapt a little and perform wasteful, seemingly pointless activities to satisfy some protocol or to fulfill a government's legal requirements. The object of Scrum is not to be perfect but to be able to adjust and adapt.

Of all the impediments a Scrum team may face in its infancy, bureaucracy is one of its biggest enemies. It's anti-Scrum by nature. A Scrum Master and Scrum sponsor need to do whatever they can to ensure that the beast stays out of the pilot team's protective bubble. This may mean talking and influencing C-level executives by demonstrating how the impediments of bureaucracy are stopping your team from providing the value that is important to them.

Other Impediments

There are literally hundreds of things that can be an impediment to the Scrum team. From laptops all running major updates simultaneously (thank you, Washington state-based software company) to two team members having an issue with each other to other major issues. Remember, an impediment is any obstacle that impedes progress toward the goal.

I strongly advise that all nontrivial impediments be recorded on the impediment list after they are brought up in the Daily Scrum. Then the Scrum Master or sponsor can see them, and the team can see that the issues are not forgotten.

What is a trivial versus a nontrivial impediment? If it was easily solved by one or two team members or a one-time thing like the Wi-Fi network going offline until someone rebooted the network router, it's not worth recording. Any issue that's easily resolved with a quick call, email, or some basic problem-solving efforts is trivial. Nontrivial issues relate to systems, processes, hardware, software, supplier, or other matter not rectifiable from within the Scrum team.

Not all impediments are able to be solved, but an attempt must be made to resolve them as much as is possible. You may have to struggle with a little bureaucracy or distributed teams like Drummond just from the nature of your work. Minimizing these issues is far better than shrugging your shoulders and pretending they don't exist. Even minimized, these impediments will affect your team's velocity.

Using what you've learned from the OODA Loop process, you can look deeper to identify what may be the underlying illness to the symptoms being described by the team. Maybe they are minor aches; maybe it's pneumonia and requires intense intervention. Observe, orient, decide, act, and then see what feedback you receive from your attempt to eliminate the impediment. If the first attempt didn't work, you may need to try something else.

METRICS AND INCENTIVES

Use of Metrics

When identifying and eliminating impediments, some are obviously interfering with your team's velocity and cohesiveness. However, other impediments might be built into your organization. Back in chapter 5, I mentioned some of the potential issues with having a star culture. A self-organizing team where everyone feels like they're contributing leads to a healthier team, in my opinion. I've met few people that disagree with this idea. That said, I'm often asked about how to measure the team's performance and create incentives. Should incentives be based on individual or team performance?

Metrics are beneficial. There are metrics in Scrum such as velocity (estimation points per Sprint) and the happiness metric (a proxy for engagement, which we'll cover in the next chapter). I recommend that the Product Owner pay special attention to at least two metrics: value and quality. How you measure value and quality will depend on your organization and product. Value, as discussed, could be as simple as gross sales or something more nuanced. Quality can be measured a variety of ways, depending on the product.

Another handy metric that's sometimes difficult to calculate is the length of time a PBI spends in the Product Backlog. Specifically, this metric measures the average number of days, weeks, whatever from the time an item is added to the Product Backlog to the point it's done and in the customer's hand. If you are able to capture this metric, it will give you a time trend you may consider improving.

There is a limit to the number of metrics you should choose to measure. Some metrics don't tell you anything of real value, like hours spent on a task (we're measuring Sprints and points, so why would hours matter?), while other metrics might give you misleading information. But more than the quality of metrics, as humans, we can only pay attention to so many pieces of information. Various studies have put the number of things we can focus on at any given time somewhere in the range of three to seven. There's still some debate around this, but a good rule of thumb is somewhere around three to five items.[67] One metric is too narrow to give you context and depth, while having too many can make you feel overwhelmed.

Overwhelm is real; it's called cognitive load or basically the amount of things we are able to pay attention to at one moment—our brain's RAM.

---

67 Clara Moskowitz, "Mind's Limit Found: 4 Things at Once," Live Science, April 28, 2008, https://www.livescience.com/2493-mind-limit-4.html.

For instance, once when I was working in IT security for a pension fund, I was measuring various alarms like DoS attacks and failed log-in attempts. Important things to measure, but I was getting close to a thousand a day, each one delivered to my email inbox. I felt so overwhelmed by these mostly trivial items that I set up a filter to move them all to a subfolder. Not the best solution, but at least my inbox was clear.

Now that you have metrics, how do you create incentives?

That's the tricky part. Which metrics do you make targets, and how do you create incentives for (I refuse to use the buzzword "incentivize") those targets?

When it comes to metrics, I believe that a variety of key metrics can tell an important story. However, when it comes to targets for those metrics, I believe in Goodhart's law, which was proposed by economist Charles Goodhart and best phrased by British anthropologist Marilyn Strathern when she wrote, "When a measure becomes a target, it ceases to be a good measure."[68] Measure revenue, but make it a target, and it may overshadow profitability. Measure weight loss, but if you solely focus on the scale's number, you may lose muscle mass and diet unhealthily. The TV show *The Biggest Loser* has been criticized by health advocates for the unhealthy way competitors rapidly shed fat to win a large prize.

Incentives

If we're not using metrics as targets, then the question becomes what to use as an incentive. Here's where I'm going to create some enemies: I believe most incentive systems don't work. Wherever I've seen incentive systems tried, I've seen those who benefit from incentives exploit loopholes or otherwise engage in activity counterproductive to overall team health. This includes client stealing, lying, backstabbing, or cheating the numbers. Our case study of Enron in chapter 5 is partly a demonstration of out-of-control incentives, as is the story of Wells Fargo employees opening new accounts in the names of existing customers in order to reap the financial bonuses tied to opening those accounts.[69]

---

68 Marilyn Strathern, "'Improving Ratings': Audit in the British University System," *European Review* 5, no. 3 (July 1997), 305–21, https://www.cambridge.org/core/journals/european-review/article/improving-ratings-audit-in-the-british-university-system/FC2EE640C0C44E3DB87C29FB666E9AAB.

69 Josh Barro, "Wells Fargo's Scandal Is a Cautionary Tale about Incentive Pay," Business Insider, September 9, 2016, https://www.businessinsider.com/wells-fargos-scandal-is-a-cautionary-tale-about-incentive-pay-2016-9.

I've seen incentives fail in my own company. We bill our clients hourly and sell pools of hours. Let's say a client purchases a pool of eighty hours a month with one of our consultants. Some clients weren't using their full bank of eighty hours. Maybe they would only use sixty hours of the consultant's time. One way to look at this is as free money—we got paid for twenty hours we didn't work. But that felt wrong. I obviously wanted our clients to feel they were getting their money's worth and using the hours they purchased.

To counteract the tendency to wait to be called upon, I created an incentive. For each hour a consultant spent at a client's office, the consultant would receive a small financial bonus. In other words, my consultants would get extra pay just for logging hours at our client's site. And it worked! Our consultants began utilizing our clients' pools of hours more effectively, and our clients felt like they were receiving more value for their money. Except . . .

My consultants are sometimes needed in the home office working with other tasks unrelated to direct client work. With the incentive in place to visit clients, I couldn't get them to do anything else. I can't blame them; it's human nature. They went where they were rewarded to be. Fortunately, this was a reversible decision, and I learned my lesson.

Most incentive systems either don't work or provide side effects to the desired outcome. Because metrics and incentives are completely unique to your business, you will have to weigh the pros and cons of creating incentives. Just keep in mind Goodhart's law. I believe having no incentives is the best way to go, but not all industries can afford to go that route, especially if your competition is offering employees lucrative bonuses.

If you create incentives, you have to be wary of false positives. It's a term often heard in medical circles where someone tests positive for a disease or a pregnancy even if they don't have the ailment (or blessing, as it were).

Perhaps the worst example of false positives—of incentives gone bad—comes from the Colombian army. When I interviewed a retired colonel, he shared a literal war story. Up until very recently, Colombia had been fighting a civil war with guerrilla rebels. One of the metrics military command chose to use was rebel bodies. Morbid as it sounds, divisions were rewarded for their confirmed kills. They had quotas to meet, and these targets for the division were broken down to the units and even individual soldiers. A soldier could earn leave time. An officer might get higher training or be able to study abroad. Incentives were based on body count just like your local car dealer measures cars sold.

This worked, too. They killed a lot of guerrilla rebels. Unfortunately, they also killed many civilians, dressed them up to look like guerrillas, and counted them toward their quota. Some studies have estimated that possibly up to ten thousand civilians were killed over a decade of fighting.[70]

The moral is, if you choose to use incentives, be careful what you use. Like we saw with Wells Fargo and the Colombian Army, whatever you use as an incentive will be achieved. Whether it's achieved in a way that's ethical or good for the company is another matter.

Instead of Incentives . . .

My philosophy is to pay people above average, create a team-focused culture, give them rewarding work, and occasionally offer them a reward just because of something they did particularly well. This is more than just my gut-thinking behind this. In his landmark book *Drive*, Daniel Pink made an argument that what motivates us aren't "carrot and stick" types of rewards. After our financial needs are reasonably satisfied, we are motivated by purpose, autonomy, and mastery.[71]

Scrum has these three elements practically baked-in. With a strong goal, a team has a purpose to work toward, the hands-off approach of the Product Owner gives the team autonomy of owning how to do the work, and they pursue mastery in their individual roles as they work toward cross-functionality.

Incentives may actually slow things down. In his book, Pink shares one study where participants were asked to solve a problem of mounting a lit candle on a wall in such a way that it wouldn't drip wax everywhere.[72] They were given nothing more than a candlestick, a box of tacks, and matches. One group was timed for averages (control), while another group was given financial incentives—the winner with the fastest time was promised the highest prize of twenty dollars. The group of participants who were give financial incentives were, on average, three minutes *slower* than the control group.

This isn't to say that all people working in Scrum are full of sunshine and happiness. It's still work with the inherent debates, stress, frustration, and other team members acting in irritating ways. But I believe that Scrum teams, overall, are more motivated and happier than those in traditional bureaucracies.

---

70 Joe Parkin Daniels, "Colombian Army Killed Thousands More Civilians Than Reported, Study Claims," *The Guardian*, May 8, 2018, https://www.theguardian.com/world/2018/may/08/colombia-false-positives-scandal-casualties-higher-thought-study.

71 Daniel H. Pink, *Drive: The Surprising Truth about What Motivates Us* (New York: Riverhead Books, 2009).

72 Ibid., 41.

Despite all of this evidence, you may still want to use incentives. Maybe you need them in your industry in order to be competitive. Some companies have tried offering team incentives instead of individual ones. This might seem like a good solution, but there is a danger here, too. Some team members may feel motivated to achieve the incentives, and others may not; or some team members may just think they are working harder than others, which leads to resentment.

The danger with team-based performance incentives is the risk of free-loaders (or free riders, as they are called in economics)—that is, somebody not pulling their own weight. Whether they are loafing or just appear to be loafing, the ripple can cause the incentives to backfire. Who wants to work hard when others who are "phoning it in" are going to share in the same reward? Maybe the above-average workers will continue to work hard, but it's unlikely that they won't hold grudges.

In short, incentives might work if, along with metrics, they are well balanced and designed carefully. Proceed with caution.

BURNDOWN CHARTS: VISUAL PROGRESS AND PROJECTED COMPLETIONS

While discussing metrics, it's a good idea to mention the burndown chart. Let me be clear, however, that the burndown chart (or "burn chart") is not a metric but rather a visual representation of the points remaining on a backlog. It's a good way to show the team's progress and how far they have to achieve the goal.

A true burndown chart starts at the number of points estimated for the Product or Sprint Backlog on the y-axis, while time is represented on the x-axis. For Product Backlogs, a burndown chart showing the number of points remaining begins to show a trend. If the product as refined at the start has a total estimate of a thousand points, and the team is completing an average of eighty points per Sprint, you can draw trend lines that descend to a projected completion date. In this case, if each Sprint was two weeks long, then the Product Backlog will be completed around twenty-four or twenty-six weeks from the start.

A Product Backlog burndown chart can be updated at the conclusion of every Sprint, while a Sprint burndown chart can be updated during the Daily Scrum, so the team can see the progress they're making with the completion of each task and item as well as whether they're on track to complete the items in the current Sprint.

9.1. Sprint Burndown

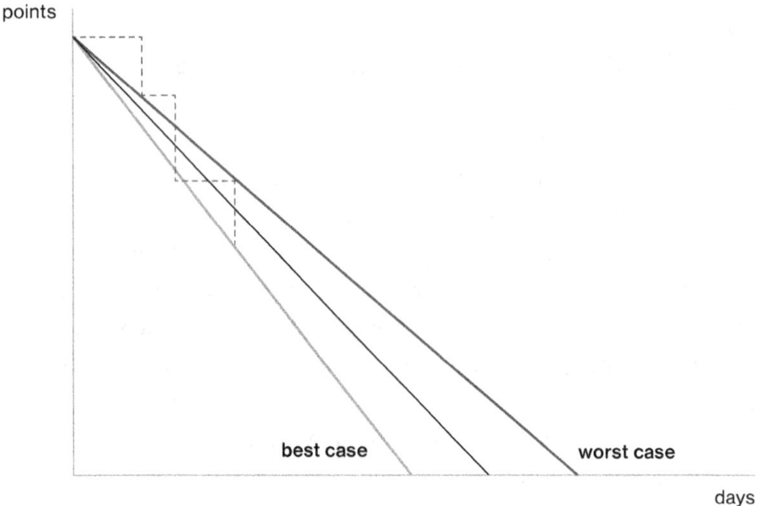

A Product Backlog is not a static list of items, though. New things are added as new ideas and needs arise and as further refinement and Spikes are completed, which add to the total points. There are two ways to handle these changes. One, just add them to the negative *y*-axis. If you started with one thousand points and add three items totaling another hundred, expand the chart so the bottom of the initial burndown bar ranges from one thousand to negative one hundred. Some teams opt for the inverse chart: a burnup chart. Like the name suggests, you start with zero points and then show the points completed with every task or Sprint, as the case may be. With every Backlog revision, you would just adjust the target line up.

Metrics and charts help to tell stories about the work done. They indicate speed, efficiency, and trends. But some things can disrupt trends, and metrics can show issues. You might have a problem. Fortunately, chances are somebody in Agile has already experienced a similar problem within the same context. You need a Scrum Pattern, and that's what we'll cover next.

YOUR SCRUM PLAYBOOK

- Scrum is not Agile; it only reveals where you are not Agile yet.
- *Shu-ha-ri*—know and practice the fundamentals until you fully understand them before making changes. It refers to the path from beginner to master.
  - *Shu*: repetition of the forms and discipline of the master so as to internalize the forms that were created.
  - *Ha*: having disciplined ourselves to follow the forms exactly, we can now begin to innovate, breaking or discarding forms that don't work for us.
  - *Ri*: now we can begin to fully customize our process to make it our own practice, acting in accordance with our individual creative technique.

IMPEDIMENTS

- Can be anything that can derail or "impede" a team's velocity and progress toward the established goal.
- Identify them as a team during the Daily Scrum.
- Explore the disease behind the symptoms.
- Keep the list of impediments in full view of the team and stakeholders.
- The Scrum Master is responsible to look for cures.

COMMON IMPEDIMENTS

- Bad Scrum
- Lack of focus
- Lack of psychological safety
- Distributed teams
- Lacking clear architecture
- Manual testing
- Manual delivery
- Bureaucracy

METRICS AND INCENTIVES RECAP

- Metrics provide a means of measuring the team's effectiveness.
- Too many metrics can be detrimental.
- Most incentive systems don't work as intended.

Playing Your Hand

- ○ If you haven't already done so, start and keep an impediment list where the entire team can see it.

Answer these questions:
- ○ Based on what you now know, how has the Scrum framework already revealed where you're not yet Agile?
- ○ Which of the common impediments can you identify within your organization without talking to the team? What other impediments can the team identify?
- ○ Where does your team feel frustrated, demoralized, overwhelmed, unsafe? What steps can be taken to minimize these issues?
- ○ Which metrics feel appropriate toward understanding your progress, keeping in mind the concept that metrics, once changed into targets, tend to fail?
- ○ Carefully consider intended and unintended consequences of any incentives offered. Most incentive programs have a tendency to backfire and/or lead to corruption of the team atmosphere.

CHAPTER TEN

Scrum Patterns and Tactics: Call, Fold, or Raise?

Happiness is not the absence of problems; it's the ability to deal with them.

—Steve Maraboli[73]

Watch a craftsperson administer his trade for any length of time, and I guarantee you will be impressed. Whether the craftsperson is a cabinetmaker, welder, blacksmith, or mason, I marvel at their speed and quality of their work. More interesting is how they solve problems. For example, a cabinetmaker installing cabinets in a kitchen often deals with the same sets of problems: a wall out of plumb, uneven floors, or dips in the wallboard. These problems are so frequent that the cabinetmaker can make quick work of them. They have a vast knowledge of tricks of the trade that they've learned from mentors and their own experience. An issue that might flummox a homeowner for an entire afternoon is but a small inconvenience for the veteran craftsperson.

Humans are great at seeing and creating patterns in our lives. From weeks, seasons, and morning routines to literal patterns in fabric, we like finding correlation and measure. This is partly why we see animals in cloud formations. If I cut a square of patterned fabric, taped it to a large piece of blank paper, and gave it to an eight-year-old child, chances are they could come close to extending the cutoff pattern onto the sheet of paper. Crudely, maybe, but effectively.

We are craftspeople, and our craft is Scrum. Just like the craftspeople mentioned above, we've encountered the same issues frequently while strategically implementing our trade. No matter how well-thought-out and planned our

---

73 Steve Maraboli, *Life, the Truth, and Being Free: Anniversary Edition* (Port Washington, NY: A Better Today, 2014), 64.

strategies may be, we need specific tactics—our tricks of the trade—in place to support that strategy. Referencing our poker analogy, your strategy could be tight—valuing caution above all else and taking few risks. A supporting tactic would be a predetermined plan to fold in certain conditions, depending on the strength of your hand. An experienced craftsperson or poker player is adept at noticing these patterns, and references their arsenal to deal with them.

Scrum implementation strategies are no different. They, too, require an arsenal of tactics to ensure Scrum is implemented and that every team has the resources, knowledge, and skill to execute the strategy. As you implement Scrum and your team grows accustomed to working with each other and within the new framework, there are going to be problems as everyone is learning and adjusting. Just like opportunities, problems require making quick decisions. You already have the tools; you can process a problem through an OODA Loop. But what if it's similar to a problem that's been encountered a hundred or a thousand times by other organizations implementing Scrum? In other words, there's a chance that the problem you're facing has already been encountered and solved. These are called patterns, a term first used in Scrum by James Coplien and Neil Harrison's 2004 book.[74]

Before we go any further, let's work with a definition. A Pattern is a solution to a problem in a particular context. If you solve a problem in one context, the same solution might not work in another context. For the cabinetmaker, the solution for uneven floors might be different if the floors were made of wood instead of concrete. Context is important when it comes to applying patterns.

Patterns are not an end-all solution to a particular problem, however. They are a starting point that you can build off of. Because Scrum is about people—culture, teamwork, and emotions—patterns are also about people. Because we're not perfect, patterns aren't either. A good coach can help you solve your issues, but you're going to have to do the work and intuit some of the decisions that are right for you. It's no different with patterns.

There are over ninety different patterns as of this writing. They have been discovered in the process of using Scrum by a variety of authors. You may face a problem for which no pattern yet exists. Your team might develop a repeatable solution. Congratulations, you've discovered another pattern! Please let the Agile community know.

We don't have room or time in this book to cover all of the patterns in detail—mainly because an excellent book that covers patterns exclusively has

---

74 James O. Coplien and Neil B. Harrison, *Organizational Patterns of Agile Software Development* (New York: Wiley, 2004).

recently been released: *A Scrum Book*.[75] While you can look up the patterns in the book or online, let's go over a few concepts regarding patterns and review some of the more common ones, so you can begin using them in your work.

Specifically, we will be looking at eleven patterns in three different groups: patterns to make your team stable, patterns to help you get predictable outcome, and patterns to help you improve your team's performance. This sequence of stable, predictable teams with improved performance is based on Jeff Sutherland's work.[76] First is stability, and with stability comes predictability. When you've achieved a level of stable predictability, your team can then focus on improving performance—getting faster. These are also the three areas where you, the *shu*-state reader, are most likely to experience problems. Like many changes, most failures occur in the early stages when problems, setbacks, and frustrations are highest. These particular patterns will help you not only solve problems in these areas but also use Scrum even better.

STEP ONE: GETTING STABLE

Have you ever watched a large ship get launched? It's a spectacular sight. A multi-ton behemoth is kept in dry dock until the big day arrives. For many large ships, it's a public spectacle with spectators and sometimes press coverage for especially significant ships. The ships are held on a skid platform that, once a hydraulic system is activated, pushes the ship into the water. It slides on cradles, which fall away as the ship enters the water. The ships bob, sway, and cause a small tsunami as thousands of liters of water are displaced. Most launches go perfectly, thanks to careful engineering. But sometimes a cradle doesn't move with the rest and the ship hits the water lopsided, causing it to capsize. It's rare, but it has happened.

Launching a new team is similar to a ship launch. It's a big deal, waves can be felt, and there are a lot of unpredictable parts because—well, because we're people. Unless you were a small organization to begin with and had many people in multiple roles instead of departments, chances are your team—even if they know each other—is working together for the first time. Beside getting used to Scrum, they're getting used to each other. Personalities, work and

---

75 Jeff Sutherland, James O. Coplien, and the Scrum Patterns Group, *A Scrum Book: The Spirit of the Game*, ed. Adaobi Obi Tulton (Raleigh, NC: Pragmatic Bookshelf, 2019).

76 Jeff Sutherland, Neil Harrison, and Joel Riddle, "Teams that Finish Early Accelerate Faster: A Pattern Language for High Performing Scrum Teams," *2014 47th Hawaii International Conference on System Sciences* (January, 2014): 4722–728, https://ieeexplore.ieee.org /document/6759182.

communication styles, and individual levels of expertise all rolling together at once. Oh, and we're shifting the culture at the same time through behavior change. No wonder we have issues. Hopefully they're a band of eager, optimistic, and supportive volunteers in a mixed implementation like we discussed in chapter 3. Even in that, the best of situations, finding team stability will take work.

Stable Teams Pattern

If you've ever worked in a department for any length of time, you might have had the experience of being "relocated." Maybe management wanted you closer to a supervisor, a restructuring occurred, or they were brushing aside a problem-employee by making everyone change so that person would not be singled out (passive management). Or maybe you were on a tight project team. You got to know each other and felt like you had each other's backs. But then the project ended. Tomas is asking you to join his project, and you know nobody else there except that weird guy, Felipe, who you wish you didn't know.

We've all been there, either in our jobs or in our school classrooms with forced lab partners. Teams change. It's a part of life. But if you're dealing with team changes during implementation, you have a long journey ahead of you.

Despite the Scrum experts' recommendations, some organizations still try to make Scrum work with various team members switching in and out or, worse, with a team that's "trying" Scrum part time while the rest of their time is spent in their original roles. "Stable" means all team members are working at all times on the same thing—you don't work two days on one project, one day on another, and you are not part of several teams. You're part of one team, and that team is stable. This avoids multitasking and reduces waste that multitasking causes.

If you're a fan of professional team sports, you've noticed the problem with unstable teams. Your favorite team finally meshes and puts together a great season, possibly making it to the playoffs or even the championship. And then managers or greedy agents screw everything up. New, "better" players are introduced next season, and the team tanks.

Psychological researcher Bruce Tuckman wrote about four stages of team development: forming, storming, norming, and performing.[77] Teams go through these stages, each one taking time and emotional energy, until they reach a stage

---

77 Bruce W. Tuckman, "Developmental Sequence in Small Groups," *Psychological Bulletin* 63, no. 6 (1965), 384–99, https://psycnet.apa.org/doiLanding?doi=10.1037%2Fh0022100.

of performance. Tuckman explains how each stage effects the team, from being very reserved to having turmoil (storming), until the team members resolve any differences and get used to working together. Without reading this academic study, you probably can relate to these stages even if you only experienced them in your youth soccer or basketball team.

Each time a new member is introduced, teambuilding begins again from scratch. This might not sound like a big deal, so let's bring in the big boys: NASA.

One NASA study showed that flight crews with experience working together made fewer errors than new crews.[78] In an interview with *Harvard Business Review*, Harvard Professor J. Richard Hackman had this to say about that study: "[NASA] found that fatigued crews who had a history of working together made about half as many errors as crews composed of rested pilots who had not flown together before."[79] That's a significant finding. One of the reasons proposed in the study is that crews who knew each other were more likely to communicate.

The Stable Teams Pattern[80] creates higher predictability and performance and reduces waste that comes from lack of communication, conflict, and training. Once a team is formed, it doesn't change. Like we saw with the Colombian Special Forces in chapter 5, the teams were formed and units did everything together: basic and advanced training, meals, meetings, everything. While they are together, there are a lot of things going on with the team under the surface. It is not only about the work. They also have to figure out how they behave and determine their social structure.

Once you have created a Scrum team, don't change it for any reason if you can possibly help it. No "borrowing" a member for a side project or switching departments, and avoid even firing people. It's that critical. Only by having teams work consistently together can you ever hope to receive the fourth stage—performance. Give your team time to work out how they work and get a feel for each other's personalities. When they stay together and stabilize, the real progress in Scrum can begin.

---

78 H. C. Foushee, J. K. Lauber, M. M. Baetge, and D. B. Acomb, *Crew Factors in Flight Operations: III. The Operational Significance of Exposure to Short-Haul Air Transport Operations*, Technical Memorandum No. 88342 (Moffett Field, CA: NASA-Ames Research Center, 1986).

79 Diane Coutu, "Why Teams Don't Work," *Harvard Business Review*, May 2009, https://hbr.org /2009/05/why-teams-dont-work.

80 Sutherland, Coplien, and the Scrum Patterns Group, *A Scrum Book: The Spirit of the Game*, 82–85.

Colocated Teams Pattern

We've already discussed the impediment of distributed teams in the last chapter. It's a problem whose only real solution is colocating the team. Drummond had office teams in two cities and a team in the drilling fields, but sometimes the problem with distributed teams isn't as obvious as it was with Drummond.

Have you ever needed something from a coworker in another department all the way on the other side of the office? Did you walk over to her? Probably not unless you were already going there. You could have called her, but you probably took the less intrusive route of email. It's quick, not intrusive, and avoids interruption and possible social awkwardness. But emails are so impersonal and seem to not lead to strong relationships by themselves. Emails also get to the point without the possibility of other important topics arising.

In another situation, if you needed something from your buddy in the next cubicle, you might just call out, "Hey. You have a second?" And you are probably more likely to talk to Juanita in the next cubicle than you are Maria on the other side of the office, no matter how critical Maria is to the project, right?

In the '70s, while studying worker proximity, MIT professor Thomas J. Allen made an interesting discovery: team members who are close to each other communicate more frequently. Not necessarily earth-shattering news, but Allen took it a step further. By measuring the distances between workers and their weekly interactions, he noticed a stark correlating relationship: the frequency of communication declined exponentially the farther away the workers were. The magic distance for frequent communication seems to be around fifty meters.[81]

This distance is probably shrinking as we grow more and more attached to our digital devices. But even frequency of communication seems to be relative to distance even in other mediums. "The more often we see someone face-to-face, the more likely it is that we will also telephone that person or communicate by another medium," Allen explains.[82] Allen is not alone in his research. *Agile Manifesto* signatory Alistair Cockburn has called this the Bus-Length Communication Principle, where "Communication between people drops off radically as soon their (walking) distance from each other exceeds the length of a school bus."[83]

---

81 Thomas J. Allen, *Managing the Flow of Technology: Technology Transfer and the Dissemination of Technological Information Within the R&D Organization* (Cambridge, MA: MIT Press, 1984).

82 Allen, *The Organization and Architecture of Innovation* (New York: Taylor & Francis, 2007), 58.

83 Alistair Cockburn, *Agile Software Development*, 102.

The Colocated Teams Pattern[84] is simple: in order to achieve team stability, team members should work as close together as possible. Obviously, I don't mean huddled together in one cubicle—an interesting mental image—but within that school-bus length of walk.

As with Drummond, I know that this is sometimes a near impossibility, but it must be strived for. Consultant Donald Reinertsen has even said, "Colocation is the closest thing to fairy dust that we have to improve communications on the development team."[85] There is nothing that facilitates a high-performance culture like team members working closely to each other.

If it's impossible to have team members share the same physical space, a second runner-up is enabling conversation via technology. The second-best thing you can do after face-to-face communication is videoconferencing—but this has to be a good stable system. For instance, if you have poor wireless data coverage, you can't use Skype on your phone to communicate—it will break down, and any possible communication leads only to frustration. That frustration will lead to even fewer interactions.

If team communication is an issue, run this pattern. Get them in one room or area. Even GoTelecom had to reorganize team members so they were better grouped together. With teams spread between two cities, Bogota and Medellin, they had to reorganize. If both teams A and B were split between the offices, they traded team members so they could stay in the same office. Team A members moved to team B and vice versa. If that type of reorganization is not possible, use all the technology available to facilitate open communication—even if they end up talking about the weather.

Yesterday's Weather Pattern

Of all the corporatese buzzwords that have graced the lips of managers over these past few decades, perhaps the most irksome for Scrum is the idea of a "stretch goal." At its essence, setting aggressive goals and challenging yourself or your employees and your organization to go beyond what might seem feasible are noble ideas. If you're not familiar with the concept, it's basically this: when setting goals with an employee or department for the next month or quarter, you take a goal that you know is achievable and make it more

---

84 Sutherland, Coplien, and the Scrum Patterns Group, *A Scrum Book: The Spirit of the Game*, 50–54.

85 Donald Reinertsen, *Managing the Design Factory: A Product Developer's Toolkit* (New York: Simon & Schuster, 1997), 113.

ambitious. If you believe 4 percent improvement in revenue is achievable, you may set a stretch goal of 10 percent.

More than just management lingo, though, it's natural for us to want to outdo our last performance. If your high bowling score is 198, you'll try to break 200. If you shot eighty-two on the golf course last weekend, you'll want to break the eighty-stroke barrier the next weekend. If you earned $80,000 last year, you'll want to earn $90,000 this year. Is that such a bad thing? It can be.

Stretch goals or other aggressive objectives should be avoided by all but the healthiest of organizations. For most organizations, researchers advise setting goals for small wins. Management Professor Sim B. Sitkin had this to say: "Small wins work by building momentum, energy, and resources, and fostering learning that will allow a firm to take on bigger, more ambitious goals later."[86]

Yesterday's Weather Pattern[87] addresses how to predict what the velocity in the next Sprint will be. Unlike departments (especially sales) who look at past performance and increase quotas and metric targets (a no-no. Remember Goodhart's law?), this pattern focuses on what the team was already able to accomplish.

People use weather as a metaphor. Weather patterns change, but are usually predictable and hold to certain temperature ranges throughout a season. Well, not in Bogota, Colombia, where the weather is pretty much the same and the only difference is that it's either raining or not raining. In Germany, on the other hand, there are seasons—summer daytime high temperatures of about thirty to thirty-five degrees Celsius and around minus-twenty Celsius in the winter. If I asked you to predict today's weather—and you weren't a meteorologist—you'd probably look at yesterday's weather for clues. If yesterday was thirty degrees, today we will most likely have something around that temperature plus or minus a few degrees. It's just about impossible we'll go to minus-twenty today if it was thirty yesterday. The old saying, "Everybody complains about the weather, but nobody does anything about it," rings true. Weather might be good or bad, but its patterns are predictable overall, with few drastic changes.

It's the same in scrum—the velocity of the last Sprint is usually similar for the Sprint to come. If you completed five PBIs in the last Sprint, with a total of a hundred points, plan on a hundred points in the next one.

---

86 Sim B. Sitkin, C. Chet Miller, and Kelly E. See, "The Stretch Goal Paradox," *Harvard Business Review*, January–February 2017, https://hbr.org/2017/01/the-stretch-goal-paradox.

87 Sutherland, Coplien, and the Scrum Patterns Group, *A Scrum Book: The Spirit of the Game*, 324–25.

The only thing you have to take into account when using this pattern is that you should balance out variance. Because the team is stabilizing, your points may have more drastic peaks and troughs. In that case, use the average of the last three Sprints completed eighty-five, one hundred and five, and ninety-five points, respectively, you can take the average of those three Sprints—ninety-five points—and set it as your target.

"But Fabian," you say, "I thought Scrum was about getting faster. How can you get faster if you keep shooting for the same target?" Ah, I'm glad you asked. As you will see in a few pages, you actually want to plan to finish early (see the Interrupt Buffer Pattern, which accounts for emergency situations). If things go well, the estimates were accurate, and the team is approaching stability, you will begin completing the PBIs early. When this happens, the team can begin working on the next PBI in the Product Backlog.

STEP TWO: GETTING PREDICTABLE

While stabilizing the team, getting them used to working together, and increasing the level of communication, the work and even workspace issues and problems often arise. Maybe you're in a new location or repurposing a new one. In addition to that change, your new Product Owner is getting used to a new way of planning work by defining and refining the Product Backlog and estimating the PBIs with the team. In other words, there's a whole lot of new activity. If the PO used to be a PM, she's a proverbial fish out of water.

These changes and getting used to them can cause issues in the Scrum Artifacts and Events, especially the work done during a Sprint. Let's look at some patterns that address come common problems in this context.

Definition of Ready Pattern

Imagine if you were a baker specializing in wedding cakes. You get a call from an enthusiastic bride, who gives you these instructions: "I want a white cake with chocolate buttercream frosting for my wedding. It should feed a hundred people." You begin taking notes, when she blurts out this question: "How much will that be, and when do you need the deposit?"

You don't have to be a baker to know that the information given is not enough to begin the work, let alone quote a price. A cake with the description can be as basic as a sheet cake or as complex as triple-terraced cake mimicking the Coliseum in structure, complete with chocolate and gladiator-like figurines for the bride and groom.

We covered the definition of "ready" in chapter 6, but, to reiterate, a PBI is ready when the Product Owner has clarified it to the point that the team understands the work necessary to bring the PBI to *done* so it adds value to the user. As with *done*, the entire team must define what *ready* means, and *ready* must be achieved no later than Sprint Planning. For our baker, if the bride-to-be hasn't defined enough detail by a certain date, the baker will refuse the order. If the Product Owner hasn't achieved *ready* for an item by Sprint Planning, it can't be included in the Sprint.

The problem the Ready Backlog Pattern[88] solves is one where the Developers are performing tasks they shouldn't. For example, if Item A depends on Item B, and you haven't completed Item B yet, Item A is not ready to go into the Sprint. You can't put it into a Sprint if it has not sufficient detail for the team to know what to do with it. So, again, the definition of "done" means the team has to know when something is done, and that usually means that the end user can use it, and the definition of "ready" means a backlog item is ready to go into Sprint Planning.

In short, the Ready Backlog Pattern ensures that the following six criteria are completed before a PBI is ready from Sprint Planning:

1. The work is immediately actionable by the team. Enough detail is provided with the PBI that the team can begin work without any additional information.
2. The planned deliverable has value. The PBI must have value that meets a client's need.
3. The Product Owner and Developers have discussed the item in refinement.
4. The item has been estimated and points assigned.
5. The item must be testable when it's completed.
6. The team has sized the pieces appropriately. Each item has been sized small enough that it can be completed in one Sprint, ideally along with additional PBIs.

This problem is most noticeable if any of the Developers have to do research in order to get the information they need to start working. Research, market or otherwise, is the Product Owner's wheelhouse. If there's a situation, other than a defined Spike, where team members are doing any kind of research,

---

88 Ibid, 316–19.

the Product Owner either doesn't understand or is unwilling to do her job. The team can approach the Product Owner for clarification, but they should never have to do research during a typical Sprint.

Good Housekeeping Pattern

This pattern has nothing to do with the popular magazine of the same name, nor is it strictly limited to your first thought—that banana peel in your top desk drawer next to the five-year-old lip balm—but workspace tidiness is an element.

The Good Housekeeping Pattern[89] was once called Clean Code and had to do specifically with programming. In a sense, if you're working on a particular function or find a bug that needs correcting, it's better to fix the bug rather than document it to be done later. Strike now while the iron is hot, as the adage goes, because later, after a hundred other thoughts have passed through your mind, you may forget exactly what you were going to do.

This pattern is no longer just about bugs in code; now, it's about tidying up in general—and that includes your workspace. With a messy work environment, you tend to waste time and energy either finding what you were working on, identifying where you need to start working again, or both. Work environment would include your physical workspace—a desk, cubicle, welding station, etc.—or a virtual workspace with digital project folder, desktop screen, or coding environment. The pattern is about maintaining a clean product or work environment at all times.

This pattern also has roots in Lean and the Toyota System, specifically what is called the 5S System: Seiri, Seiton, Seiso, Seiketsu, and Shitsuke. If your Japanese is as rusty as mine is, they have been redefined in English as Sort, Set in Order, Shine, Standardize, and Sustain.

The 5S system, at its core, is simple: at the end of each day, the workspace should be cleaned, any equipment should be replaced in its spot (everything has a spot, right? Marie Kondo is watching), and the work itself should be left in a done state. That way, if you or anyone else works on the product, you (or she) knows exactly where to begin. If the task or product was not completed, then at least leave some documentation to yourself or your team about what was remaining.

When work environments are messy, or you return to a product unsure

---

89 Ibid, 374–76.

where you left off, time and energy are wasted as you have to "sink" yourself back into the work. You're basically sitting there wondering, "Where did I leave off?"

Using the Good Housekeeping Pattern will stop velocity from grinding to a halt due to lack of organization.

Swarming Pattern

Have you ever watched ants in action? Whether a large dead bug or a half-eaten peanut butter and jelly sandwich, they're a flurry of activity. In the course of a day, a colony of ants can reduce that sandwich to nothing as they pack it away somewhere in their colony.

But what would happen if there were two sandwiches on either side of their hill? Five? Six?! I'd be willing to bet that all the sandwiches would be much more intact than the single sandwich. Which is fine for ants. They're not trying to achieve any production goals—they'll collect the same amount of sugary goodness either way.

We're not ants. (Just in case you needed me to make that clear.) Then why do we tend to sometimes act like them? We're not just working for work's sake like the ants. We're trying to deliver our sandwiches . . . er . . . PBIs. We're delivering value. Instead of attacking one PBI as a team, the tendency is to work on multiple PBIs. If there are five PBIs in the Sprint, a new team might try to work on three simultaneously, if not all five.

The Swarming Pattern[90] basically means that the team only works on the first priority PBI with maximum team effort. The team "swarms" around PBI priority one and focuses on it until it's done.

The problem is that when you take on too many items, you're multitasking. I think your knuckles are still red from the last time I mentioned multitasking, but let me gently remind you that you can multitask by taking on several projects, *or* you can multitask on several items at once in the same Sprint. Trying to complete two, three, or more PBIs at the same time leads to unfinished work, dilutes your efforts and focus, and slows the team down.

Here's how it works. During the Sprint, one person takes the next PBI in the sequence of priorities. He then becomes the captain of that PBI. Everybody then helps the captain while he's working on that item, and he directs the team toward its completion Whoever takes the next priority PBI in the Sprint becomes the next captain, and so on.

---

90 Ibid, 127–31.

Now some associate this swarming with the idea of a Kanban system. Practitioners of Kanban try to minimize work-in-progress (WIP). In essence, they believe the queue for WIP should be around two or three items at any given time. In Scrum, the WIP limit is one. That's all.

Now this has extreme results. The issue is that in actual real-world practice, sometimes it is difficult for everybody to work on priority one. Sometimes the nature of the work itself doesn't permit everybody to work on that same task. In those situations, the next group of people will be working on priority number two with a new captain.

Other times, priority number one could be blocked because the team is for some reason facing an unresolved impediment. Again, the team would switch to priority number two, but the ideal scenario is everybody works on priority one until it's finished. With this pattern, you will never have uneaten sandwiches.

Managing Interruptions: Interrupt Buffer Pattern

It's January 1. The night before, in an alcohol-fueled state of optimism, you vowed that you were going to finally run in a marathon. This, despite the fact that the only running you do is when you're late for the bus. You plan to start your training program, but this first day, your mom calls—her plumbing is leaking, and she asks you to help. No problem. You intend to start the next day, except your boss asks you to take on a special task. No running that afternoon either. Eventually, the one thing you wanted to accomplish that year has been thwarted by constant interruptions.

You can try to minimize interruptions in life, but they're almost as guaranteed as death and taxes. It's no different when it comes to planning your Sprints. Instead, we must make room for interruptions.

Let's say you and your team have been flying through your Sprints. You've had a couple early stabilization issues, had to move some teams around, and maybe had an issue with *ready*, but now you're starting to find your groove. Your client, a bank, is ecstatic with each new release of the online platform you've created for them. They're happy with the progress. What could go wrong?

Now it's Tuesday morning, the second day of a Sprint after you and the team just planned a hundred points for your current four-week long Sprint, when your client calls in a panic.

"It's down. It's all down!" he says.

You can practically feel his spittle hitting you through the phone. "What's down?"

"The platform! Our customers can't perform any transactions!"

You take a deep breath, trying to release the tension building in your neck, and look at your desk calendar. "No problem. We'll be finished with our current Sprint first week of December. We can add it to the Backlog."

Obviously, that's not what you're going to tell your panic-stricken client.

Let's say you use four-week Sprints, and your velocity is a hundred points and you just completed Sprint Planning. So that means you now have a full plan for the next four weeks, and that plan has a hundred points. But then you get the bank's call. How do you fit that in?

As we've talked about, in Scrum, you don't want to change the Sprint goal in terms of quality or quantity, ideally. The Sprint is protected. At the same time, you want to be able to tell your client, "Okay, no problem. We're going to fix it." But obviously you can't do that with a Sprint already planned, right?

If you work on the problem right away, your team is focused on it, and they don't do anything else. Now you have a problem. Since you have spent time and energy working on the problem that was unplanned, you are not able to achieve the Sprint goal of a hundred points.

The Interrupt Pattern Buffer[91] is what allows you to plan for interrupts. Chances are that the interruptions you see from the client, a boss/management, or some other emergency is frequent enough that you have a feel (an estimate) for how much time an interruption takes. At the same time, using Yesterday's Weather Pattern, you have an average of your Sprint velocity. Now you can create a buffer for interruptions.

If you average a hundred points, estimate the number of points to reserve for interruptions. Maybe it's twenty points. When using this pattern, plan on eighty points. If there are no interruptions (unlikely), then continue working on the next Product Backlog Item once the Sprint's goal is completed. Easy.

But what if you have a major interruption? What do you do if the bank's system takes fifty points to solve? The solution is to stop the Sprint. When the interruption uses all of the buffer and you can't achieve the Sprint's goal, you have no other option. The Product Owner stops it, which sends a flag to the rest of the organization that something is wrong.

When the interruption is dealt with, you can continue working on the PBIs you had planned, but the goal is no longer achievable. The next Sprint Planning takes into consideration the PBIs unfinished due to the interruption.

Now you can go train for your marathon.

---

91 Ibid, 157–60.

Fix Problems Immediately: Whack-the-Mole Pattern

Smokey Bear has had a long, illustrious career in the United States reminding people that "Only you can prevent forest fires."[92] The public-service spokes-bear was created to remind people that forest fires are harmfully destructive, and he starred in a number of TV commercials and instructional videos on fire safety. It makes sense. Forest fires are easier to extinguish before they start. Making sure a campfire is completely out is a lot easier than dousing a square kilometer of inferno.

But we've all had our share of organizational fires. Problems that might have been noticed and even addressed in a meeting go ignored. Maybe some programmer in 1984 looking at lines of code realized we might have an issue in the year 2000 since he was taught to only use two digits to indicate the year. Had his concerns been brought up and addressed, the world might have saved a lot of technical debt they earned over the Y2K scare.

Often these problems are pushed aside. Whether they're a bug in the coding that is still workable, or a manufacturing defect, solving them is delayed due to the pressures of business, time, or money concerns. The problem is that unresolved problems often cost more time—and sometimes money—to fix later rather than right away. Solving later doesn't always cost more, but it happens enough that it makes sense to put out the proverbial campfire before you burn the forest. Software engineer and CEO Steve McConnell says, "A small mistake in upstream work can affect large amounts of downstream work. A change to a single sentence in a requirements specification can imply changes in hundreds of lines of code spread across numerous classes or modules, dozens of test cases, and numerous pages of end-user documentation."[93]

The Fix Problems Immediately Pattern (my name for it. The Patterns Group named this one the Whack-the-Mole Pattern[94]) is how to address problems. Basically, address and fix all problems as they arise.

The question then becomes how to do this during a Sprint? Unlike the Interrupt Buffer, this is not a client or management interruption but an issue with the product itself. So the first solution is for the Developers to attempt to fix the problem within a specified amount of time they choose. In any situation, the Product Owner should be notified that there's an issue. If the

---

92 "Story of Smokey," Smokey Bear, accessed January 10, 2020, https://smokeybear.com/en/smokeys-history?decade=1940.

93 Steve McConnell, "An Ounce of Prevention," *IEEE Software* 18, no. 3 (May/June 2001), 5–7.

94 Sutherland, Coplien, and the Scrum Patterns Group, *A Scrum Book: The Spirit of the Game*, 377–81.

problem is not resolved in the time they estimated, the Product Owner should get involved. Depending on the severity of the problem, the Sprint may have to be stopped.

Why all the fuss? Can't a small problem wait until tomorrow? Not if it can be helped. Though little damage will probably be done between today and tomorrow, sometimes just the lag time between one day and the next (or next week, over the course of a weekend) can make it difficult for us to get into the issue again. Similar to the Good Housekeeping Pattern, it's best to finish it while everything you were doing—and possibly all the solutions you've tried—are still fresh in your mind. Later, during the Sprint Retrospective, you can review these issues to try to prevent them from happening in the future.

In short, fix those problems, put out your embers, or (if you must) whack your moles.

STEP THREE: IMPROVING PERFORMANCE

A quick recap: as you've implemented Scrum, you've learned the basics of the 3-5-3 structure, and now you've learned patterns to help you stabilize your team and get predictable by keeping people moving through the issues and dealing with problems that might come up. As the team continues to stabilize, and their behaviors get better during the "getting predictable" step, their performance and functionality will steadily improve.

Because constant feedback and improvement is part of the Scrum ethos, it makes sense that we have patterns designated to that pursuit of excellence.

Scrumming the Scrum Pattern

I've said it before, and I'll say it again: Scrum will not make you Agile; it only shows you where you are not. As you continue through the cycles, problems come up, lessons are learned, you get feedback, and the Scrum Master is working to resolve nontrivial impediments. But are those lessons really learned, the problems fixed, and the feedback addressed if you don't change your ways?

Read any significant management publication, and you will eventually come across some statistic regarding employee engagement. While there are always numerous factors, one that seems to pop up again and again is the employees feeling like nothing changes. The suggestion boxes grow moss and cobwebs, and the paper slips yellow and curl with age. Suggestions were considered, promises made, then promises were broken along with the trust. It's not that management is evil or doesn't care (at least, not most management) but that change is just as hard for an organization as it is individually—if not harder. Did you stick with the marathon training?

But Scrum is different in so many ways. It has a way to improve constantly practically built-in to the system if the users will only choose to use it. That's where the Scrumming the Scrum Pattern[95] comes in. In the last chapter, I mentioned the quote where an empty impediment list means you're not looking hard enough for ways to improve. It's true. There's always something that can be improved in the process, in how the team works together or in the work environment itself. What can be improved can come from the impediments or other metrics such as the Happiness Metric, which we will cover in just a bit.

Here's how it works. Of all the things covered in the Sprint Retrospective—remember, you're providing psychological safety so everyone feels free to share—the problems and issues you encountered during the Sprint are rife with improvement opportunities. Chose one item, and only one item, to improve in the next Sprint. It might be your biggest impediment or some feedback about team communication or how the team worked together.

Why only one item?

Imagine if you went to a doctor with joint pains. She first checks for the usual suspects: hairline fractures, arthritis, muscle tears, and so forth, but finds nothing. She concludes that your issue can be solved with over-the-counter supplements. You leave her office with a list of three items: Omega-3 supplements, vitamin B complex, and a mineral. You begin your regimen, and three weeks later you feel like a new person. Which one did the trick? Did they all help? Was one useless? Or was one giving you all the benefits while the others had no effect? You can't know.

That's why you select one item to improve, so you can see how effective the change you made is. It may need further review and adjustment. That's okay. Just like you are now producing multiple results for your client, you're also producing multiple opportunities to improve. Decide (quickly) on a solution and review its results in the next retrospective.

Incremental improvements—the one thing to improve from the Sprint Retrospective.

---

95 Ibid, 440–44.

Teams That Finish Early Accelerate Faster Pattern

I have a friend who, when he travels via commercial airlines, hates checking baggage. He does all he can to cram everything into his carry-on and backpack. Somehow he has been able to do this even for a six-day trip, but not without hassle—and forget the chance of buying souvenirs. That's the issue with packing too much. There's no room for error and no chance to add.

Maybe you've had an overambitious Saturday where you hoped to accomplish ten chores on your to-do list but were only able to accomplish five and felt defeated and exhausted, and ended up considering the pros and cons of hired help. This is "muri," or overburden, the enemy of Scrum we discussed in chapter 6. It seems to be hard-coded in human nature to underestimate and overcommit. It's no different when it comes to Planning Sprints.

The Teams That Finish Early Accelerate Faster Pattern[96] is a simple one: don't cram too much work into one Sprint. Or, more elegantly, plan for room to grow and improve.

This ties into Yesterday's Weather and Interrupt Buffer Patterns, and harkens back to our review of how Sprint Planning goes. Here's a quick refresher—the Product Owner sets the priority for the Product Backlog and meets with the Developers. In part two of the planning, I often find the Product Owner pushing for more PBIs to be included than the team feels they can handle, at least while they're in the early stages of implementation. That's why the Scrum Master is there to mediate and facilitate negotiation. His job is to remind them that they need to allow room for problems, interruptions, and growth.

When there are minimal problems and interruptions and the team completes all of the PBIs for that Sprint, they can begin the next PBI on the backlog. That is how they are able to increase velocity. Not only that, but they aren't dealing with the stress of trying to complete more than is possible. Much like my friend's carry-on, that can make a person feel like they're about to explode.

Happiness Metric Pattern

When I was first learning Scrum, I went to Argentina to work with one of the experts there. He was teaching people that the objective of Scrum was for workers to be happy. I added that people are also more productive, because that is what I had understood. To my surprise, he disagreed.

---

96 Ibid, 351–52.

"No," he said, "the aim of Scrum is that people are happy, and if they are more productive that is good, but it doesn't really matter."

I was flabbergasted. That didn't make sense to me, and it took me a while to understand. Maybe it's my industrious German roots showing. Years later, when I was training with Jeff Sutherland in Boston and heard him talk about the Happiness Metric Pattern,[97] I remembered what the Argentinian had taught and felt a little irritated thinking everyone in Scrum is concerned about happiness to the exclusion of everything else.

I asked Jeff, "Can you explain that to me? Why is happiness so important?"

Jeff quoted a Harvard study showing the correlation between happiness and engagement and productivity, and then told me, "Happiness is a tool to have a more productive and engaged team. It's a lead indicator."

The problem was two different perspectives. The Argentinian thought happiness was the end goal (remember Goodhart's law?), and productivity was an unimportant—good if it happened but not critical—byproduct. Jeff focuses on productivity, and he uses the Happiness Metric as a gauge—a means to an end. If happiness goes down, you can assume that very soon productivity and engagement will go down, too.

The topic of happiness in a work environment can be a touchy, difficult subject. In the Scrum community, many people talk about happiness and how the "team has to be happy." So much so, it's a wonder that we're not sometimes viewed like some sort of hippie commune. So many people talk about how the team has to be happy. That is not our objective. The objective is to be productive and produce more value faster. However, if you can do that by being happy and engaged at work, is that a bad thing? Work doesn't always have to feel like work.

Unlike my Argentinian friend, I see the Happiness Metric as a means to an end. One recent study shows how workers who feel happy are about 12 percent more productive.[98] Meanwhile, researcher and Harvard lecturer Shawn Achor has said that "happiness raises nearly every business and educational outcome: raising sales by 37%, productivity by 31%, and accuracy on tasks by 19%, as well as a myriad of health and quality of life improvements."[99] In other words, there's virtually no downside that I'm aware of.

---

97 Ibid, 426–39.

98 Andrew J. Oswald, Eugenio Proto, and Daniel Sgroi, "Happiness and Productivity," *Journal of Labor Economics* 33, no. 4 (2015), 789–822.

99 Shawn Achor, "The Happiness Dividend," *Harvard Business Review*, June 23, 2011, https://hbr .org/2011/06/the-happiness-dividend.

Using the Happiness Metric is simple and it ties directly to Scrumming the Scrum Pattern. During the Sprint Retrospective, you ask the team members how happy they felt during the Sprint on a scale of 1–5 or 1–10, whichever you prefer. If anyone answers less than the top number, follow up with a question like, "How might you have felt happier?" or "What could have brought that three to a four?" This way you are able to have a number of items to improve on the board. The team then decides by consensus on one item to improve in the next Sprint.

Why all this fuss? Well if the metrics aren't enough and the word "happiness" makes you feel as warm and tingly as the Grinch on Christmas Eve, then here's another word for you: engagement. If productivity is all you care about (I'd ask that you reassess your life up till this point), then the Happiness Metric Pattern is one you will want to use consistently. Workers might say, "happy," but their work says, "engaged."

These patterns may seem similar, and in some ways they are, but each pattern here—and all the other ones developed by the Pattern Group—are not isolated quick fixes.

This chapter served as a quick overview to the world of patterns and the vastness of community thinking. Chances are that if you're dealing with issues in Scrum, somebody else has already had the same issue. See, there are advantages to *not* being an "early adopter." We who've gone before you have worked out many of the bugs.

By working through these three pattern steps, your team begins to stabilize, your Sprints and velocity grow more predictable, and the overall performance in value added and employee engagement climbs. Maybe other departments have begun to take notice. While they're working crazy hours trying to make up for previous planning errors, your team is taking an extended lunch and playing a little badminton, while their metrics are surging forward with unmistakable success. What's next?

Scaling through the organization!

YOUR SCRUM PLAYBOOK

Even in the best of situations, problems will be encountered when implementing Scrum, just like the carpenter installing new cabinets and discovering the walls are not plumb. You can look to patterns to help you find solutions faster.

- A pattern is a solution to a problem in a particular context.
- Patterns are starting points to solve problems, not the solutions without adaptation.
- There are currently more than ninety known patterns, detailed in the book *A Scrum Book.*
- Patterns can be categorized into groups; for example: make your team stable, get a predictable outcome, improve team performance.

MAKE YOUR TEAM STABLE
- Stable Teams Pattern
    - Recognize the four stages of team formation: forming, storming, norming, performing.
- Colocated Teams Pattern
    - Keep team members close in geographical proximity, ideally fifty meters or the size of a bus.
    - If colocation is not possible, incorporate videoconferencing with a stable, quality server.
- Yesterday's Weather Pattern
    - Eliminate stretch goals and instead set frequent, small wins.
    - Use the velocity of the last Sprint to estimate the expected velocity of the next Sprint.

INCREASE PREDICTABILITY
- Ready Backlog Pattern
    - Understand what "ready" means.
    - The team should not need to do research in order to work on the item.
- Good Housekeeping Pattern
    - Maintain a clean product or work environment at all times.
    - Use the 5S system: Sort, Set in Order, Shine, Standardize, and Sustain.

- ▸ Swarming Pattern
  - — Work on the first priority PBI with maximum team effort.
- ▸ Interrupt Buffer Pattern
  - — Plan Buffer points into each Sprint to account for interruptions.
  - — If Buffer points aren't used, they can be applied to the next PBI.
  - — Only when there are not enough Buffer points to address the interruption should the Sprint be stopped in order to address the emergency.
- ▸ Whack-the-Mole Pattern
  - — Address problems as early and completely as possible—put out the fires before they become infernos.

IMPROVE PERFORMANCE

- ▸ Scrumming the Scrum Pattern
  - — During the Sprint Retrospective, choose ONE item to improve in the next sprint.
  - — Review the results in the next Sprint Retrospective.
- ▸ Teams That Finish Early Accelerate Faster Pattern
  - — Don't plan too much work for one Sprint.
  - — Ties back to Yesterday's Weather Pattern and the Interrupt Buffer Pattern.
- ▸ Happiness Metric Pattern
  - — Happiness is a lead indicator of productivity.
  - — Assess team members' level of happiness by asking them during the Sprint Retrospective.
  - — Use answers to fill in things to improve and work on one of those items during the next Sprint (Scrumming the Scrum).

Playing Your Hand

- ○ Identify a current problem your organization is facing.
- ○ Identify the pattern that addresses that problem.
- ○ Implement the pattern steps as adapted for your situation.
- ○ Assess the results.

CHAPTER ELEVEN

Scaling Scrum: Playing with Multiple Hands

The key to making things affordable is design and technology improvements, as well as scale.
—Elon Musk[100]

I first encountered Scrum years ago. When I finally accepted its superiority with the Ecuadorian project, I decided to switch my business model. Though I was a top consultant in traditional project management in Central and South America, I saw the benefits of Scrum and an emerging need within the market. Despite my enthusiasm, at times it felt as if I were peddling a cure-all snake oil—at least, that's how some companies made me feel. My team and I had to convince people to let us start a pilot program with Scrum, so they could see for themselves how well it worked.

Now, companies call us asking us to help them implement Scrum or wondering if it will fit in their industry. Even more than that, we often find that companies already have one or two Scrum teams reaching the performing stage. They want to know how to scale it to the rest of their organization.

Scaling is about more than just making Scrum bigger. Oftentimes, when someone hears the word *scale*, it brings back memories of an art or design class where you were resizing an object, either making a large object small in a sketch or model, or making a small object—like a cell—large. While scaling Scrum is along the same idea, it involves much more than simply cloning a pilot team over and over again.

I find that organizations approach scaling with the idea that, if the pilot

---

100 Justin Bariso, "This New Interview with Elon Musk May Completely Change How You Think about Elon Musk," *Inc.*, August 22, 2018, https://www.inc.com/justin-bariso/this-new -interview-with-elon-musk-may-completely-change-how-you-think-about-elon-musk.html.

team is producing X outcome, two Scrum teams will produce 2X, three will produce 3X, and so on. When you add more teams to a product, however, you make the lines of communication and coordination more complex. Done well, you can have three teams producing 3X, if not more. Done poorly, you will have a dismal performance.

Scrum is different from traditional work, but once a team really *gets* it and develops a feel and rhythm—moving from *shu* toward *ha*—it becomes second nature, and they can't imagine working without Scrum. Scaling requires much more care. Shifting your culture into alignment with Scrum's values is a long road. Scale too soon, and the road could crumble. The lightweight framework of Scrum scales well. But then again, any unresolved issues or cultural misalignments will scale, too. Address your issues and misalignments first. If you scale when it's not needed, you could add unnecessary layers of bureaucracy that only slow your teams' velocity.

In this chapter I will help you decide if you should even consider scaling Scrum, and I will discuss the common issues around scaling, how to solve those issues, and how the Scrum at Scale framework works.

THREE RULES FOR SCALING SCRUM

Rule One: Don't Scale

Are you thinking about scaling? My first advice to anyone in your shoes is this: DON'T.

In a chapter talking about scaling Scrum, telling you not to might sound odd—and it is, but with good reason. I've seen too many companies attempt to scale something that doesn't need to be scaled in the first place. I've also seen companies who rush into scaling before their pilot team has stabilized. I never want to be the wet blanket for a company on fire for Scrum, but I do want you to do it in a way that benefits rather than harms you. The decision to scale Scrum is a decision that should be made after no other options are left.

The simplest way to implement Scrum is to have only one cross-functional team producing a product. You can have multiple Scrum teams, each producing a unique, stand-alone product. In that case, there's also no need to scale. The reason scaling exists is not to have multiple Scrum teams but to help manage knowledge, coordination, and communication between those teams.

You can have multiple Scrum teams *without* scaling. Did you read that, or did you skip past it? Read it again. Teams working on separate products or separate modules of the same product with no dependencies do not need a formal scaling structure.

Of course, you, like most companies, want to grow. I can't think of any company who plans to shrink their profit and growth, saying, "I think we'll do a little less this year." Naturally, the desire is to grow, and it may seem like scaling is the next step. But scaling Scrum for the sake of scaling can lead to worse results. Yes, I said "worse." Any scaling must be strategic and avoided until it makes sense.

I recommend refraining from scaling until you have no choice. This makes scaling sound bad. It's not. Many large corporations are scaling Scrum as we speak, including "Amazon, GE, 3M, Toyota, Spotify, Maersk, Comcast, AT&T and many other companies . . . in different domains."[101] It works, but it's a difficult bridge to navigate. Get really good at using Scrum. Let your pilot team or teams find their rhythm and catch their stride, producing more value than they thought possible. Then, if the teams have interdependencies and communication issues, you may want to consider scaling, but only after you follow rule two.

Rule Two: Remove Interdependencies between Teams

If your product is complex enough, you may need to have two or more teams working on the same product. This does not necessarily require scaling. Remember bad architecture? It's an impediment to your teams' velocity when there's any kind of dependency between teams.

If Team A can't complete their Sprint without Team B completing a PBI first, you have an interdependency issue. Like we discussed with the bad architecture impediment, first make sure your product is as modular as possible. Like we saw with our fictional One Gallon company and Saab's Gripen fighter jet, standardizing interfaces can save interdependencies. If you can remove them, great; you don't need to scale.

I'll admit, though, that even in the One Gallon and Gripen examples, eventually the parts have to create a functioning vehicle—a fuel-efficient car or a lethal bird of war. Modularity will only take you so far, so consider if the Story Map could be refigured to allow zero interdependencies. If not, and your teams and complexity are growing, then scaling is the next step.

---

101 Jeff Sutherland and Scrum, Inc., *The Scrum@Scale® Guide: The Definitive Guide to Scrum@ Scale: Scaling that Works*, version 1.05 (November 26, 2019), p. 19, https://www.scrumatscale .com/wp-content/uploads/Scrum@Scale-Guide.pdf.

Rule Three: Scale If You Absolutely Must

Obviously, sometimes scaling is your only option. When you have multiple teams working on the same product, even with minimal dependencies, sometimes you will still need the level of organization, coordination, and communication best offered by a scaled structure.

Scaling is best done organically, in my opinion. What do I mean? Just as living organisms grow via cellular mitosis—the reproduction and splitting of cells—Scrum should grow in the same matter. It's the bottom-up or mixed implementation we discussed in chapter three. A pilot team is formed, ideally made up of willing, eager volunteers perfecting their craft and learning the fundamentals. It might start with a team of five. As the product grows, you add more team members until your team gets too big, so you split into another Scrum team. Other departments and managers take notice to see how they can be a part of it. As more and more people are added to the same product, the Product Owner's role increases, and more Scrum Masters are needed.

The other way to scale Scrum is as we saw in the top-down approach. That's how Drummond did it, as we'll see at the end of this chapter. They took their division and created an executive Scrum team and scaled downward. This is difficult because everyone is learning an entirely new way of working all at once. I said difficult, but it is possible.

When scaling, teams will change. Just like our splitting cell, some members will stay with the original team; others will start the new team. I've adamantly stated not to change teams, but you may find that, with scaling, this is unavoidable while maintaining each team's cross-functionality. Many within the Scrum community shoot for a team size of under seven if at all possible. A Harvard University study published in the psychological journal *Sociometry* puts the ideal number around five or six (actually, the study's graphical intersection was around 4.8, but dividing a person into tenths is inhumane). They measured team dynamics around feelings of satisfaction, productivity, problem-solving, and efficiency of communication.[102] In my own experience, teams of five to six people seem to work well. Some teams may only need three members to be able to produce their product end-to-end. You will have to decide on the best practice for your situation.

---

102 J. Richard Hackman and Neil Vidmar, "Effects of Size and Task Type on Group Performance and Member Reactions," *Sociometry* 33, no. 1 (March 1970), 37–54, https://www.jstor.org/stable/2786271.

CROSS-TEAM SYNCHRONIZATION

When an organization scales too soon, or scales without having ideal communication processes in place—when teams have interdependency or need more coordination—communication and effectiveness break down. Getting good at Scrum with teams that have solidified through Tuckman's four stages of development (forming, storming, norming, and performing) is the first priority. Communication is difficult enough in any organization. It's easily complicated by throwing strangers together in a massive effort to immediately create a scaled Agile organization. Some organizations formalize all communications; others try to make communication a free-for-all with no barriers.

Getting teams to communicate effectively *and* efficiently, while staying synchronized at the same time, is challenging. If the perfect cross-team synchronization existed, it would optimize four areas of good communication:

1. **Communication saturation**, where all necessary communication would reach all who needed it without gaps in information or understanding.
2. **Communication Channels** would allow for quick communication with the right people without being too numerous to handle—an overloaded email inbox, for instance. And . . .
3. **Decision Latency** would be kept to a minimum for fast decisions.
4. **Degree of Separation** minimal—the fewer removed people are from each other organizationally speaking, the faster and better the communications.

In essence, when striving for cross-team synchronization (CTS), you want to saturate communication—max out information without spending more time than you need, minimize communication channels, and alleviate excessive decision latency.

Over mankind's tenure, many organizations have attempted to facilitate synchronization through various models—from the rigid hierarchies of the Roman armies to the flat, no-boss structures of some modern start-ups. Each has its inherent pros and cons.

11.1. Hierarchical Structure

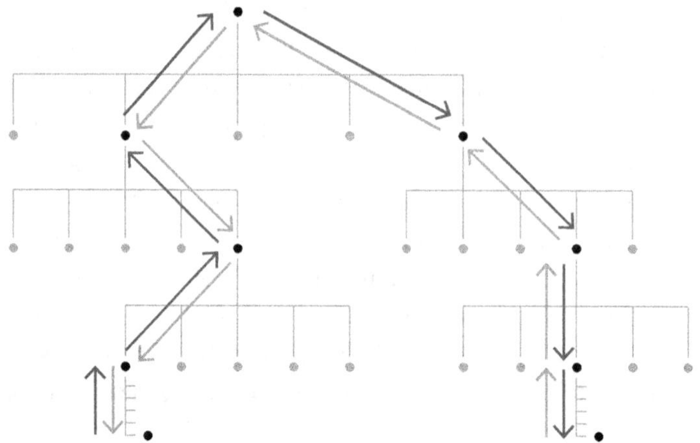

Hierarchical Structure

Have you ever heard about six degrees of separation—the idea that everybody in the world is only separated by six levels of people? For instance, I know a man who went to school with a girl whose cousin married a man who was one of former US President Clinton's aides. So I'm separated from Bill Clinton by four degrees. Does that mean I could manage to get a meeting with the man? Most likely not.

Is the six degrees idea true? I don't know. Maybe someday someone will show that some Bushman in Kenya is actually seven degrees separated from a Buddhist monk. The point is that, the further we're separated from someone, the less accessible they are and the more watered-down the communication becomes.

In the traditional hierarchy, a model that's been around since the days before Christ, you have one leader, assistant leaders, assistant-assistant leaders, and end with the lowest positions. For the Roman army, this started with the emperor and ended with the centurions.

The hierarchical structure has endured because it mostly works even if it works inefficiently. It handles one of our four requirements for CTS quite handily: communication channels are clearly defined. You can talk to your supervisor and teammates, but to discuss things with another department, you have to go through your boss or attend an interdepartmental meeting.

With regards to the other three areas of team synchronization, many hierarchical structures do not work. As you can see in the diagram, even in a relatively shallow structure of four levels, cross-team communication requires going up and back down—eight degrees of separation. In other words, because of rigid channels, you're more separated from that guy in accounting than you are from President Clinton. And if there's any technical aspects to the issue, understanding suffers. Reaching consensus by having department heads or executives sign off on anything takes far longer than the five hours promoted by the Standish Group's findings. In a world that demands companies respond faster, the hierarchical structure is like a ninety-year-old man playing on a high school basketball team—he might shoot well, but he can't get to where the ball is.

That said, there is one area where they could be very good: decision latency. Even with the multiple layers, rigid communication channels mean fewer people needed for decisions requiring consensus. When no consensus is needed, this structure has the potential for an advantage. Despite this, its heavy-handed bureaucracy often causes even this potential advantage to disappear.

11.2. Flat Structure

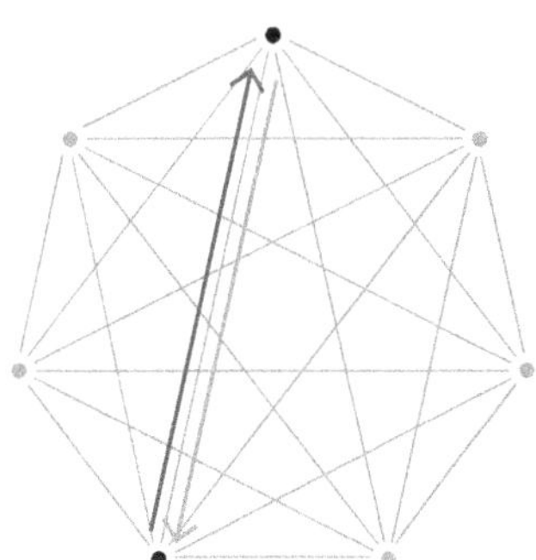

Flat Structure

Anthropologist Robin Dunbar said, "there is a well-established principle in sociology suggesting that social groupings larger than 150–200 become increasingly hierarchical in structure."[103] Robin is famous for his idea that we can't effectively sustain working relationships with more than one hundred and fifty people. It makes sense. This could be why armies like the hugely successful Roman army of a millennia or so ago had units of about one hundred and fifty soldiers.

---

103 Robin Ian Macdonald Dunbar, *Grooming, Gossip, and the Evolution of Language* (Cambridge, MA: Harvard University Press, 1999), 72.

What does this have to do with cross-team synchronization? Well, one trend is to buck the model of the stuffy, old bureaucracies by having very little structure. Employees can talk to whomever they like, and any bosses in place are more like friends with open-door polices.

For a small start-up team, this structure can be ideal. Everyone knows what everyone else is working on; it handles our three CTS quite nicely. Communication saturation is a given, because there are multiple opportunities to give and receive information. Communication channels are manageable with the small team, and the decision latency is close to zero.

But few small-teamed companies dream of staying small. As they grow, they are increasing the number of people and complicating the number of points of communication. The total number of communication channels is determined by the formula $n(n - 1)/2$, where n is the number of people in a group. A team of three people has three points of communication. Our magical team number of five has ten channels. At seven, you have twenty-one channels, as shown in the diagram above. That's twenty-one points of people exchanging information. It grows geometrically. It's not far-fetched to think our team could grow from ten to fifty people in a short time. At fifty, without formalizing CTS, you have 1,225 channels of communication. Now we can see why the Roman armies easily defeated tribal hordes.

Not only will the channels increase, but if everyone on every team can talk to everyone else, you probably will have more communication than is needed, but at the very least, the teams will be spending more time communicating and less time performing work. I'm not talking about idle chitchat but work-related discussions not properly synchronized and channeled, which can kill your team's output.

As the team continues to expand, decision latency begins to suffer. Not only do you have multiple points of input, but if any decision requires consensus, the chances of making it quickly are as likely as a snowball surviving a day in the Amazon.

11.3. Network Structure

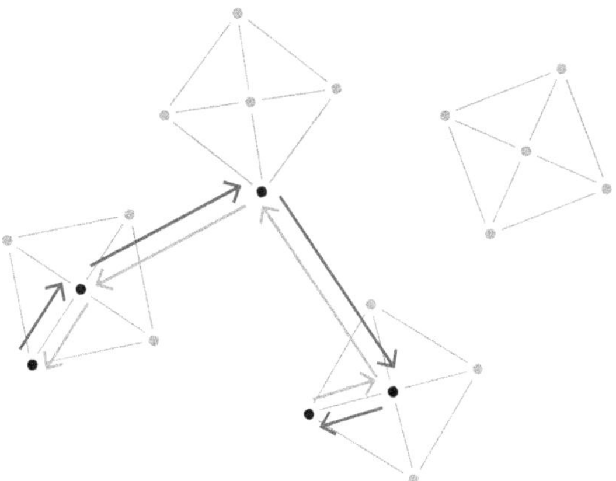

Network Structure

You can see how both structures—hierarchical and flat—aren't quite nailing our three areas for strong CTS. So what's the solution? A network. Instead of a hierarchy of different levels of leaders, a network of teams and teams of teams.

Each team of teams is connected to other teams. One or several people on each team act as a connection—a hub—to other teams of teams almost like the neurons of the brain. Just like a computer network, this network of teams has multiple hubs for communication and coordination.

One way to think about this is by comparing it to something you use every day: the internet. The internet is, at its core, just a computer network. Its architecture could have been set up in a way where everyone's computer would also act as a server with trillions of channels of communication. But the parents of the modern internet—the captains of military IT teams and scores of university academics—wanted the network to survive disasters like cyclones and war. Today, we see a network of nodes—vast areas connected by switching hubs. If one hub goes down, traffic is rerouted. It may slow down, but the internet hasn't ever gone completely down (knock on wood).

One company that has created their own network structure is the Chinese giant Haier. It used to be a titan of the bureaucratic model, but soon managing the behemoth monster grew too cumbersome—far too wide and deep to effectively manage. Instead, they created microenterprises. As one *Harvard Business Review* article put it, "Large corporations often consist of a few dominant businesses ... These tightly integrated entities and their monocultures make a company vulnerable to unconventional competitors and blind it to new kinds of opportunities. To avoid that risk, Haier has divided itself into more than 4,000 microenterprises, or MEs, most of which have 10 to 15 employees."[104]

This is the ideal model, in my mind, and a perfect basis for optimizing our three areas for CTS. Communication saturation is obtained through both formal and informal channels, the number of channels is kept to a minimum with smaller teams, and decision latency stays low when the team is given the authority to make most decisions. This is the type of structure with which we scale Scrum. The details of the how we achieve this CTS will be covered later.

A (VERY) BRIEF SCRUM@SCALE OVERVIEW

Many options exist for scaling Scrum, and I've examined many of them. I've studied Large Scale Scrum (LeSS) with creator Craig Larman, Scaled Agile Framework (SAFe) with creator Dean Leffingwell. I have also looked into Nexus from Ken Schwaber, Disciplined Agile Delivery (DAD) created by Scott Ambler and Mark Lines, and the so-called Spotify model created by Henrik Kniberg (and according to Sam Newman, "not even Spotify uses the Spotify model anymore"[105]). In my opinion, the best approach to scaling Scrum so far is Scrum@Scale®,[106] or S@S for short (both mean "Scrum at Scale"), because it best optimizes the four areas of cross-team synchronization.

S@S is the newest development in Scrum. The guide was only just released a little over a year ago as of this writing. Prior to this formalized method of scaling, many organizations were trying to scale Scrum with an assortment of methods. Many of them had started using Scrum in bottom-up and mixed implementation, and they hit the tipping point—other teams in the company wanted in. So they tried creating multiple teams but didn't know how to synchronize them without adding to the bureaucracy. Others might have had a core executive team and tried coordinating the Scrum teams. Teams' velocity often slowed. Most made valiant efforts, but all ended up being more hierarchical and bureaucratic than Agile.

Jeff Sutherland and his team, in an effort to meet this growing need for a scalable version of Scrum for these organizations, created *The Scrum@Scale Guide*[107]—and in January 2018, I was invited to visit Jeff's team in Boston,

---

104 Gary Hamel and Michele Zanini, "The End of Bureaucracy," *Harvard Business Review*, November–December 2018, 50–59.

105 Sam Newman, *Monolith to Microservices: Evolutionary Patterns to Transform Your Monolith* (Sebastopol, CA: O'Reilly, 2019), 64.

106 Scrum@Scale is a registered trademark of Scrum Inc.

107 Sutherland and Scrum, Inc., *The Scrum@Scale® Guide*.

along with a handful of other Scrum professionals, to review and comment on the first *Scrum@Scale Guide.* You may download the guide for free here: https://www.scrumatscale.com/scrum-at-scale-guide/.

If you've already read the guide (and really, if you haven't yet, why not? It's free), here's a quick refresher of what S@S is and how it functions. S@S is a set of scaling principles where Scrum teams can coordinate and network to accomplish the same goal.

As the official guide states, Scrum@Scale is

- ▸ Lightweight—the minimum viable bureaucracy
- ▸ Simple to understand—consists of only Scrum teams
- ▸ Difficult to master—requires implementing a new operating model[108]

I couldn't agree more. Instead of a bulky bureaucracy managing teams, S@S is at its essence nested Scrum teams. I like to think of it like a fractal (though, to be clear, it's not a fractal, as the structure is sometimes asymmetrical). Your pilot team may consist of five people. As you scale, the team may split into more teams—up to a group of five total teams—which is just a team of teams. Each team is acting like a single member of a core Scrum Team.

The difficulty in mastering this can't be emphasized enough. Adding layers of coordination and multiple teams all working on the same product without carefully facilitating communication potentially lead to issues. On one end of the communication spectrum, you have overcommunication (more time spent communicating versus working). Venture too far to the other end of the spectrum, and you'll see a sharp increase in decision latency (communication kept to a minimum at the expense of expediency), as we discussed in cross-team synchronization.

Scrum of Scrums (SoS)

To keep things simple, we'll start with the Scrum of Scrums (SoS) which is the simplest form of scaling. This is a team of teams, for all intents and purposes. With a pilot team, you had three to nine team members producing value for a client in the form of a product. SoS can be thought of as a team of Scrum teams working together to deliver that same value. Where S@S can be made up of one or multiple product teams in an organization, the SoS is the framework for

---

108 Ibid, 2.

multiple teams to work on and deliver one Product Increment together.

Beyond the SoS approach, things get far more complex. The guide does well to explain the basics of complex S@S structures, but just like a college textbook might go into theoretical nuclear physics, it is best not to experiment on your own without a qualified expert. Scaling Scrum beyond a SoS takes experience, and because each organization has unique issues, I advise you to hire a trained, knowledgeable expert who has sufficient qualifications, is respected within the Scrum community, with years of experience, and doesn't contradict *The Scrum Guide*. In other words, don't try this at home.

Just like a Scrum team has three roles, so does S@S. Whether you have to coordinate three teams on one product, or you have twenty-five teams working on three products, the roles don't change. They grow, as you will see.

11.4. SoS of Five Teams

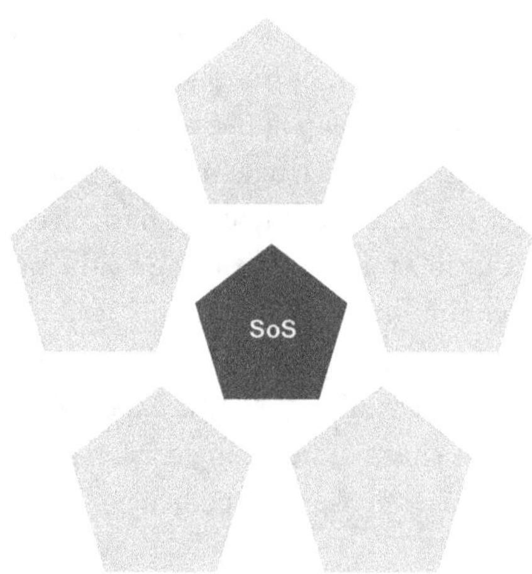

Product Owner Team (POT)

The Product Owner role does not change. For each product, you still have only one Product Owner. This is true for SoS as well. The role is the same as it is for Scrum: create a Product Goal; populate, refine, and prioritize the backlog; and focus on the *what* part of the product—synthesizing the client's needs with the market as well as the company's vision. You may have one Product Owner for a time performing their role for multiple Scrum teams. In S@S, the Product Owner role scales from the top down. In other words, one Product Owner for the SoS may be fine for a time, but eventually the work will be too much for her. As her workload increases, she may need assistant Product Owners. It's important to note that the Product Owner is not a boss. Her role is to manage the product, not the people.

Chief Product Owner (CPO)

At some point, and it varies depending on a number of variables in your organization—product complexity, number of PBIs, refinement workload—the Product Owner will need what I call assistant Product Owners: team members who assist in her role. The guide suggests that our Product Owner be called a Chief Product Owner, but that's up to you. Her role is unchanged other than coordinating with her assistants to facilitate the job of synchronizing, prioritizing, and refining a master Product Backlog throughout the other layers of the SoS structure.

Scrum of Scrums Master (SoSM)

No Scrum team is complete without a Scrum Master. In every case I'm aware of where an organization tried to remove a Scrum Master from a team, or split his duty across two or three teams, team performance has suffered and velocity has dropped. And just like the core team needs a Scrum Master, so does an SoS.

The Scrum of Scrum Master (SoSM) is not a separate team "overseeing" the other teams like a supervisor; he's one team member. An SoSM works to remove any impediments that are unresolvable at the team level, works to help the SoS go faster through the retrospective and constant improvement, ensures that the scaled events are taking place, and works closely with the Product Owner Team to coordinate releases.

If Product Owners are scaled top down and helpers added as needed, Scrum Masters are scaled bottom up. Every layer of scale needs Scrum Masters to facilitate Scrum and assist the teams.

Scrum of Scrum Events

SPRINT PLANNING, SPRINT, SPRINT REVIEW, AND RETROSPECTIVE
When operating in a scaled framework, the Sprint becomes the heartbeat of the entire organization. Every Sprint is synchronized, with each team performing their roles. The Product Owner Team, SoSM, and SoS start and end

the Sprint together under a unified definition of done. During planning, the Product Owners pull PBIs from the enterprise Product Backlog. The first parts of Sprint Planning begin with the Chief Product Owner, Product Owners, and team representatives gathered in one room pulling items from the enterprise backlog. This is followed by breakout sessions where the team and their Product Owner decide which specific items will be worked on. Finally, Developers decide how they will do their work splitting the items into smaller tasks.

The Sprint Review is one event with all the teams present. Together, they have achieved one Product Increment, not multiple increments, which would mean the teams were not integrated.

The Sprint Retrospective happens first at a team level, as it did with the pilot team. Then the teams may have representatives—especially those who experienced issues and are best able to articulate them—have a large Retrospective to discuss the processes and improvements for the next Sprint.

SCALED DAILY SCRUM

There is some disagreement about the function of SoS. Some say it is not formal, other than that a representative or Scrum Master from each Scrum team meets in a Scaled Daily Scrum with one of the team's Scrum Masters acting as the Scrum of Scrums Master (SoSM) for that event. Others hold to the idea that the SoS itself is a team of teams. I'm in the latter group—the SoS is a Scrum team of teams. Like all high-performing teams, they must coordinate and communicate.

The Scaled Daily Scrum is a standing event held at the same place and time each day, just like with the Daily Scrum. First, the individual Scrum teams all hold their Daily Scrums. Then a representative from each team meets at the SoS level. As with the Daily Scrum, the scaled version discussed three things: what their team did yesterday, what they plan to do today, and what impediments are in the way.

Not every industry leader agrees with this. They see it as a waste of time and a rigid structure that is against the spirit of Agile. I disagree. Not only are the Daily Scrums and their scaled counterparts helpful, but I believe they prevent waste.

My company saw a sharp increase in demand a few years ago, and I couldn't hire new people fast enough. I'm a little ashamed to admit this, but, in the chaos, we stopped doing the Daily Scrum for a while. Yes, even I practiced bad Scrum once. It seemed to make sense in the craziness of the moment. We couldn't spare any time, so we were saving, right? Except, we only made things worse.

At the end of our Sprints, we realized we weren't achieving the Sprints' goals. We weren't seeing what people were working on, what they had done, or any of the issues that were surfacing. It was so chaotic, we were approaching it with an all-hands-on-deck approach. During the Retrospectives, we eventually realized that our focus was on putting out fires instead of accomplishing goals. We were busy, not productive. We had violated a Scrum principle, and it showed in our lack of productivity.

Just as the Daily Scrums allow you to all be on the same page—just a quick check-in—each day, the Scaled Daily Scrum does the same. The other argument is that, as you scale, it takes too much time. But does it? Even in a large organization with a highly complex product requiring a Scrum of Scrum of Scrum of Scrums (SoSoSoS)—four levels, or three layers of depth (which is what I think should be enough for almost any product)—would contain roughly 625 team members total. The Daily Scrum events would be four, one for each level starting with the team. At fifteen minutes maximum per Daily Scrum, that's only an hour of communication in an eight-hour day, and it doesn't involve all 625 team members. Let me put it another way: many traditional managers spend *hours* in meetings each day and talk about the same issues over and over again with little progress. With S@S, we talk for up to one hour max a day, and then get things fixed immediately. Which would you prefer?

Executive/Meta Level

Even in an entirely Agile organization, you need a team that runs the functions of the company, including the human resources, finance, long-term planning, and all other executive functions. But the agility of Scrum doesn't stop at the glass door where you have bureaucrats on one side and Scrum teams working on products on the other. They are much more intertwined than that.

Within the C-level suites, we find two iterations in line with the Product Owner (Steve Jobs) and Scrum Master (Sheepdog)—two teams that champion and support the framework.

EXECUTIVE ACTION TEAM (EAT)

The Executive Action Team is comprised of executives from various divisions or disciplines. They meet regularly and are responsible for maintaining the Scrum protective bubble for the Scrum part of the organization in situations where the entire company isn't Agile. They support the Scrum Masters and are the last stop for removing any impediments that couldn't be removed at the team or SoS levels. Most importantly, they maintain their own backlog, what the guide calls an "Organizational Transformation Backlog (a prioritized list of the agile initiatives that need to be accomplished) and see that it is carried out."[109]

EXECUTIVE METASCRUM (EMS)

The executive that owns the organization's vision and sees that all the teams are aligned with the vision is called the Executive MetaScrum or EMS. They meet on a regular schedule, too—at least once per Sprint—and the Chief Product Owner (or one for each product in larger organizations) is in attendance. They review the Product Backlog and determine if any changes are needed in strategy, resource management, or implementation.

That summarizes the core essence of *The Scrum@Scale Guide*. As with all things Agile and Scrum, the guide is organic and subject to its own refinement as new approaches and understandings develop around Scrum. If you're serious about scaling Scrum in your organization, I suggest you learn the core concept of scaling as you navigate the complexities involved along with the nuanced needs of your own company.

And if you are seriously considering scaling, here are some of my "rules" regarding the process.

A TALE OF TWO CYCLES

Both the Product Owner and Scrum Master Cycles are discussed in *The Scrum@ Scale Guide*. However, I wanted to separate these items from our review because, to me, these are the core of what makes Scrum@Scale superior to other methods of scaling Agile frameworks.

Product Owner Cycle

The Product Owner steers the proverbial ship. While the executive/meta levels handle the heavy lifting of Product Goal and product life cycles, marketing, etc., the Product Owner is piecing together the various inputs, orienting herself to the dots scattered before her, making the connections, and casting a vision for the team.

---

109 Ibid, 8.

The Product Owner Cycle is the process that drives the teams' work forward. In our pilot team, the Product Owner handled the *what*: what to work on, in what order to work on it, and what the client needs or wants. As we scale Scrum, that individual role and its cycle scale, too. The steps in the cycle are simple: vision, prioritize, refinement, and release planning.

The Chief Product Owner is still working on crafting a strategic Product Goal that can be succinctly communicated along with the *why*, as in, why the organization exists to pursue the goal as she keeps a pulse on the marketplace. As the role scales, she now must communicate that vision and the priorities, and ensure alignment through the levels of teams, each with its own unique contribution of value to the Increment.

The Product Backlog is the same. Whether we're talking about a simple car prototype or a massive global enterprise software system, she starts with the map, talks to the client, and gets the input she needs to determine the order and priority.

At an enterprise level, those priorities might be larger than before. The items will most likely be larger, depending on the number of team levels, each level refining the item into smaller slices until they have PBIs at the team level that meet the definition of *ready* for their next Sprint.

The next step in the cycle is release planning. The goal of this planning is for the Product Owner to forecast product releases. Whereas a Product or Sprint burndown chart can be used to project a trend or when a task or item will be completed, release planning goes out a little further or about one to six months.

Scrum Master Cycle

If the Product Owner steers the ship, the Scrum Master is keeping the engine room operational and, I don't know, melting iceberg-like impediments. The Scrum Masters or the Scrum of Scrums Masters are present in every team, fulfilling the same role for the individual teams as those chosen to be the SoSM are doing for the team of teams—facilitating communication, adhering to Scrum time boxes, and, most importantly, removing impediments.

The Scrum Masters are taking care of the teams. Their organization from individual team SMs through the EAT work together as a unit to complete the Scrum Master Cycle. The cycle is made up of three core functions: continual improvement, cross-team coordination, and deployment.

The continual improvements involve not only ensuring the teams get better at Scrum but also removing all impediments. Any problem, frustration, or challenge is another indicator of where the team is not yet Agile and can be seen as a symptom to a cure. These are opportunities for the teams to improve. These all start at the team level. If the team's Scrum Master can't remedy the impediment on his own, he or a representative raises it to the next level at the Scaled Daily Scrum. If that team can't resolve it, it goes to the next level—all the way to the EAT if necessary.

Working to solve cross-team efforts often involves coordinating similar processes across multiple related teams. In other words, getting the teams to talk to one another. One team might have a process similar to another—database management for instance—and the potential is for islands of information to develop. The Scrum Master Team helps to facilitate the conversations. As mentioned, there needs to be a balance between formal communication and informal lines.

The final step is deployment. The SoS or (SoSoS, etc.) releases the product as a team—one team and one Product Increment. Since the *what* of the Increment is determined by the Product Owner Team, the purpose of deployment is to ensure the *how* of the product work is flowing smoothly and to integrate the work of the various teams so their items work together.

CROSS-TEAM COORDINATION

The Scrum Masters are responsible for cross-team coordination—maintaining the synchronization between the teams. They do this by facilitating the coordination or creating the processes or mechanisms that make synchronization possible. As we saw with cross-team synchronization, with Scrum scaling approaches, some companies tried different things to optimize the three areas of CTS.

One solution is to allow cross-team communication to occur only through Scrum Masters. The request goes up two levels and down two levels, and then it has to go back the way it came. Did you ever play the game called telephone where you start off with a phrase that, by the time it made it to the other side of the room, no longer made sense? Yeah, it's going to be like that. But even if you kept the communication 100 percent accurate, you're adding to the decision latency. If Juan is waiting for an answer from Federico, and there are four levels, it may be a day before he gets his answer. When you're moving at the speed of Scrum, that kind of delay is costly.

The solution is a little of both, as we saw in the network structure. The formal communication facilitated by the Scrum Masters can minimize the interruptions that cause focus to falter. Many organizations facilitate formal types of conversations by creating clubs or guilds for common interests. This might be all the Oracle database engineers getting together to discuss emerging technologies, tactics, etc. Because the organization has cross-functional teams, you are pooling together a number of people from different teams. This form of communication can help facilitate informal conversations without adding to the latency of hierarchy or the chaos of multiple channels.

In addition to formal communications, I suggest you help to foster informal communication when possible. Maybe add some water coolers (hydration is important) and central coffee and tea stations. These are good old-fashioned contact points for people to "bump into each other." One company I worked at had only one copier for the entire floor. Often there'd be a line of people waiting to make copies. What modern managers might see as a waste of time was helpful. By standing in line, conversations sparked. Yes, often they revolved around the weather and sports scores—not bad for team building—but they'd often spark work-related conversations between departments that yielded ideas and solutions that might not have otherwise occurred.

As you scale, decision latency and communication channels will increase; there's no getting around it. The key is to experiment with both formal and informal modes of communication until you find the intersection of tolerable latency without overcommunication. That sweet spot on the graph is what we're aiming for.

How They Cycle

I already mentioned how the two cycles scale: the Product Owner Cycle from the top down, and the Scrum Master Cycle from the bottom up. This is more than just a way of organizing the process. If the Sprint is the heartbeat of S@S, these cycles are the circulatory system—the blood—of the process.

Think for a minute about your home or office's thermostat. If you have the thermostat set to twenty-two degrees, and it falls below that setting, the thermostat detects the change, sends a signal to the heating system, and the room heats up. Eventually the room reaches the set temperature and the thermostat sends a signal to the heating system to shut off. What would happen if it never turned on? You'd feel very cold. If it never shut off, it might get so hot you have to open the windows, shut off the circuit, and call a technician to fix it.

While this makes sense in the heating and air conditioning industry, it's missed in companies. The Product Owner and Scrum Master cycles are the two parts to our system: action and feedback on that action. The Product Owner Cycle focuses on the product and the work, while the Scrum Master

Cycle focuses on the process and the people. If the MetaScrum makes an executive decision that goes top down, the EAT is collecting feedback from the base-team level on how that decision affected them. These two cycles allow for those leading and those following to be on the same page to minimize gaps in information and understanding.

The Cycles Intersection

Think back to how we covered the basic Scrum cycle—a goal inspired the items and priorities of the Product Backlog, which translated to the Sprint Backlog by means of the Sprint Planning. Then the team began their cycles of the Daily Scrum until the Sprint's time block completed. They held the Sprint Review with the stakeholders, and then the cycle completed with Sprint Retrospective, which fostered changes in the next Sprint. In this cycle, the Product Owner and Scrum Master worked in unique but complementary ways.

The two cycles complement each other in the same way. The Scrum Masters and the Product Owners each work on the Product and Process in a synchronized movement. In the Sprint, the two cycles intersect at two points: release feedback and process review.

Product release and feedback. This is essentially the Sprint Review at a higher level. All the teams have completed their individual PBIs, coordinated through the *what* of the POT and released for feedback. The feedback is used to further refine the backlog with any further request or changes. Meanwhile, in the Scrum Master Cycle, we are looking at ways to improve the deployment methods to better facilitate future releases.

The next step is the process review—the loop in the OODA Loop feeding back into every level to determine if there were any process issues, team dynamic problems, or communications. This is much like the team-level Sprint Retrospective. The two cycles focus on their respective roles in making improvements both to the work itself and to their adherence to core Scrum elements (three artifacts, five events, and three roles). Any issues in communication, unresolved impediments, or other issues are discussed at this juncture.

Transparency and Metrics

Remember when you rolled your eyes at me when I was going on about the importance of transparency? Well, it's just another one of the reasons you shouldn't scale until you must. When you embrace the values and shift your behavior at the pilot level of Scrum implementation, true transparency will take time to fully develop. It takes a high level of honesty and psychological safety to show work, raise issues, and critique work without any agendas.

We just discussed metrics in the previous chapters, so I'll only reiterate that no metric should become a target. That said, the metrics you choose to measure your organization's performance will be unique to the company and the product. Jeff Sutherland suggests that you have the following metrics:

- Productivity (e.g., change in amount of working product delivered per Sprint)
- Value Delivery (e.g., business value per unit of team effort)
- Quality (e.g., defect rate or service downtime)
- Sustainability (e.g., team happiness)[110]

Drummond Company: A Scrum@Scale Case Study

Scrum has been done to death in the software industry, where projects often have low cost of change and high uncertainty—those conditions ideal for the rapid feedback and iterations of Scrum—but as we've seen, it's just as effective for hardware applications.

Drummond Company is one of America's largest coal and gas companies. Their Colombian gas drilling operations require a huge amount of resources and planning before they even break ground on what could be a well that produces nothing. If software is made for Agile, drilling seems to be made for traditional, waterfall management. All the things needed to successfully drill a well take enormous amounts of planning: geological tests and surveys, government permits, moving hundreds of pieces of equipment, coordinating drilling teams. And because Colombia only ended their civil war a few years ago, they need the protection of armed security teams in the remote regions where disgruntled guerrilla rebels might still be encamped.

That's where our paths crossed. Before I converted to Scrum during that Ecuadorian telecom project, my team and I had been consulting with Drummond and other companies. I worked with Drummond to create their project management office, or PMO, years ago. Even then, concerns about communication and collaboration among their different teams seemed to be a challenge. Later, I stayed in touch, though I had converted to Scrum. It never occurred to me that they might have a use for Scrum. Like many

---

110 Ibid, 16.

others in Agile, I easily saw the value of Scrum in software and other complex environments with high uncertainty and a relative low cost of change, but when I thought about the mining industry, it seemed like traditional project management might be the best fit.

But one day I got a call from Alberto Garcia, my contact at Drummond, while he was still a vice president. After some small talk, he started asking some questions.

"You're training people in Scrum now, right?" he asked.

"Yes. I've been training for a few years now."

"I read Jeff Sutherland's book. We have an issue. It's the same one you noted with our PMO last time you were here. Do you think Scrum could help us solve these issues?"

I didn't know, yet I was intrigued by the idea. "Yes, I think so. But where do we start?"

I had seen where Scrum could help other nontech industries. Drilling seemed so old and ingrained, but maybe Scrum could work here, too. I love the challenge of trying to solve difficult puzzles, so I agreed to see what I could do.

Alberto and I met several times, looked at the operation, and identified the two issues in his gas mining division: communication and collaboration. He was right; the PMO and I had discussed this before, and it was still an issue. The main office in Bogota had issues collaborating and communicating with a remote office and their teams in the field—the ones who did the hard work of locating and drilling wells. Each team and office had few issues with internal communication; only when they tried to coordinate with distant offices did issues arise. Critical information was not reaching the teams in the field in time, leading to costly delays. The trick was solving these two issues and allowing them to produce more value faster. Actual drilling takes the same amount of time, no matter what you do—drills can't go through soil and stone any faster. So we had to focus on the steps that led up to the auger turning.

We created a Scrum team with Alberto—with his extensive knowledge of both the industry and the product—as the Product Owner and a head administrator, Arnovi, as the Scrum Master. Because Alberto was also the head of the gas drilling division, the top-down implementation was the way to go, though not ideal for the reasons mentioned in chapter 3: pushback and resistance.

In essence, we ended up creating an Executive Action Team. At the executive level, though, a Scrum team is still a team with just more executive functions of oversight and delegation. It still requires a Product Owner, a Scrum Master, and the Developers to determine how the work will be done and to create value. That was Drummond's first Scrum team. Because it was cross-functional with the administrators from every part of the operation, and they were now communicating on a regular cycle, things began changing.

Each area of the division became a separate Scrum team. The division comprised of somewhere around fifty or so people, so developing an overly complex S@S framework was unnecessary. The teams each worked on their part of the product: Corporation Issues, Operations, Exploration, Engineering Surface Facilities, and a Planning Team that handled all permits and adherence to government regulations.

The EAT decided on a two-week Sprint as the rhythm for their drilling. As the teams began communicating and the Product Owner and Scrum Master cycles started, the issues—the impediments to being Agile—quickly emerged. Engineer teams were frustrated because they were waiting for well supplies. The team responsible for the supply chain were attempting to minimize inventory by ordering only what was needed for each section of operation attempting to facilitate a just-in-time strategy. They didn't know that their attempts to keep inventory costs down were actually increasing costs when teams had to wait. Now that they weren't separated by departmental walls, they understood each other and were able to balance the inventory costs in a way that kept the teams well-supplied.

Exploration and operation teams began communicating through formal and informal channels to get faster and to smooth the transition between doing surveys and tests and actually breaking ground on the first test well.

Distributed teams was a serious impediment, with one team in the main offices and other teams sometimes in various locations out in the field, but each day the Daily Scrums and Scaled Daily Scrum happened first in person among the teams and then via a videoconference system. Conversations went like this.

"What's your team working on today?"

"We were going to begin casing well three, but we haven't received the materials, so we're going to start prepping four instead," the operations representative might say.

Then the planning team representative could look at the issue, expedite it, and make the necessary adjustments to ensure that type of delay was avoided in the future.

When they started, they had one simple Sprint goal: finish drilling one well each Sprint. They were eventually able to drill two wells per Sprint. Before they began using S@S, their fastest well was producing in an average of nineteen days. Now they were averaging six days per well, and their costs became more predictable, going over budget by only an average of 2 percent.

When I asked Alberto to comment on how Scrum had helped him and his team, he said, "Scrum has been a successful implementation for our organization and will be implemented in other specific oil and gas operating teams: drilling, stimulation and completion, construction of production facilities." I'd say they were able to scale successfully.

Where you go from here is up to you. If you were eager to scale your Scrum operation, perhaps I've given you pause. Just like Scrum requires full commitment rather than approaching it as if it were a toolbox of techniques and tactics, S@S requires a strong desire to see it through and push past the scaling impediments that might be exclusive to your company. It takes time, dedication, a firm hand, and a willingness to embrace the culture.

I don't want to discourage you from scaling any more than I would discourage my son from learning to ride his bike. When you're ready, go for it! Just watch for traffic and wear a helmet.

YOUR SCRUM PLAYBOOK

When considering whether or not to scale Scrum, there are many important elements to keep in mind. Scaling exists to help manage knowledge, coordination, and communication between teams, so it doesn't make sense to scale until it becomes absolutely necessary.

THERE ARE THREE RULES FOR SCALING SCRUM:
- Rule one: don't scale.
    - You can have multiple Scrum teams producing independent products—no need to scale.
    - Important to let pilot team(s) find their rhythm first.
    - Have two or more well-functioning teams before making the jump.

- Rule two: remove interdependencies between teams.
    - When you can remove all interdependencies by taking a modular approach, you don't need to scale.

- Rule three: scale if you absolutely must.
    - Scaling should be done organically.
        - In a bottom-up or mixed implementation approach, teams grow to a point of needing to be divided into additional teams.
        - In a top-down approach, an executive Scrum team is formed and scaled downward.

WHEN SCALING, COMMUNICATION IS A TOP PRIORITY IN FOUR SPECIFIC AREAS:
- Communication saturation—everyone gets the information needed without gaps.
- Communication channels are streamlined and easily managed.
- Decision latency is kept to a minimum.
- Reduce degrees of separation between one person and another.

SCALING FRAMEWORKS
- The traditional hierarchical structure does a good job with clear communication channels and maybe decision latency but struggles with communication saturation and degrees of separation.

- ► A flat structure in which there is no hierarchy can work for smaller groups, but it begins to break down the larger the group becomes.
- ► To solve communication issues in both structures, use a network structure in which there is a network of teams and teams of teams.

A team of teams has representatives (hubs) connected to the other teams, which brings us to S@S.

ELEMENTS OF SCRUM@SCALE

- ► Lightweight—minimum viable bureaucracy.
- ► Simple to understand—consists of only Scrum teams.
- ► Difficult to master—requires the implementation of a new operating model.
- ► Scrum of Scrum (SoS) is the simplest form of scaling and a framework for multiple teams to work on a Product Increment together.

Elements of S@S

- ► Product Owner Team (POT)
- ► Scales from the top down
- ► Same role as in basic Scrum
- ► Comprised of Chief Product Owner and a Scrum team of Assistant Product Owners.
- ► Scrum of Scrum Master (SoSM)
- ► One team member
- ► Ensures Scrum goes fast
- ► Removes impediments that are unresolvable at the team level.
- ► Scaled bottom up
- ► Scrum of Scrum events
- ► Sprints are synchronized
- ► Sprint Reviews are done with all teams present.
- ► Sprint Retrospective happens first at the team level, then representatives go to a larger Retrospective for the next Sprint.
- ► Scaled Daily Scrum
- ► Teams hold individual Daily Scrums.
- ► Representatives from each team meet at the SoS level for a scaled Daily Scrum.
- ► Executive Action Team (EAT)
  - — Comprised of executives from various divisions or disciplines.
  - — Responsible for maintaining the protective bubble around the

Scrum teams.
- Support the Scrum Masters.
- Maintain an Organizational Transformation Backlog (a prioritized list of the agile initiatives to be accomplished).
- Executive Meta-Scrum (EMS)
  - The executive that owns the organization's vision and alignment.
  - Meet at least once per Sprint with the Chief Product Owner in attendance.

Thermostat for S@S
- Product Owner Cycle
  - Still manages the goal, prioritization, refinement, and release planning.
  - Must also communicate and ensure alignment through all levels of the team.
  - Release planning can extend out over longer periods—one to six months.
- Scrum Master Cycle
  - Still facilitating communication, ensuring adherence to Scrum time boxes, and removing impediments.
  - Focus is on taking care of the teams.
  - Three core functions are continual improvement, cross-team coordination, and deployment.
  - Scrum masters are responsible for cross-team coordination.

Product Release and Feedback
- Essentially the Sprint review at a higher level
- Looking to refine the backlog, deployment methods, or better facilitate future releases

Process Review
- Determining if there were any process issues, team dynamic problems, or communications

Recommended Metrics for SoS
- Productivity
- Value delivery
- Quality
- Sustainability

Playing Your Hand

- ○ Carefully consider whether you really need to scale.
- ○ Ensure that your Scrum teams are already highly proficient at Scrum.
- ○ See if you can break your project into independent modules (S@S is not needed).
- ○ Recruit the assistance of an experienced Scrum expert to help you proceed further.

CHAPTER TWELVE

Cashing Out: Final Words

There is no such thing as a free lunch.
—attributed to Robert A. Heinlein

By now, you know about the game of Scrum. Unlike the inflexible strategies of waterfall planning—analyzing possible scenarios and pretending you have access to unknowable future information—you've learned to place calculated bets on the cards you've been given, taken each hand one at a time, and gotten better at improving each Sprint—after all, we're playing poker now, not chess.

Scrum is more than just reading this or other books, getting the gist, going about seeing what works and what doesn't, and making changes to suit your needs. It's a study of people and processes based on the cutting edge of what has worked. Teams of the best minds have continually refined the framework based on real-world feedback, and top global companies have recognized the value of Scrum.

The transition to Scrum is like the new industrial age. Instead of the heavy-handed management of early labor during the industrial revolution, we're creating teams of people who don't need carrot-and-stick motivation because the vision, challenge, and nature of their work is enticing. We are living in truly exciting times, but it takes a disciplined mindset of you, the *shu* state reader, to understand and master the basics of Scrum so you can move on to the eventual mastery of *ri*.

Let's review where we started and then dream about where Scrum can take us.

THE ROAD SO FAR

When I was that boy with my new Batman figurine, seeing the capitalist world of marketing and possibility for the first time, I felt like I was seeing everything for the first time. It was a bit overwhelming, shocking, and inspiring.

Perhaps you felt this way about Scrum. Maybe this book landed in your hands because a boss bought it and ordered you to read it. You turned the pages out of dutiful obedience or fear of termination—but maybe you saw how this might make your work better. What if issues that you've been griping about for years were finally solved? What a concept!

Or maybe you read this book because you've seen the writing on the wall. Your company is at risk of being left behind—the horse-and-carriage of a new age. Either learn the new ways of doing things or risk being left in the dust by your competition.

Whatever the reason, you made it this far. Possibly you've been a go-getter and have already formed your Scrum team, or maybe you're still unclear of exactly how to start, but you want to. A desire to start and learn is the best place to be when pursuing any endeavor.

Reviewing the History

Along this journey, you have learned about where Scrum started. First, the two researchers talked about the new product development game where they compared teammates to the scrums of Rugby field. Then the cocreators, Jeff Sutherland and Ken Schwaber in the '90s, started the first Scrum project, which together they formulated and refined into a framework. Their work, in part, helped facilitate the creation of the Agile Manifesto.

One of Scrum's figurative parents is the Lean of Toyota and its philosophies of minimizing all forms of waste and inefficiency (the three enemy Ms of Scrum: *muda, mura,* and *muri*—not to be confused with mega-corporation 3M) and a commitment to long-term benefits over short-term gains.

While Scrum borrows from the best of the Toyota system, it's eclectic borrowing a good portion of inspiration from the OODA Loops of John Boyd. Specifically, we looked at how many managers and even leaders skip the second O—orient. Beyond observing and deciding, orienting involves taking a step back to connect the dots of many sources to ensure you're not assuming your biased opinions are cold, hard facts (they're not).

But in the end, Scrum exists to produce value quickly, among other reasons. And it has demonstrated that it does this and more. From my Ecuadorian project, to the hallways of Salesforce, Saab's fighter jet, and thousands of companies of every size, the Scrum framework has shown it is more than theory—it's a practical solution that is revolutionizing industries.

Committing to Scrum

Scrum requires a full commitment. The going will be tough. With all change, resistance isn't necessarily hardest in the beginning; sometimes it's most difficult when you're in the midst of change. That's the valley—the point at which the thought of quitting is most tempting. As noted entrepreneur Seth Godin put it, "Never quit something with great long-term potential just because you can't deal with the stress of the moment."[111]

If you're already making a product whose bugs or release are backed up, you can dive in with Scrum, work to populate a backlog, assemble the team, and begin righting the ship. If you are about to start a new product, then you're in a prime position. Remember that Scrum is ideally suited for complex environments where the cost of change is low and uncertainty high, and where David Snowden and his Cynefin framework explained the processes of sensing the way forward through attempts and feedback.

Once the decision to move forward with Scrum has been made, stay the course. It will help you find your way to agility, but that doesn't mean bending to the demands of a rigid bureaucracy.

Waiver in your commitment, and suddenly value decreases, velocity slows, and team engagement withers. You have sailed into the dangerous waters of Frankenscrum or Stunted Scrum—a hybrid that attempts to take the best parts of Scrum and marry them to the worst parts of traditional models. It might seem pretty on paper, but that pig is just wearing makeup.

In an existing company with an existing culture and framework, your first unofficial team member is the Scrum sponsor. Find a strong one like Alberto Garcia at Drummond, not a weak one like the IT head at Big OG. Perhaps you are the sponsor. If so, good! Read on.

Shift Your Culture

No longer the realm of seemingly eccentric, Silicon Valley developers, Scrum has emerged in the mining and manufacturing industries, and has begun cropping up even in the military complexes of the world.

With Scrum's pillars of transparency, inspection, and adaption—looking back, you probably can see these pillars underlying the structure of everything you've learned—you start to move forward. This means discovering your organization's big vision, if you didn't already have one, and then the

---

111 Seth Godin, *The Dip: A Little Book That Teaches You When to Quit* (New York: Penguin, 2007), 64.

actual values proofed by your daily behaviors. Were they in alignment with Scrum's values of commitment, courage, focus, openness, and respect, along with healthy doses of psychological safety, trust, integrity, and honesty? Maybe you found your entire organization was in good stead here, or, on the other end of the spectrum, you might have found you're sliding in the ruts made by Enron.

But the entire company need not change. Start with your team in a separate bubble separated from dodgy office politics and frivolous ten-page reports. Start living the values—maybe like Salesforce did through constant modeling and language change. Reward ideal behavior, address behavior, and hold your peace when tempted to dive into positional authority to get things accomplished. Whatever work culture you had before, you're creating a team separate from that—the team needs to know that this is serious. Ideas—even seemingly out-there ideas—will be discussed seriously, critiques won't be mean-spirited, and talking will be encouraged.

You are on the path, and that matters most. Slow, persistent, and consistent progress is best.

Scrum Elements: 3-5-3

Before your first Sprint, you've begun deciding how the 3-5-3 structure—three roles, five events, three artifacts—will look in your company. Working with the first few members of your team, specifically the Product Owner and Scrum Master, you've set your Sprint length and begun going through the Story Mapping process to begin determining the first few priorities on the first artifact—the Product Backlog. The rest of the artifacts, including Sprint Backlog and Increment, can be learned by doing.

Similar to our tactical Colombian Special Forces troops, Scrum events start, have a duration, and then end—they are like missions that make strategic, tactical progress toward achieving your objectives. You are now familiar with all the Scrum events: Sprint, Sprint Planning, Daily Scrum, Sprint Review, and the Sprint Retrospective; and you have a good understanding of what each event entails.

Bringing the Players Together

Scrum is more than processes and strange terms. Like any business framework, it's about people. Until we reach an age where robots are building things for other robots, we will have to deal with all the joys, challenges, and ups and downs of working with and for people. Business management, after all, is far more about psychology than math.

Maybe by this point you have a Product Owner in mind, or you already discussed it with her. The Scrum Master is next—someone who has a firm grasp of Scrum from an existing company, or who will undergo more training and ideally be teamed with an expert to coach along your coach. You have your Steve Jobs and Sheepdog.

Then you begin forming your team. Again, if I could wave a magic wand, your ideal team members will be enthusiastic, curious volunteers who have the necessary skills to make the product from start to finish—sketch to testing. They will be the ones who answer "yes!" when invited to work on the product.

Like our Colombian force, the team goes through Scrum training together, and they estimate Product Backlog Items together, so they spend most of their working time—you guessed it—together, even if they are in a virtual setting. They begin going through Tuckman's four stages of team development and are forming a high-performance team. There are no superstars here. We're building a team according to the High-Performance Commitment Model in chapter 5. The players have buy-in through the process of Sprint Planning, and by living the values, they develop a team-based commitment culture, which allows everyone to work for the good of everyone else.

Playing the Game – First Cut to Winner-Takes-All

Nothing is more exciting for me than to complete training with a brand-new team and be there helping them as a coach on that first morning. Everyone's a little uncertain. They all nodded in unison during the training and laughed and smiled as they practiced our in-class exercises when they began "getting" Scrum at a deeper level. By this point, they *know* Scrum in theory. It's the "in practice" part that makes them a little nervous.

How it unfolds is varied from client to client, but the Product Owner has had time to work with me and/or the Scrum Master and the team in place before the first Sprint Planning. If it's a new product, they've gone through the experiment canvas as a team and decided on their minimum viable product to test. Sometimes, they're focused on making an older product better.

With the Product Backlog partially populated with PBIs, and assuming the estimation has been done with the team (using Planning Poker and the Fibonacci number sequence, as discussed in chapter 6, or some other method), they're ready to begin Sprint Planning in three phases. In part one, the Product Owner proposes how to increase the product's value, and then the Scrum

Team decides on a Sprint Goal based on the backlog priorities. In the second part, the Product Owner negotiates the "what" with the Developers. And in the third part, the Developers discuss how to do the work and place their tasks on a board for transparency.

They start their work and run into issues. Each Daily Scrum (same time, same place, every day) the team members answer their three questions: What did you do yesterday? What are you doing today? Are there any impediments in your way? We discussed the common impediments new teams encounter and how the Scrum Master (sometimes working with the sponsor) can alleviate them.

At the end, they've produced something of value that's testable. The client can experience the product and provide the priceless feedback during the Sprint Review. Lastly, the Sprint Retrospective is where, in the beginning, a lot of things will have seemed to go wrong.

Then we run our Scrum Patterns to make the team more stable and predictable, and to get them performing better. We check the Happiness Metric and, using a process of consensus, decide on the one item to improve in the next Sprint.

The process continues. The Increment grows. The team's velocity gets faster, and they begin producing some remarkable outcomes.

As the culture continues to shift—as Scrum helps you align your team's values—decisions are made quicker, especially reversible decisions. With decision latency lowered, things just keep getting faster.

Maybe along the way, the product grows in scope or complexity and more team members are needed. You have to decide if you want to scale or not. First you look for ways to remove interdependencies or to simplify. But when you have no other choice, you now have the basic understanding of Scrum@Scale, which is simply synchronized teams working together. Simple but not easily mastered. Scrum@Scale is growing and adapting just as each team does after a Sprint. As more and more case studies like Drummond emerge, Jeff Sutherland and his trusted team will revisit the framework just as they continue to do with Scrum.

NEXT STEPS

There's an old story about a retired man walking along a beach in a warm, sunny community along the ocean. The man notices a boy off in the distance who is bending over and then throwing things into the sea. As the man approaches the boy, he notices the low tide has stranded hundreds of sand dollars on this stretch of the beach. The boy is throwing them back to the water.

"My friend," the old man says. "What are you doing?"

"These sand dollars will die if they are left on the beach. I'm saving them."

The man smiles at the boy's enthusiasm, but with the wisdom of his age, he knows the futility of the boy's efforts. "Son, look around, there might be thousands of them. You can't make a difference."

The boy stops for a moment and meets the man's gaze as if thinking. Then he bends down, picks up another sand dollar, and chucks it into the waves. "For that one, it made all the difference in the world."

We just reviewed a lot of what we've covered. You've learned a lot in this book. It's easy to see, with all these nuances in implementation and mastery, how some lose their way. Bad Scrum is not just an enemy of the organization that attempts it, but it threatens the existence of Scrum. Just as people might emerge from cults with paranoia of all spiritual leaders, workers emerge from Bad Scrum experiences and fill their blogs and social media with all the evils of "Scrum." Beware the false prophet.

One of the beautiful things about Scrum could also be its undoing. Because Jeff and Ken believed in Scrum's ability to do amazing things in the world, they didn't protect its name. With altruistic intentions, they made the core information of their work freely accessible. And it worked. Scrum started as a smoldering ember in a small circle of software companies and, like fire, caught quickly among the dry reeds of the frustrated traditionalists. Then the logs of the hardware industry began to smoke and are now catching as well.

But along the way, others sought to benefit from this wave by changing Scrum, calling it something else, trademarking their new monster, and creating their own branded certifications. Worse are those who advertise certifications in Scrum but teach something far removed from any recognition of the original intention. Sometimes they teach bad Scrum for greedy reasons, and other times it might just be ignorance. Some so-called Scrum experts, trainers, and teachers are flying flags of their own designs.

In other words, the Scrum community—and in a larger sense, the Agile community—is comprised of many good people working for the benefit of everyone. Like any community, however, there are those who seek to serve only themselves even at others' expense. Our community is not perfect.

So when seeking advice, knowledge, or education, be cautious.

I believe that Scrum is more than a framework, more than a career, more than just a path for entrepreneurs and capitalists to make more money quicker while having the added benefit of "happy" teams. I believe that Scrum has the power to change the world.

The world is getting better, and a lot of evil from centuries past has faded away. But we have a long road still ahead of us. Many societies are still plagued with corruption and bureaucracy. Relief monies for those impacted by disasters are absorbed by tyrants under the guise of administration and regulation. I believe Agile and specifically Scrum can turn the tide.

Imagine if all red-taped barriers were stripped away, and the best minds and teams were permitted to work on issues like surviving climate change (or reversing it); curing cancer and other debilitating diseases like Alzheimer's, multiple sclerosis, and heart disease; manufacturing houses that can withstand any storm, cars that have zero carbon footprints, and renewable energy sources that are cheaply obtained. Picture a framework allowing the best and brightest in your company or society having the freedom to collaborate and solve problems you didn't even think were problems because they were engaged with their work.

That's the power of Scrum. Will we get there? I don't know. But I'm working on it one team at a time. And for those teams who are willing to let me help, it makes all the difference in the world. Beyond the scope of businesses and organizations, Scrum is a helpful framework for transforming families and individuals. I've used the Scrum frameworks even in personal pursuits like Muay Thai training.

My life's mission is to help people become a better version of themselves. Spreading the word of Scrum and ensuring that teams, companies, nonprofits, and megacorporations are using it to its full benefit is part of that mission. When businesses and organizations build better teams, everyone benefits. I want you to see results that far outweigh your expectations. Those results come through the Scrum cycle: problem-solving, feedback, learning, and continual improvement. As part of my mission, my team and I are more than happy to discuss the possibilities for you and your team. If we can help in any way, please contact us:

Scrum Network   Tel: +573223945643
Carrera 64 No.103c-40 ScrumNetwork.com
Bogota, Colombia   info@scrumnetwork.com

FAQs

Is Scrum a part of Agile?

As mentioned in the book, Agile is a mindset based on values and principles that form the Agile Manifesto. Scrum is a framework within the Agile mindset. A metaphor I like is that Agile is like ice cream, and Scrum is chocolate (or vanilla—whichever is your favorite!). There are other frameworks within the Agile mindset such as Kanban and Extreme Programming (XP), but Scrum is the most popular one, with 52 percent of Agile adopters using it.[112]

Is Scrum a methodology?

This is a common misconception. Some people don't realize there are subtle but distinct differences between words like *framework*, *model*, and *methodology*. Scrum is not a methodology; it is a framework. A methodology gives you step-by-step instructions like a recipe, for example. If you follow steps A, B, and C, you will always get result D. In a framework, you are given a structure to operate within, but that leaves some of the "how" of completing specific parts very open to your specific context and circumstances. There is no Scrum recipe to follow. You have the freedom to adjust the "how" to your specific situation.

Should I get Scrum Master certification?

Whether or not you get Scrum Master certification depends on what you want to do with it. As of the time of this writing, Scrum Master skills are in high demand and there's a lot of competition, so being certified in this skill set can help you find quality employment. Having quality training and reputable certification to help bear evidence to that skill set can mean a huge difference in your salary expectations. However, like many professions, you can acquire the skills and knowledge without receiving a certification; the caveat is that demonstrating you possess those skills and knowledge is more difficult.

---

112 VersionOne CollabNet, *13th Annual State of Agile™ Report.*

Where/When can Scrum be used?

In general, Scrum can be used in projects with high uncertainty and low cost of change or in complex environments. Remember the Cynefin (pronounced KUH-nev-in) framework discussed in chapter 2? That framework allows us to identify problem complexity, and aids organizations in finding solutions and making decisions for those problems. Use the Cynefin framework to determine if Scrum is the best fit for your product or situation.

How can I introduce the idea of Scrum in my workplace?

Being an evangelist for any change is difficult (just ask any real evangelist). After I converted to Scrum, convincing organizations to follow suit was difficult. There are several things you can do to introduce Scrum. One way you can generate interest is to find a preexisting problem in your company that is ideal for Scrum as a solution.

You can go a step further and give someone this book. Drummond was exposed to Scrum by the sharing of a book much like that. I often give away books that I think would help the receiver.

What can I do if Scrum is not working?

When people say Scrum is not working, I find that they are usually not applying it correctly. If it's not working for you, I would start by looking at the 3-5-3. Are you using the three artifacts, five events, and three roles as laid out in *The Scrum Guide*? When Scrum isn't working, in every case we've seen, the team wasn't implementing the 3-5-3 elements completely. We see this a lot; we call it the "Scrumbut . . ." They say they use Scrum, *but* they have a Project Manager. Or they use Scrum, *but* they have three-month-long Sprints. Or they use Scrum, *but* they do a *Daily* Scrum *once a week*. They're not using Scrum—they're using some elements of Scrum, but they are doing it incompletely. It's Frankenscrum or Stunted Scrum; it's not Scrum.

When should we scale Scrum?

First, you should determine if scaling is even necessary. I've found that often companies are trying to scale either before they're ready to, or when they don't even need to scale. You should only scale if you need several teams working on the same product and they can't work independently (without interdependencies) to produce the product.

Many companies want to scale too quickly, thinking that scaling will offer a solution when the smaller team is not working. If you have one team working with Scrum and they have problems, when you scale, you will also scale the problems. I'm continually amazed by this common misconception that problems will vanish if you add more people to it.

To scale, make sure the 3-5-3 elements are working well in your pilot teams before you even think about scaling. For more information on scaling Scrum, read chapter 11.

Are there pain points in Scrum – and how can I minimize them?

Yes, of course, there are lots of pain points in Scrum. We call them impediments. The three most common impediments are distributed teams, unstable teams, and lack of psychological safety. See chapter 9 for more information about these impediments and how to solve them.

Where can I get support with Scrum?

Feel free to reach out to me and my team:

Scrum Network	Tel: +573223945643
Carrera 64 No.103c-40	ScrumNetwork.com
Bogota, Colombia	info@scrumnetwork.com

Is there software or a tool I can use for Scrum?

Of course, there are plenty of software platforms that can help, but I advise proceeding with caution. Don't believe that software alone will help you solve your problems. Software is just a tool. If you buy a Ferrari and you don't know how to drive, the Ferrari is useless. If you have problems using Scrum and you get some fancy software, it's not going to get better. It will get worse, because you still have the same problems but now you have problems and software.

Before you look at tools, you should make sure you have some mastery of Scrum. That said, there is a lot of software available. We have developed a Planning Poker app, Planning Gorilla (www.planninggorilla.com). In addition, there is other software that can help you use Scrum, including Trello, Microsoft Planner, AirTable, or Microsoft Excel, and other Scrum-specific software that can help, such as Jira from Atlassian (*after* you're good at Scrum).

What's the difference between the different certification bodies?

There are many entities that certify for Scrum. The main difference between them is in reputation and quality of the certification. The first question to ask is why somebody would want to be certified in the first place. Usually, it is to show that he has at least a basic, solid understanding of a topic. It's similar to choosing a university. Get a business degree from Harvard, and nobody will question the veracity of your education. Get a business degree from the Business School of the National University of Mongolia, and you will be questioned because they have no reference point for that school's level of quality (I'm sure it's a fine school). It's more or less the same when it comes to Scrum certification bodies.

There are currently three highly reputable certification bodies. The Scrum Alliance was the first entity that offered certification. Scrum Inc. was founded in 2006 and is supported by Jeff Sutherland, one of the cocreators of Scrum. Scrum.org was founded in 2009 and is supported by Ken Schwaber, the other Scrum cocreator. These three entities all carry a high reputation within the Scrum community. The Scrum cocreators do not support any certification body outside of these three as of this writing. In my own experience, to this time, I also haven't seen any other entity that could demonstrate the same high-quality certification as these three.

Acknowledgments

You've read about the power of Scrum to help teams create amazing work. The work of this book would not be possible without a team of my own—it takes patience, work, research, editors, friends to bounce ideas off of, and copious amounts of encouragement. I appreciate all of this (and more) that my team provided.

Thank you to Monica for your insistence that this book be written and your encouragement to create this work. I am grateful to Luis for the details of the case studies. Thank you, Maryem Romero, for the translation of this book into Spanish so that this work can reach its wider audience. Camilo Rodriguez and Joaquin Botero: thank you for your review of the Spanish version of this book.

To Jeff Sutherland: my thanks for inspiring me in Scrum and being my mentor in this area of my life. I am grateful for the excellent discussions I have had with James Coplien about Scrum Patterns, those with Jon Kern and Ryan Lockard about Agile, and those with James Grenning about Planning Poker. These conversations inspired me and shaped my thinking. Thank you, Kiro Harada, for inspiring me with your work in the Scrum Patterns Group (and the Japanese whisky). I also want to extend my deep gratitude to Alberto Garcia and Arnovi Viloria for helping me with the Drummond case study. To anyone I didn't name, thank you for your help (you know who you are).

I want to thank the whole RTC team for making this book possible. I would like to especially thank James for his work in distilling a three-hundred-and-fifty-thousand-word transcript into a readable book.

About the Author

For more than twenty years, Fabian Schwartz worked in the tech industry as a program manager, developer, tester, project manager, and trainer. He has also taught IT and project management at South American and European universities for the past fifteen years.

Over the past decade, he has translated his love of training and efficiency into a thought leadership and public speaking role and has taught Scrum to more than forty thousand people. After becoming an early advocate of Agile, he became an expert in all facets of Scrum, having pioneered Scrum outside of software.

Fabian is the cocreator of "The Scrum in Hardware Guide" and has worked directly with Dr. Jeff Sutherland, cocreator of Scrum. Fabian has an MBA from Macquarie University in Australia as well as degrees from Germany and the UK. He has pursued continuing education from Stanford University and Harvard Business School.

Fabian has helped many businesses throughout Europe, Australia, and the Americas—from small start-ups to Fortune 100 companies—leverage Agile and achieve goals more effectively. He is the leading Scrum trainer in Colombia and is the only trainer certified by the three leading certification entities.